Reforming Latin America's Economies

Other books by the Author

SEEKING GROWTH UNDER FINANCIAL INSTABILITY (*editor*)

FROM CAPITAL SURGES TO DROUGHT (*Co-edited with S. Griffith-Jones*)

ECONOMIC REFORMS IN CHILE

FINANCIAL CRISES IN 'SUCCESSFUL' EMERGING ECONOMIES (*editor*)

REFORMING THE REFORMS IN LATIN AMERICA

Reforming Latin America's Economies
After Market Fundamentalism

Ricardo Ffrench-Davis

First published in 2005 by
PALGRAVE MACMILLAN
Houndmills, Basingstoke, Hampshire RG21 6XS and
175 Fifth Avenue, New York, N.Y. 10010
Companies and representatives throughout the world.

PALGRAVE MACMILLAN is the global academic imprint of the Palgrave Macmillan division of St. Martin's Press, LLC and of Palgrave Macmillan Ltd. Macmillan® is a registered trademark in the United States, United Kingdom and other countries. Palgrave is a registered trademark in the European Union and other countries.

ISBN-13: 978–1–4039–4945–5 hardback
ISBN-10: 1–4039–4945–X   hardback

This book is printed on paper suitable for recycling and made from fully managed and sustained forest sources.

A catalogue record for this book is available from the British Library.

Library of Congress Cataloging-in-Publication Data

Ffrench-Davis, Ricardo.
    Reforming Latin America's economies : after market fundamentalism / Ricardo Ffrench-Davis.
        p. cm.
    Includes bibliographical references and index.
    ISBN 1–4039–4945–X (cloth)
        1. Latin America – Economic policy. 2. Latin America – Commercial policy. 3. Chile – Economic policy. I. Title.

HC125.F479 2005
338.98—dc22   2005046301

10 9 8 7 6 5 4 3 2 1
14 13 12 11 10 09 08 07 06 05

Printed and bound in Great Britain by
Antony Rowe Ltd, Chippenham and Eastbourne

Contents

List of Figures

List of Tables and Box

Tables

Preface

During the last decade and a half Latin America has implemented deep economic reforms. In broad terms, they have been guided by the one-size-fits-all recipes, inspired in the so-called Washington Consensus.

This book searches into three major issues that are at the core of the predominantly neoliberal approaches adopted by reformers during the last fifteen years. We focus on macroeconomic, trade and financial reforms and policies. As shown through eight chapters, the approaches taken in these three areas have a significant responsibility in explaining the disappointing outcomes achieved with respect to growth and equity. Across the whole text we take a policy-oriented approach, offering alternatives for dealing with macroeconomic, trade and financial challenges faced by the region. In the last part, the ninth chapter illustrates a significant move toward *reforms to the neo-liberal reforms*, in the return of Chile to democracy in 1990.

Low average GDP growth, high real macroeconomic instability and inequitable income distribution have overwhelmed the positive achievements, such as sharply reduced inflation, reduced fiscal deficits, and expanding exports. Actually, in 2005 (as compared to 1990), the average Latin American is farther below the economic well-being of citizens of developed countries and some other emerging economies.

This book is, principally, a product of the last twelve months. Nonetheless, I have been integrating the valuable knowledge that, I believe, I reaped in coordinating research projects at ECLAC and participating in its institutional reports. Those research projects resulted in collective volumes published by The Brookings Institution Press (*Financial Crises in Successful Emerging Economies*, 2001), Palgrave/WIDER (*From Capital Surges to Drought*, 2003, co-directed with Stephany Griffith-Jones), and Palgrave/ECLAC (*Seeking Growth under Financial Volatility*, 2005). I acknowledge the support of the Ford Foundation and UNU/WIDER in the financing of those projects of ECLAC.

Participating in collective discussions and writing sections during the preparation of the ECLAC biennial reports of 2000 on *Equity, Development and Citizenship*, of 2002 on *Globalization and Development*, and of 2004 on *Productive Development in Open Economies*, and for the contribution of ECLAC on *Growth with Stability* to the Financing for Development Summit (Monterrey, 2002), were highly fruitful for me.

I acknowledge my indebtedment to José Antonio Ocampo, Andras Uthoff, Daniel Titelman, Manuel Agosin, Renato Baumann, Ricardo Bielschowsky, Roberto Bouzas, Robert Devlin, José María Fanelli, Roberto Frenkel, Stephany Griffith-Jones, Daniel Heymann, Jorge Katz, Bernardo Kosacoff, José Luis Machinea, Manuel Marfán, Deepak Nayyar, Joseph Ramos, Helmut Reisen, Jaime Ros, Andrés Solimano, Barbara Stallings, Joseph Stiglitz, Heriberto Tapia, John Williamson, and several unfairly omitted staff and participants in research projects and seminars of ECLAC. I have benefited also greatly from the highly substantive working meetings of the "Macroeconomic" and "Capital Account" Task Forces of the *Initiative for Policy Dialogue* launched and directed by Joseph Stiglitz.

The major part of this book was written for this publication. The rest proceeds from two sources. In 1998 I finished preparing a collection of papers, previously printed between 1991 and 1998, that was published by Palgrave Macmillan (*Reforming the Reforms in Latin America*, 2000). One of its chapters, on trade reforms, is partially reproduced here (chapter IV), duly revised, extended and updated. The other source is parts of papers published since 1998, written with valuable and generous co-authors. I appreciate the permissions granted by Manuel Agosin, José Antonio Ocampo and Heriberto Tapia, to use and adapt pieces of our joint works. I also appreciate the corresponding authorization from Brookings Institution Press, CEPAL Review/ECLAC, FONDAD and Palgrave/WIDER.

Heriberto Tapia has provided a notably efficient and enthusiastic support in all stages of the preparation of this typescript. Finally, I acknowledge the support of CIEPLAN (Centre for Economic Research on Latin America) for this publication.

When closing this book, Latin America is back to a sharp economic recovery. I hope to contribute, with this analysis and policy proposals, to a transit away from short-timed recoveries (as they were in 1994 and 1997), and to place the region firmly on the road to sustained growth-with-equity.

I have been awarded the Chilean prize on the "Humanities and Social Sciences, 2005."

Ricardo Ffrench-Davis
March, 2005

I
Reforming the Reforms: Why and How

Introduction

Latin America lived through a period of deep economic reforms during the 1990s, framed by the so-called "Washington Consensus." Dramatic changes affected the relative importance of the State, which saw its sphere of action diminished amidst deregulation, massive privatization, the reduction of public investment and expenditure, giving broader space for the working of private agents. One of the crucial objectives of reforms has been to improve the environment for productive activities and to achieve a sustainable higher GDP growth. Two purposes commonly stated by neo-liberals have been the achievement of a "market friendly" environment and "right prices." Throughout this text it will become evident that reforms have failed in both aspirations: productive activities – firms, entrepreneurs, labor – have faced, frequently, an *unfriendly* domestic scenario, with wrong outlier macro prices such as exchange and interest rates. It is evident that there is need to be *market-friendly* and to have *right prices* for a market economy to achieve development. The crucial point is that priority must be granted to productive activities and employment; it is impossible to have, in general, good consumers that are bad producers. In contrast, frequently, priority to purely financial activities has resulted in outlier exchange and interest rates and volatile aggregate demand, all providing a most *unfriendly* environment for productive activities. Here we are concerned about how to be efficient in fulfilling those two desired conditions and additionally having a market performance that leads to growth-with-equity.

These reforms were conducted under pressures from international financial institutions, some governments (for instance, the US Treasury) and those economists following the recipe, in strong fashion, of a neoliberal approach. It was a time of the supposed "end of history," with a naive interpretation that there was a *unique* road to a market economy, in a globalizing world that limits drastically the room for choice. Within the voices taken into account by authorities and the trainings requested, financial dimensions took a predominant place at the expense of other economic and social dimensions. Broadly speaking, notwithstanding heterodoxies and contradictions, among the emerging economies (EEs), Latin American countries (LACs) were the most active implementers of neoliberal reforms (NLRs).

One and a half decades of intensive and profound reforms have left a mix of successes and failures. It is evident that there are clearly positive results in several areas. Outstanding are the eradication of hyperinflation, more balanced public budgets, a rise in the share of exports in GDP, reduced room for bureaucratism, and less microeconomic decisions taken centrally. Notwithstanding, the net balance, in terms of growth and equity, has been notoriously poor. In all, the net outcome is "disappointing," using an expression summarizing an evaluation by John Williamson (2003b), the outstanding economist that coined the expression "Washington Consensus" in his well-known publication of 1990. GDP per capita hardly rose 0.9% per year, while in the USA and the whole world it increased 1.8% and 1.1%, respectively, between 1990 and 2004. Fifteen years after 1990, wages averaged a level below that of 1980, the number of poor people was higher, and investment ratios were as low as in the 1980s. In addition, accountability has been absent. There are impressive flaws in the design of reforms and in the capacity to recognize failures and correct them timely. In this book we examine the evolution of reforms, policies and results, and seek to reform them, starting from the present situation. That is why we label our proposal as a *"reform of the reforms."* We will focus in the more outstanding features of macroeconomic policy-making, trade liberalization, capital flows and financial reforms that contribute to explain why growth performance has been poor on average.

In this chapter, in section 1 we summarize the results achieved. In section 2 we describe, first, some major features of neo-liberalism, that underlied the actual implementation of the Washington Consensus; then, we highlight the main analytical features of our approach. Section 3 outlines the content of the chapters that follow.

1. The outcome of reforms since the 1990s, and the challenges by 2005[1]

Year 2004 posed a record annual growth rate since 1980, bringing back widespread optimism among international and national authorities. Also year 1997 was a peak year and of notably intense optimism. This year, together with 1994, had been the two best after 1980. This peak came after economic reforms that had proceeded at a fast pace across Latin America along the 1990s. By early 1998, an optimistic mood prevailed among public and private leaders in LACs, and in financial and official institutions abroad. Optimism related both to recent performance and the future of the region. The predominant view was that reforms were working well.

Significant progress had been attained in several fronts. There had been a generalized recognition by regional authorities of the need of preserving macroeconomic balances. As proof of the effectiveness of this recognition, hyperinflation had disappeared, and many countries were experiencing one-digit inflation rates. Also, budget balances and fiscal savings had improved considerably. Actually, in the quinquennium before the contagion of the East Asian Crisis, the average fiscal deficit was 1.5% of GDP; a significant improvement *vis-à-vis* previous performance, and quite a positive figure as compared to that of several developed economies. Monetary expansion to finance public deficits had nearly ceased. In another front, the quantum of exports was expanding rapidly – about 50% faster than world trade – and was diversifying in terms of items exported and markets of destination. Many countries were accumulating significant international reserves. A long wave of massive privatizations had been made.

Frequently, it could be heard that, already accomplished this first generation of reforms, it was time for the implementation of a second generation of reforms, that had been left behind; this second set included areas such as education and the judicial system reforms (Camdessus, 1997; IDB, 1997; World Bank, 1997). By 1997, the predominant view was that growth had picked up. Actually, GDP rose 5.2% in that year. But also, actual growth had been similar in 1994 (5.2%, see figure II.2), just before the explosion of the tequila crisis.

[1] See descriptions, assessments and measurements of reforms in ECLAC (1998; 2002a); Easterly, Loayza and Montiel (1997); Edwards (1995); Ganuza et al. (2001); IDB (1997); Kuczynski and Williamson (2003); Morley, Machado and Pettinato (1999); Ocampo (2004); Stallings and Peres (2000); World Bank (1997).

High instability of GDP was an outstanding fact. It is a signal of real macroeconomic instability, associated with changes in the mood of risk rating agents, political authorities, international financial institutions and influential mediatic economic observers. The present influences excessively expectations about the future. There is an overwhelming short-termism that leads to pro-cyclical performance.

Development and welfare are linked to the sum of short terms. That is, average economic welfare depends on the evolution of GDP in long periods. After the meager 1.3% yearly growth in the 1980s, in 1990–97 growth jumped to 3.2%. It was a sizable improvement, but notably below the 5.6% average achieved in the 1970s (see table I.1). The two good years – 1994 and 1997 – were not enough to compensate for weak performance in the rest of that period.

When a new prolonged period of restricted supply of foreign financing (a binding external constraint, BEC) reigned since 1998, the economic performance worsened sharply. In the sexennium 1998–2003, GDP growth collapsed to 1.3%, implying an annual per capita fall of 0.4%. In general, along this period optimism disappeared, and it became fashionable to have the contradictory view that reforms had been insufficient and weak. A sharp GDP recovery, to 5.8% in 2004, once more, improved the mood of observers and authorities.

In all, annual GDP rose scarcely 2.6% during the fifteen years between 1990 and 2004 (see table I.1). Additionally, active population

Table I.1 Latin America: Gross domestic product, 1971–2004 (annual growth rates, %)

	1971–80	1981–89	1990–2004
Argentina	2.8	−1.0	2.6
Brazil	8.6	2.3	2.0
Chile	2.5	2.8	5.2
Colombia	5.4	3.7	2.8
Mexico	6.5	1.4	3.1
Peru	3.9	−0.7	3.2
Uruguay	2.7	0.4	1.8
Venezuela	1.8	−0.3	1.9
Latin America (19)			
Total	5.6	1.3	2.6
Per capita	3.0	−0.8	0.9
Per member of labor force	1.7	−1.5	0.0

Source: ECLAC, expressed in US dollars at 1980 prices for 1971–89, and at 1995 prices for 1989–2004. Preliminary data for 2004.

Table I.2   Latin America: Social indicators, 1980–2004

	GDP per capita (1995 US$)	Poverty (Millions)	Poverty (% of pop.)	Real wage index (1995 = 100)	Unemployment (% of labor force)	Population (Millions)
1980	3,687	133	38.7	102.7	7.7	342
1990	3,345	204	48.3	96.2	7.4	422
2004	3,913	228	42.9	96.8	10.0	533

Sources: GDP per capita, poverty, and population based on ECLAC data for 19 countries. Real wage regional index is based on real indices provided by ECLAC for 12 countries, weighted by labor force in each year.

Unemployment is calculated by ECLAC with information for 24 Latin American and Caribbean countries.

(the labor force, comprising all workers and entrepreneurs) also increased 2.6% annually since 1990; consequently, the mediocre output growth merely matched the additions to the labor force. As a matter of fact, output per worker in the long period 1990–2004 stagnated. This, plus a regressive bias in reforms and policies, contributes to explain the poor performance of wages: 2004 recorded an average wage lower than in 1980 and similar to that in 1990 (see table I.2). But, wages refer to the formal segment of labor markets. Actually, labor markets expelled workers from the formal to the informal segments, with more instability of jobs and falling average income of non-waged workers (ECLAC, 2004c, based on ILO data for LACs; IDB, 2004; Tokman, 2004).

Economic reforms have tended to result in a worsening of the *macrosocial* balance (as we have labeled the set of general social conditions like poverty levels, employment, social programs, and the distribution of income, voices and opportunities). In terms of poverty, after the sharp rise in the number of poor recorded in the 1980s (see table I.2), an additional worsening took place during the NLRs; now there are 22 million more of poor people than there were in 1990, and income distribution remains notably regressive (World Bank, 2003). This is partly associated to the slackness of labor markets, higher open unemployment, the low physical investment ratio (that is, productive investment or fix gross capital formation, GKF),[2] and the underrated role granted to

---

[2] GKF includes equipment and machinery, infrastructure, commercial and residential building.

reducing the equity gaps in education, labor training and access to capital markets. The hard fact is that the distribution of opportunities and of productivity has become even more skewed than before this sort of reforms (Altimir, 2004).[3] This is especially grave in the region that traditionally has been the most unequal in the World (Bourguignon and Morrison, 2002).

As a consequence, there was a double development divergence in LACs: as in the 1980s, per capita GDP did not converge to that of the developed world. In addition, within LACs, the regressive gaps between high-income brackets and low-income brackets increased. Presently, Latin America has a GDP per capita (in PPP equivalent) of merely one-fifth of that of the richer countries; and the average Latin American country records an equity gap, between the income of the richer quintile and poorer quintile of households, that is about twice as large as compared to that within the richer countries of the world. Latin America has a much larger equity gap in comparison with the "best practices" in the world. These trends are inconsistent with the consolidation of democracy and its deepening.

The meager GDP growth was associated, to a significant degree to a low ratio of productive investment (see chapter III, and Ffrench-Davis and Reisen, 1998). This is one of the areas where the reforms have performed more poorly. In the 1990s, Latin America invested six percentage points of GDP less, on average, than it did in the 1970s, and just one point more than in the 1980s "lost decade" (see figure I.1). As of 1999 it has fallen further: in 1999–2004 it averaged a ratio similar to that recorded in the 1980s. It is a shocking fact that we discuss in detail in chapter III.

Not all sectors exhibited low GKF. In general, it was vigorous in the production of exportable goods and services. That helps to explain why export volume grew 7 to 8% per year, a rather good comparative performance with respect to that of the world economy. But the rest of GDP – that is, about 6/7 – was stagnant and likely with notably low GKF, given that the sum of GKF in exports and in non-exports is equal to total GKF. Evidently, for vigorous overall growth, there is need for the rest of the economy (non-exports) to expand fast. Actually, that has happened in all really successful exporting EEs: for instance, in Korea, Malaysia, and Taiwan along several decades, and Chile in 1990–97, the output of

---

[3] That was clearly the case of Chile, during the 1970s and 1980s, when most neoliberal reforms were implemented. Some significant correction, *with reforms to the reforms*, took place with the return to democratic rule in the 1990s (see chapter IX, and Ffrench-Davis, 2002, chapter 9).

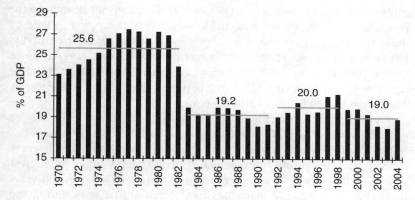

Figure I.1 Latin America: Gross fixed capital formation, 1970–2004 (% of GDP, scaled to 1995 prices)

Source: ECLAC data for 19 countries. Preliminary figure for 2004.

non-exports expanded annually around 6%; in Latin America, it scarcely rose 1% in 1990–2004 (see chapter V and table V.2). Consequently, managing to achieve a higher investment ratio in non X-GDP is one key factor missing in the production function.

Low GKF makes it harder to incorporate technical change; increases in productivity are closely associated with diverse forms of higher productive investment (De Long and Summers, 1991). An *unfriendly* domestic macro environment appears to be a crucial factor explaining that insufficiency of capital formation. The "unfriendliness" is a consequence of (i) the persistent boom-and-bust evolution of aggregate demand, associated to the strongly cyclical behavior of net capital flows and, to a lesser degree, unstable terms of trade; (ii) *wrong* macroprices (like outlier exchange and interest rates, which entrepreneurs and workers face); (iii) the weaknesses of policies directed to *complete* markets of productive factors (labor training, technology, and long-term segments of capital markets), and (iv) insufficient investment in infrastructure and public goods.

Real macroeconomic instability in EEs is one strong force behind the poor achievement of investment ratios in the 1990s. A significant, well-documented, variable underlining the drop recorded in productive investment is the output gap between actual and potential GDP (chapters II and III, and Agosin, 1998). The gap reflects the underutilized installed capacity in firms and other components of the stock of physical capital, unemployment of labor, and reduced actual total factor productivity (TFP). Profits tend to decrease while the mood of lenders becomes sombre. A notorious effect of these recessive situations, usually, has been a sharp reduction in investment ratios; for instance, a drop of capital formation in 1995, of 13% in Argentina and 30% in Mexico; in 1999 it fell 18% in Chile, and between 1998 and 2002, 56% in Argentina, and 11% in all Latin America.

It is evident that *market friendly* reforms and *right* prices are inputs for growth. However, actual poor performance indicates that *friendship* has not been effective and prices have diverged from *rightness*. For instance, it is common to observe in neoliberal reforms notably high real interest rates (i.e., Chile had an annual average of nearly 40% for over 8 years from 1975 to 1982, and many LACs exhibited outlier rates during the 1990s and the present decade; ECLAC, 1998, chapter IX; ECLAC, 2004a, chapter 3); as well, real exchange rates cyclical fluctuations are a known fact. Evidently, these outlier rates pose obstacles to accurate project evaluation for the allocation of resources, do promote speculative rather than productive investment creating larger capacity, and contribute to the deterioration of the portfolio of financial institutions.

The other relevant explanatory variable is the scarcity of the ingredients required by a productive investor. There is need for long-term financing, access to technology and capacity to absorb it, availability of well-trained labor, and infrastructure complementary to productive investment.[4] Neoliberalism assumed, and still assumes, that liberalization and privatization bring along, spontaneously, a rising supply of these ingredients of potential GDP. Usually, it does not emerge spontaneously and in the right time; hence, it is a challenge for reforms and economic policy to take account of it. It is what is called *completing* factors markets, since incomplete, under-developed or inexistent markets cannot work well: they are missing factors in the aggregate production function. This *incompleteness* is an intrinsic feature of underdevelopment and reveals a lack of enhanced systemic productive capacity or systemic competitivity.

That source of discouragement for domestic private investment has been reinforced by a change in the relative composition of FDI, from greenfield investment to acquisitions; the first one has been discouraged by the "unfriendly" environment for GKF, and acquisitions have been stimulated by privatization, depressed prices of domestic assets and depreciated currencies.

---

[4] As documented by Easterly and Servén (2003), most LACs also "witnessed a retrenchment of the public sector from infrastructure provision and an opening up to private participation" that was not fully replaced by private investment.

2. From naive neoliberalism to progressive pragmatism

a) Market fundamentalism

There are a wide variety of paths and timings chosen by LACs in the design of their structural reforms and economic policies. However, there are some distinctive features that reflect common external influences or common domestic approaches, which are at the core of significant shortcomings of the first generation of reforms across Latin America. Most reforms were performed under the umbrella of the so-called "Washington Consensus." The neoliberal fashion tackles various real problems, of great significance, that had been emerging or developed in recent decades, particularly in the 1970s and early 1980s. In the case of LACs, those economic pitfalls generated costly disequilibria, such as the huge fiscal deficits, high and variable inflation, a worsening accountability of public firms, negative real interest rates, the arbitrariness of effective protection and too many microeconomic decisions centralized by national authorities. Naturally, I share this view. However, the right changes can be made in the wrong way. That is what happened, frequently, with several of the neoliberal reforms. Usually, they have been too loaded with ideologism, depicting a poor understanding of how markets actually do work and their degree of maturity and *completeness*.

It is a significant feature that neoliberalism has an extreme faith in the efficiency of the traditional private sector and mistrust for the public sector and non-traditional forms of private organization. There is a tendency to implement reforms abruptly and to the extreme, assuming that when markets are liberalized they become *complete* rather spontaneously; this view regularly disregards crucial inter-relationships among variables, and it is too short-termist.

The predominant approach assumes that market signals flow transparently and fluidly among markets and among generations. In doing so, structural imbalances are assumed away, except those generated by state intervention. These naive assumptions lead to an underestimation of the negative effects on (i) capital formation, (ii) the utilization rate of potential GDP, and (iii) the distribution among people of productivity and opportunities. Neoliberal adjustment processes tend to generate regressive effects in face of external shocks and of one-anchor anti-inflationary programs.[5] The outcome is associated with the specific features of the set of structural reforms that have been implemented.

---

[5] For instance, lead by exchange rate peg or real appreciation, or by restrictive monetary policy in isolation.

Paradoxically, the view still in fashion, which is built on microeconomic theory and *optimization*, jumps to policy recommendations based on the *maximization* of liberalization. It disregards gradualism and intermediate positions between the extremes of indiscriminate liberalization and arbitrary interventionism; it also underrates the deep implications of the absence of complementary reforms.

In fact, typical failures have been: (i) the liberalization of the capital account, together with large external inflows, which usually has given way to cases of crowding-out of domestic savings and increased external vulnerability; (ii) trade liberalization has proceeded *pari passu* with exchange rate appreciation, contradicting all reasonable recommendations; (iii) bank privatization without prudential regulation and supervision has brought in moral hazards, and related non-transparent loans, which have produced banking crises and rescues at government expense of up to 50 per cent of an annual GDP, according to figures published by the World Bank; (iv) the absence of effective prudential regulations of public services, parallel to their liberalization or privatization.

The prevailing approach has involved the repetition of costly mistakes, particularly in the macroeconomic management, the design of trade and financial reforms, and in the weakness of efforts to *complete* markets. For example, it is impressive that the policy errors carried out in the financial reforms of Argentina and Chile during the 1970s, were replicated in many other countries of the region since the mid 1980s, and in Asian countries during this decade. They share the weakness of prudential supervision, but also the booms in short-term segments, the crowding-out of domestic savings, and financial crises highly expensive for the treasury. Comprehensive *accountability* seems to be rather absent, judging from the frequent applause for many ill-designed reforms whose objectives have not been accomplished or which have ended up in critical scenarios (recall the exuberant praises of Argentinean reforms by 1997).

In all these cases there has been responsibility for reformers, resulting from the lack of pragmatism in the design and sequencing of reforms. They should be extremely dissatisfied and revising radically their recipes. However, accountability, learning and pragmatism have been quite limited among the influential IFIs and the main political and economic leaders, in this strong wave of transformation of Latin American economies.[6]

---

[6] A recent IMF report (see Singh, et al., 2005), apparently, refers to a definition of macroeconomic balances that moves in the direction of the approach that we develop in chapter II, but the policy proposals do not reveal significant pragmatic changes.

It is clear that many outstanding specialists in the northern academic world do not share many of the traits of the neoliberal paradigm, and that well developed standard neoclassical analysis can be used to show the dangerous pitfalls of naive market fundamentalism (for instance, a short, incomplete list, should include Krugman, 1990a; Rodrik, 2003; Sachs, 1987; Solow, 2001; Stiglitz, 1994 and 2001; Williamson, 2003b).

Moreover, the actual implementation was in several cases more ideological and incomplete (in a comprehensive sense, not in the sense of more of the same) than the written "consensus" (see Williamson, 2003c). In fact, NLRs were, generally, conducted under the belief that there is a *unique* (one-size-fits-all) good policy recipe: liberalizing markets across-the-board, abruptly if possible, and until the extreme (more of the same is always good). There was no significant consideration of the fact that the selection of policies should depend (i) on the objectives democratically chosen by society; (ii) on the degree of development of domestic markets; (iii) on the degree of homogeneity of these markets; (iv) on the particular domestic macroeconomic situation, and (v) on the nature of international institutions and markets.

The spread of NLRs has been reinforced by the phenomenon (mistakenly evolved into an ideology) of economic globalization. It is beyond discussion that globalization, and especially the ability to move money rapidly from one place to the other, has limited the room for discretionary policy from governments and has taken certain policy issues virtually off the agenda. The debt crisis of the eighties brought into the forefront the economic agents linked to the financial sphere, in public and private enterprises as well as in ministries and other governmental departments, and in mass media. This situation imposed the predominance of a short-termist bias over concerns for productivity and additions to productive capacity (the *financierism* and its intrinsic *neo rent-seeking*, see chapter II). In speculative markets, as Arrow (1974) points out, a considerable part of the efforts of economic agents focuses on acquiring information leading to capture benefits at the expense of the rest of the economy (capital gains and the associated *neo rent-seeking*), and tends to lead to a negative sum redistribution, given that real resources are used in the process.

At a distributive level, indiscriminate deregulation also concentrates opportunities in favor of sectors with greater access to the financial system and more short-termist approach; in fact, usually the long-term segments of capital markets and small and medium productive firms (SMEs) have tended to loose shares in the financial markets. Macroeconomic policy-making has become to be excessively influenced, probably not purposely, by well-trained specialists in short term and liquid finance (see chapter VI).

However, the extent of this loss of room for exerting policy discretion has been exaggerated, as revealed by the effective macroeconomic activism exhibited by some LACs. In fact, still there is significant room to *make* globalization, according to domestic requirements for achieving growth-with-equity, notwithstanding the new context of increasingly integrated markets. In chapters VII and IX we illustrate the room for maneuver and the high efficiency its use may imply, with the cases of Korea and Malaysia in 1998–99 and Chile in 1990–95.

It is evident that we are not condemned to an extreme, unique, option of no room for active policies (see chapter VIII). Understanding the real working of markets, strong personality, political will for giving priority to the common good, and transparency, are crucial ingredients. It is true that they are very demanding requirements. That explains why few countries have reached development. But, indeed, it is possible.

Next, we present some policy-oriented principles that would allow to progress on the path of reforms impregnated with pragmatism, suitable for development with equity and for the enhancement of democracy. In this search for more appropriate policies we have benefited from work of diverse authors concerned about the disappointing record (see, for example, Krugman, 1990a; Stewart, 1997; Rodrik, 2003; Williamson, 2003b; Ocampo, 2004; Stiglitz, 1998). The *disappointing* market record can be improved significantly by *reforming the reforms*.

b) Our analytical approach

Criticism of neo-liberalism tends, frequently, to lack concrete policy proposals. Here we adopt a systematically policy-oriented approach.[7] Our policy-orientation is pragmatic (or realistic) in the sense of considering the actual working of markets and the response capacity of different economic agents; we search for pragmatism with a progressive bias, in the sense of being efficient in achieving our goals, that is growth-with-equity.

Reforms should not become a goal themselves, but a means for progress. An identification of the results being sought should be made; then accountability should be demanded. For instance, (i) if success in reducing inflation and imposing fiscal discipline results unable to provide stable aggregate demand and *right* macroprices to domestic

---

[7] Our alternative approach can be associated to the so-called *neostructuralism* (Sunkel, 1993), or productive transformation with equity (ECLAC, 1992; 2002a), or growth with equity (Ffrench-Davis, 2002).

producers (see chapter II); or (ii) if a domestic financial reform, implemented in order to increase domestic savings and enhance the volume and quality of investment, implies that financial savings increase while national savings decrease, and investment remains low (see chapter III); or (iii) if a vigorous export expansion does not generate a dynamic GDP growth (see chapter V).

Here we present some of the analytical pieces, policy-oriented, that contribute to explain the failures of the neo-liberal implementation of reforms under the Washington Consensus, and offer a robust alternative. We stress three features most relevant in emerging economies, which should have a determinant bearing on the design of specific policies. They relate to (i) the structural heterogeneity of factors and markets; (ii) the implications of asymmetries in instability, and (iii) the diverse links between different macroeconomic approaches and economic development (growth and equity).

Factor heterogeneity or market segmentation is one of the most typical features of developing countries. This naturally affects the transparency and flow of information, and the diverse capacity of different agents to respond efficiently to a given policy. Various dimensions of structural heterogeneity play a crucial role: among others, heterogeneity within each factor market; heterogeneity in the openness and stability of various external markets; heterogeneity between stages (expansive and contractionary) of the business cycle; variety in the elasticity of response to incentives among regions and among market segments (large and small businesses, rural and urban enterprises, infant and mature firms, consumers and producers, productive and speculative investors); heterogeneity in the time horizons and variables maximized by productive as compared to purely financial agents, heterogeneity in the degree of mobility of factors (financial funds highly mobile, while most producers of GDP tend to be immobile in the short term).[8] All these forms of heterogeneity have significant implications on the effects of the adjustment path and the feasibility of attaining different combinations of objectives (hysteresis), which implies that there is no single equilibrium but rather multiple ones.

In brief, the particular features of the transition to new equilibria make a crucial difference, and naive reforms may have an extremely long and costly adjustment period, given the presence of imperfect and *incomplete* markets. What happens during the process (hysteresis effects on the flows

[8] The issue of structural heterogeneity and its implications on economic development has been widely studied at ECLAC. See, for example, Cardoso (1977); Fajnzylber (1990); Ocampo (2002); Pinto (1970); Prebisch (1977).

of human and physical capital), together with the time involved, can have significant implications for the well-being of people.[9] We must always take into account that their welfare is the ultimate objective of economics.

Hence there arises the recommendation of contributing to improve the working of markets, enhancing the role of longer-term horizons and productivistic factors. The target is an endogenous development process guided by reforms and policies designed within the national economy and accommodated to its markets features and objectives (Fajnzylber, 1990; Sunkel, 1993). A crucial space corresponds to the application of a productive development policy. This includes systematically developing and *completing* factor markets, guiding the allocation of resources towards investment in physical and human capital, deliberately improving the distribution of productivity and opportunities across society, and promoting the acquisition of comparative advantages.

Reforms and policies should strive to actively contribute to complete and integrate factor markets rather than increase segmentation, as it has often tended to occur with the recent style of reforms. Meso policies, such as labor training, dissemination of technical knowledge, and space for small and medium firms are at the core of spreading productivity through society. That is the most sustainable road to endogenous dynamic growth-with-equity. This is the constructive option, in contrast to inward-looking development in the more naive old ISI approaches, or outward-looking ones in the approaches based on the integration into world markets via abrupt and indiscriminate import and financial liberalization, and the fading-out of the sense of Nation.

Our approach requires a dynamic and modern private sector, together with active linkages with global markets and an efficient State. Given a framework of structural heterogeneity, achieving an efficient state – central and local governments, regulatory agencies, and public enterprises – is not easy. Furthermore, it is necessary to be selective also in the sense of dealing only with that quantity and quality of actions that the State is capable of designing and implementing with social efficiency, and focusing efforts where they will have the greatest impact. These principles help to minimize "State failures."

Financial instability has become an outstanding feature of the EEs. We distinguish two sorts of instability. One is the very short-termed, which can be faced by the producers of GDP with derivatives or waiting a short while before closing dealings in the market. But the strong globalization

[9] Several varieties of reforms might work in the sense of generating growth and welfare increase in the margin after the adjustment process is finished.

of financial volatility is of a second, damaging nature. Capital surges have not been one shot events but a process of several continued flows along a mid-term. Actually, they have taken place in medium-term cycles generated by successive waves of optimism, then followed by contagion of pessimism in international financial markets. Indeed, an essential feature of financial flows to developing countries have been strong medium-term cycles: abundant financing in the 1970s followed by a drought in flows in the 1980s; a new period of large inflows in 1990–97 followed by negative financial flows since the Asian crisis. Although short-term lending has made the cycle more severe, fluctuations in liquid inflows into stock markets, and longer-term flows, such as mid-term bank lending and bond financing have been equally important in generating these cycles. The extended term of these cycles, thus affecting expectations about macro-prices, among other variables, have generated significant allocative effects. Given irreversibility of resource allocation, sudden stops in inflows have been a common source of costly crises: for all LACs in the 1980s, Argentina and Mexico in 1995, East Asia in 1998, most of Latin America in 1998–2003 (see chapter VII).

Instability of the real economy is asymmetrical, and inevitably implies, in average, underutilized potential productivity and lower actual output. In fact, economic recovery may increase the flow of output in the present up to the full use of existing capacity, but it cannot recuperate output not generated yesterday. This obviously has significant implications for average actual TFP and GDP.

Instability also tends to be asymmetrical with regard to income distribution, since high-income sectors, more diversified and with better access to financial markets, can take better advantage of the opportunities emerging during economic booms, and then adjust more easily during recessive periods. The available data indicate that distribution has a tendency to deteriorate during recessions and to improve with recoveries, but with less strength on the latter than the former (Morley, 1995; Hausmann and Gavin, 1996). The labor market is negatively affected via the depressive incidence of instability on the investment ratio. The more *incomplete* the financial markets and the smaller the capital formation ratio, the larger will the probability be that the regressive effects predominate.

The repetition of conjunctures with significant underutilization of productive capacity results from external shocks and unsustainable domestic macroeconomic policies and outlier macroprices, as illustrated by the cases of Argentina and Mexico in 1995 (see chapter VII). The actual productivity of the total stock of factors evidently decreased in these two nations in 1995, given that this stock kept growing (although at a slower pace) while actual output decreased. Output recovered in 1996–97, giving way to widespread assertions that the crisis had been superseded fast and efficiently. This sort of wishful thinking or *neopopulism* tends to lead to a dangerous underestimation of the costs of policy mistakes and to the persistence of ideologism in the design of reforms. Always, the present value of recoveries, as well as of drops in output and welfare, should be considered in assessing performance of a reform, a policy or an adjustment process. There is a worrisome tendency to underrate the significance of instability and underutilization of capacity (Stiglitz, 1998).

In the last two decades, as shown above, policies have been taking place in a framework where capital formation is comparatively very low. It is a well-established empirical fact that there is a strong correlation between physical investment and growth, resulting from the interrelation of capital accumulation, productive employment and the absorption of technical progress (chapter III, and Schmidt-Hebbel, Servén and Solimano, 1996). Hence, careful attention should be devoted to the effects of given reforms or policies on investment ratios and productivity growth (Katz, 2001). In this book we examine in detail effects of trade and financial reforms, of capital flows and macroeconomic management, on capital accumulation and its rate of use and overall productivity.

3. A policy-oriented menu on macro, trade and finance

Besides this introductory chapter the book is divided into four parts.

Part One (chapters II and III) reviews the main macroeconomic principles that, in our view, should guide economic policies in EEs to achieve sustainable economic growth with equity.

Chapter II analyses the link between the macroeconomic framework and economic growth. The core of the chapter is the discussion of alternative approaches in macroeconomics. On the one hand, the financieristic or neoliberal approach emphasizes macroeconomic balances of two pillars: low inflation and fiscal balances, together with full opening of the capital account. We can call it *financial macroeconomic balances*. This financieristic approach assumes, either that that is enough for achieving productive development in a liberalized economy, or that it becomes enough with the addition of microeconomic reforms. As mentioned, several LACs were successful after 1990 in reducing inflation to one-digit figures, and balancing their fiscal budgets. However, economic activity was notably unstable; in the period covered, overall changes in GDP were led by ups-and-downs in aggregate demand, and these responded to shifts in net capital flows. Similarly, in the 1990s, East Asia continued to fulfill the two conventional pillars – low inflation and fiscal surpluses – but lost the third pillar, of sustainable macrobalances for the real economy. Therefore, most EEs were implementing a financial or two-pillar macroeconomics at the outset of the Asian crises, with the euphoric support of specialists in microfinance. A *financieristic* rather than productivistic approach had become binding.

We emphasize that an alternative, appropriate definition of macroeconomic balances should include a comprehensive set of fundamentals. That is, alongside low inflation and fiscal responsibility, which are indeed, crucial variables, it should include a balanced real economy, that is, an aggregate demand consistent with the productive capacity of the economy and a "sustainable external balance." This implies, first, a high rate of use of productive factors (capital and labor), since a low rate of utilization discourages investment in human and physical capital, hampering future growth and macrosocial balances. The way in which a persistent gap tends to negatively affect the speed of expansion of the production frontier and actual productivity is illustrated by examples from the lost decade (the 1980s) up to the lost sexennium (1998–2003), including the Tequila effects and the East Asian contagion.

At the same time, a balanced real economy must avoid vulnerability to costly external crises, by keeping sustainable external deficits and net debt, low net liquid and short-term liabilities, non-outlier real exchange rates and price-earnings ratios in stock markets, and strong prudential regulation, supervision and transparency of the financial system.

Naturally, broader macroeconomics goals require more and better policy instruments. Chapter II concludes with a review of complementary domestic macro policies to achieve a sound real macroeconomics, in five key areas (monetary, exchange rate, and fiscal policies, the regulation of capital flows, and the supervision of the financial institutions). An outstanding feature in all of them is a strong counter-cyclical character, in a framework of globalized markets.

The need for effective measures to ensure that capital inflows enlarge productive investment and are consistent with a sustainable macroeconomic environment is emphasized: the composition, the level and deviations from the trend of the volume of flows are crucial. The explanation rests on the diverse capacity to react of different markets and agents, and on the asymmetries intrinsic to instability already discussed. In periods of surges (as opposed to a stable trend), liquidity constraints for consumers tend to be released faster than for investors, given the weaknesses of long-term segments of capital markets. Also, consumers can react faster than productive investors since the latter need to identify, design and develop new projects, which is a time consuming process; given the irreversibility of investment, favorable expectations assumed at a particular time by long-term investors must be taken as sustainable for a longer horizon.

Chapter III presents a brief historical overview of growth and investment in Latin America. One major conclusion is that it is impossible to achieve sustained growth without a substantial increase in capital formation. This result contrasts with the opinion of some academics and policy-makers for whom what matters for growth is only an increase in productivity. We prove that what they usually measure as productivity gains is, to a great extent in volatile economies, a rise in the rate of use of existing productive factors.

In order to move toward a macroeconomics-for-growth we need to have a systematic clear differentiation between economic recovery and the generation of additional capacity. This has been a common misleading factor for both leftist and rightist governments in Latin America. That pitfall leads, not only to neglect of the importance of investment from the point of view of public policies, but also stimulates the private sector to run a *destabilizing intertemporal adjustment*. Indeed, interpreting that a mere recovery is a sustainable growth of potential GDP, supported by a high TFP, leads the population to feel richer and to start consuming the future, while not being really richer. Sharply distinguishing between creating capacity and using existing capacity should be guiding our macroeconomic policy.

Subsequently, we focus on the influence of the macroeconomic environment for capital formation, emphasizing the role of macro prices such as the exchange rate, interest rates and import tariffs, and the management of aggregate demand. The significance of a *productivistic* as opposed to a *financieristic* environment is stressed.

Part Two (chapters IV and V) focuses on trade reforms and policies. This is an area where structural heterogeneity plays a key role, which explains why one of the main achievements of economic reforms – the significant export dynamism – has not been accompanied by overall GDP growth. Indeed, GDP is compounded by tradable and non-tradable sectors. And within tradable sectors, there are in turn exportable and import-substituting sectors; still, for most LACs, exports are a minor proportion of GDP.

Chapter IV reviews the trade reforms implemented in LACs in recent years. A sharp increase has been recorded in the neutrality of trade policy, drastically reducing the dispersion of effective protection; the reformers have foreseen that this would result in more competitive firms, higher productivity and rising export-oriented production of tradables. We stress that, in order for trade reforms to be successful, it is necessary that the present value added by the creation of new activities (mostly exportables) exceeds the present value subtracted by the destruction of existing ones (mostly importables). This tends to require an increase in exports greater than the decrease in import substitution; consequently, with an expansion of the share of tradables in GDP. Additionally, it is expected that export activity will have positive spillover effects on the rest of the economy, which will depend upon the degree of diversification and the quality of value-added in goods and services exported; and international competitiveness must be attained through a continuing increase in productivity rather than by low wages and rising subsidies or tax exemptions.

The analysis of trade reforms shows that most LACs adopted abrupt import liberalization together with a weaker export promotion (or non-existent, beyond the direct impact of tariff reductions on imported components of exportables); this implies a sharp contrast with successful East Asian experiences. Indeed, significant inconsistencies have prevailed, particularly the coexistence of import liberalization with exchange rate appreciation; usually, real interest rates have also been extremely high, discouraging investment and the restructuring of output. In addition, a scant comprehensiveness has characterized policy sets, with weak or negligible efforts to improve factor markets, such as labor training, technology, infrastructure and long-term segments of capital markets. The shortcomings or *incompleteness* of these markets during the transition, have been a significant deterrent for private investment. Overall, negative pulls appear to have been stronger than positive pulls on investment during the transition to post-reform equilibria.

Most LACs have given priority in their governmental programs to export-led development. In chapter V we analyze how dynamic exports may contribute to sustained GDP growth. Once again, however, what matters is the net aggregate effect of economic policies on both exported GDP and non-exported GDP. Since exported GDP (net of imported inputs) still represents only about one-seventh of total output in Latin America, the challenge is to get export dynamism-cum-growth of non-exported GDP.

In LACs, exports have had unstable prices (we know with certainty) and (presumably) they have weak linkages with the rest of the economy (non exported-GDP). There is a role for (i) the level and stability of the real exchange rate (we know that RER instability deters non-traditional exports, and, hence, diversification); (ii) a sustainable macro for growth, and (iii) for factor market completion in enhancing productive linkages. One relevant component of Latin American exports is their reciprocal trade. Intra-regional exports tripled in the seven years up to 1997, covering then one-quarter of total exports of goods, but since then have been affected by swings in regional output. If attention is focused on growth and shares of non-traditional products (more intensive in value-added), both are notably higher in intra-regional trade. These goods and services face distortions and incomplete domestic markets, which preferential regional trade agreements (PRAs), in an environment of *open regionalism*, can contribute to removing progressively and efficiently. PRAs are significant for these products rather than for traditional exports, for which extra-regional markets will remain the main source of destination. In this sense, regional trade contributes to a more dynamic productive transformation of the domestic economies, and can complement policies directed to enhance systemic productivity.

Part Three (chapters VI, VII, and VIII) deals with international finance, which has played a leading role in defining business cycles in Latin America. Indeed, from the debt crises of the 1980s, external crises and subsequent recoveries have shaped the pattern of economic instability of most LACs. Figure I.2 shows that, for the average LAC, generalized booms and recessions were led by sharp changes in aggregate demand;

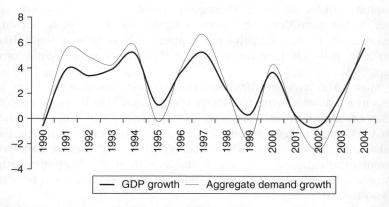

Figure I.2   Latin America (19): GDP and aggregate demand, 1990–2004 (annual growth rates, %)

Source: ECLAC data. Includes 19 countries. Preliminary figures for 2004.

with the exception of 2004, those changes were led by sharp shifts in the supply of external financing.

The high costs generated by business cycles in EEs are thus related to the strong connections between domestic and international capital markets. This implies that an essential objective of macroeconomic policies must be how to reap the benefits from external savings, but reducing the intensity of capital account cycles and their negative effects on domestic economic and social variables.

In this sense, our approach challenges the common assertion in the economic literature that the only correct way to conduct policy is with an open capital account. Chapter VI reviews the analytical foundations of the role of capital flows in development and the issue of capital account opening, discussing the contribution it can make to capital formation and macroeconomic stability through different channels. It is stressed that the conventional arguments are based on assumptions that are often unrealistic regarding the functioning of international capital markets and their interaction with EEs. Therefore, careless capital account liberalization can be destabilizing source of shocks.

The intertemporal character of financial transactions, the incompleteness of markets and the predominance of short-termist agents contribute to making finance one of the most imperfectly functioning (for our purposes, which are achieving growth with equity). This explains why the association between capital flows and domestic economic activity has been an outstanding feature of EEs during the past quarter century. Indeed, in a framework where both supply and demand of capital are led by private agents, the volatile dynamics of capital flows has been the result of the interaction between (i) the nature of (domestic and foreign) agents driving financial markets – short-sighted "by training and by reward" – and (ii) a process of pro-cyclical domestic adjustment, allowed by passive macroeconomic policies. Indeed, during booms there tends to be a contagion of over optimism that pushes asset prices up (creating bubbles), which in turn, stimulates additional capital inflows since for the most influential financial operators, the more relevant variables are not related to long-term fundamentals but to short-term profitability.

Thus, it is the market itself which generates incentives for EEs to enter the *vulnerability zones* during booms, inducing deviations of macro variables from sustainable levels (liquid external liabilities, deficit on current account, real exchange rate, real estate prices, etc.). The longer and deeper the economy's penetration into those zones, the higher the likelihood of crisis and its severity. Hence, improved information, financial sector regulation and comprehensive prudential macromanagement of financial flows constitute a public good for which there is a shared role for governments on the supply side (creditor nations) and on the demand side (debtor nations).

In chapter VII, we describe the external crises experienced since the 1990s by Latin America and East Asia. Latin America enjoyed a booming expansion of capital flows during 1991–94 and subsequently in 1996–97. These inflows overcame a binding external constraint that was responsible for the severe economic recession and low domestic investment of the 1980s. Nevertheless, these inflows also had undesirable effects on exchange rates, balance on current account, and control over the money supply, resulting in vulnerability to negative external shocks. The costs were felt in late 1994 (Tequila crises) and in 1998 (the Asian contagion).

We argue that the impact of the Tequila effect did not spread more widely to other countries in 1995, mainly due to several positive external shocks experienced by the region, associated with terms of trade improvement, highly dynamic growth of world trade, devaluation of the US dollar and, in addition, IFIs/US timely massive intervention. Nevertheless, the global impact was significant in that Latin America saw negative growth rates up to March 1996, while domestic investment fell substantially. The negative effect was clearly stronger in those countries, such as Argentina and Mexico, considered more successful by financial markets that had applied more permissive policies toward the heavy volatile capital inflows, and had experimented greater exchange rate appreciation between 1991 and 1994. On the contrary, Chile, other country classified as successful, as previously mentioned, applied effective policies deterring volatile inflows and actively intervened to moderate exchange rate appreciation; thus, it was able to remain immune to the Tequila effect.

After a period of financial euphoria, international financial markets were heavily hit by the Asian crisis that started in 1997 in Thailand. It is quite remarkable that the East-Asian economies – with superior macro policies in previous decades – succumbed to crises in the 1990s, when they adopted policies similar to the Latin American policies. The East Asian crisis showed that the two regions faced common destabilizing external forces. The common factor was that, starting in the early 1990s, several East-Asian economies started opening their rather closed capital accounts, to liquid and short-term financial flows. The opening of the capital account was undertaken at the time the surges in the supply of capital to the so-called emerging markets' economies were taking place. Capital inflows caused actual and expected gradual exchange rate appreciation that in turn encouraged the use of additional inflows to finance rising current account deficits, while external liabilities accumulated with mismatches in the maturity structure of the balance sheets of domestic financial intermediaries. As a consequence, these economies moved in a rather similar way with LACs toward *vulnerability zones*.

A new and generalized recessive adjustment was under way in Latin America since 1998 and until 2003, associated to the contagious effect of the Asian crises and the new vulnerabilities that arose in 1996–97. Once again, GDP growth experienced a downswing, productive investment was affected and the social indicators were deteriorated. Chapter VII closes examining the significant economic recovery exhibited by the major part of the region in 2004–05; we highlight that recovery, in this occasion, was not associated to a capital surge, but to sharp positive shocks in the terms of trade and volume of exports.

With chapter VIII we conclude Part Three. The experience with volatile capital flows in recent decades has left behind a track of instability and crises in EEs and particularly in Latin America. But critical episodes have also given origin to valuable lessons that can help us to understand better the process of financial globalization and to improve the future macroeconomic management.

From an analytical point of view, recent crises have shed light over a number of wrong hypotheses that became part of the "conventional wisdom" of the financial world. We summarize five wrong beliefs: (i) recovery from crises is rapid; (ii) open capital accounts discourage macroeconomic disequilibria; (iii) corner exchange rate regimes are the only viable today; (iv) financial inflows complement domestic savings, and (v) prudential regulation of banks suffices for deterring financial crises. These beliefs have misleadingly prescribed a passive approach in the management of macroeconomic policies.

In response, we have grouped a set of active policies for open economies. In all of them, the underlying principle is that usually crises are the consequence of badly managed booms; consequently the main aim of macroeconomic policies should be of prudential nature, by controlling booms before they become unsustainable. In particular, since international capital markets give rise to frequent cycles of abundance and scarcity of funding and systemic crises, policy-makers should exercise active capital account management, in order to ensure that capital inflows are consistent with macroeconomic stability, investment, and growth based on systemic competitivity. Indeed, in the last decades we have learnt that in spite of the new challenges imposed by globalization of financial volatility still there is significant room for successful domestic policies. There is no unbeatable reason why LACs cannot improve the balance between positive and negative effects of positive and negative external shocks.

In Part Four (chapter IX), we discuss the Chilean case of successful implementation of what we call a macroeconomics-for-growth. This experience is especially relevant for three reasons: (i) the Chilean economy is the only LAC that has grown at satisfactory rates since 1990, averaging 5.2% in these fifteen years; (ii) Chile led the way in neoliberal reforms, carried out under the prolonged umbrella of the dictatorship of Pinochet, in the long period 1973–89, and (iii) the case has become paradigmatic, which grants great relevance to understanding the process, its ingredients and outcome.

In Ffrench-Davis (2002) we analyzed reforms and economic policies in Chile since 1973. There we explain why average growth was short of 3% during the dictatorship (1973–89), and examine the policy variables underlying the jump to 5.2% since the return to democracy (1990–2004). The more significant change took place in the first half of the 1990s with the return to democracy. Chapter IX focuses in the deep *reforms to the reforms* implemented in macroeconomic policies. It represented a sharp move toward a macroeconomics-for-development.

Part One

From Financieristic to Real Macroeconomics

II
Macroeconomic Policies for Development*

Introduction

Macroeconomic balances are not objectives to be pursued for their own sake, but they are crucial for achieving a more dynamic development with equity. This is why it is so important to learn how these balances are obtained, how sustainable and comprehensive they are, and how consistent they are with *macrosocial* balances.

Several Latin American countries (LACs) have suffered from hyperinflation: a phenomenon that, when alive, tends to occupy such a dominant place that anti-inflationary policy often becomes the leading and absolute objective of the economic program applied. This chapter goes beyond this traumatic situation or other catastrophic events. What concerns us in particular is the interrelation between macroeconomics and growth: what macroeconomic policies should be carried out to generate growth and equity?

From the productive point of view, efficient macroeconomic policies must contribute to: (i) the use of the available productive capacity, raising the level of utilization of production factors, labor and capital, in a sustainable manner; (ii) foster capital formation, and (iii) increase productivity by furthering improvements in factors quality and in the efficiency of their allocation. These are the three cardinal elements that can generate endogenous growth and determine the economic growth rate during the transition to a new stationary level.[1]

---

* Section 2 is partly based on "Macroeconomics for growth", published in *CEPAL Review* No. 60, December, 1996.
[1] Somewhat related discussions can be found in Agénor and Montiel (1996); CEPAL (2004a); Easterly, Islam and Stiglitz (2001).

A high average rate of use of capacity implies reconciling the levels of actual aggregate demand and potential supply, attaining a suitable mix between tradables and non-tradables, and achieving appropriate macro-economic relative prices, such as interest rates and exchange rates. They are key variables for attaining macroeconomic policy objectives. Capital formation and the effective productivity of that capital are vitally dependent on the quality of those balances. LACs have had a poor record in this respect since the eighties.

If macroeconomic policies are to make the most effective contribution to development, it is necessary to adopt a comprehensive overall view (i) that systematically takes account of their effects on productive development; (ii) that reconciles the macroeconomic and macrosocial balances in a similarly integrated manner, and (iii) that gives rise to trends which are sustainable in time.

The performance of LACs has been driven by a macroeconomic environment where the main agents – government, entrepreneurs, workers, investors – have been facing sizable fluctuations in aggregate demand, economic activity, and macro prices. Significant successes in reducing inflation and improving fiscal responsibility have failed in achieving stability in the environment met by producers, both by labor and capital.

Consequently, though overall production also responds to complex processes related with micro and meso structures, macroeconomics has been one main factor behind the volatile and disappointing behavior of regional output. This is a severe failure in LACs economies, which requires a sharp correction. It is crucial to avoid or soften deep and long-lasting recessions, and to ensure a sustainable evolution of the main macroeconomic variables during boom periods: external and fiscal accounts, domestic and private indebtedness and, in general, a convergence between aggregate supply (the potential output or productive frontier) and effective demand.

This chapter focuses on the definition of macroeconomic balances, the ups and downs experienced by LACs in that field, and their overall impacts on growth and equity. Since capital flows have played a dominant role in the Latin American economies during the last third of the century, their effects are well discussed in this chapter. Chapter III documents how the macroeconomic environment affects productive investment. The analysis of the capital account management is developed in Part III of this book.

In this chapter, section 1 defines macroeconomic balances for sustainable growth, emphasizing the relative weight of real versus financial factors in economic decisions; the analysis leads to two contrasting approaches to macroeconomic balances: a two-pillars financieristic balances, and a three-pillars real macroeconomics for development. Section 2 examines why financial instability has significant real permanent effects, via the gap between the potential GDP of an economy and its actual utilization (called here output gap or recessive gap); it focuses on the positive implications of holding low output gaps. It then analyzes the evolution of the macroeconomic environment in LACs since the eighties, usually with large recessive gaps. Section 3 summarizes a set of key considerations on macroeconomic policies to achieve comprehensive macroeconomic balances, consistent with higher and sustained economic growth with equity; includes monetary, exchange rate and fiscal policies, and the regulation of capital flows. Section 4 concludes.

1. Real macroeconomic balances

There is a broad consensus that macroeconomic "fundamentals" are a most relevant variable to enhance economic development. However, there still is wide misunderstanding about what constitutes "sound fundamentals", and how to achieve and sustain them.

The operational definition of macroeconomic balances has become so narrow that in many LACs the coexistence of "a sound macroeconomics" is observed, mirrored in low inflation and small public deficits or surpluses, in parallel with slow growth and high unemployment. This section widens the view on macroeconomic balances by taking into account the macroeconomic incentives faced by firms and workers in the productive side of the economy, analyzing also the relationship between financial and real variables, and the *social* effects of macroeconomic policies.

a) A two-pillar macroeconomics

The approach that has been in fashion in the mainstream world and IFIs, even up to today, emphasizes macroeconomic balances of two pillars: low inflation and fiscal balances, with a clear omission of the overall macroeconomic environment for producers, which includes other most influential variables such as aggregate demand and exchange rates. We call it financial macroeconomic balances.[2]

This approach evidently includes other ingredients, but assumes, that the hard, relevant, proof is in fulfilling those two pillars. That leads to

---

[2] See analyses on shortcomings in the macroeconomic policies implemented in the 1990s in Latin America, in Williamson (2003b) and Ffrench-Davis (2005).

achieving productive development if the economy is liberalized, or that it suffices with the addition of microeconomic reforms. This approach is well illustrated, for example, by Stanley Fischer (1993), that after mentioning several intervening variables, concludes that "the evidence reviewed and presented in this paper supports the conventional view that a stable macroeconomic environment, meaning a reasonably low rate of inflation and a small budget deficit, is conducive for sustained economic growth". Additionally, a frequent assertion in the more recent conventional literature is that an open capital account imposes macroeconomic discipline to EEs.[3] Indeed, this approach assumes, sometimes explicitly or frequently implicitly, that full opening of the capital account would contribute to impose external and fiscal balances and automatically generate an aggregate demand consistent with productive capacity: it is well documented that that is not the usual experience in the frequent cases of external, positive and negative, financial shocks experienced by EEs (see chapter VI, and Ffrench-Davis and Ocampo, 2001).

Naturally, even though insufficient and frequently achieved in a fashion unfriendly with development, concern on those two financial balances is justified. In particular, Latin America suffered of hyperinflation processes, many times led by public deficits out of control, with very pervasive effects on economic and social development. LACs were successful in the 1990s in reducing inflation to one-digit figures, and balancing their fiscal budgets (fiscal deficits averaged, of course with diversity among countries, between 1 and 2% of GDP in 1994 and 1997, the two years preceding the two recessive shifts of the 1990s). Expansions of the money supply to finance public expenditure had become weaker or disappeared. In fact, several LACs fulfilled the main requirements of neo-liberal macroeconomic balances (see panels C and D in figure II.1).[4]

---

[3] A recent working paper of the IMF (Tytell and Wei, 2004) examines the "discipline effect" of financial globalization on macroeconomic balances, focusing on the two pillars in fashion – low inflation and fiscal balances – disregarding the other components of a comprehensive set of real macroeconomic balances.

[4] Also, economic reforms succeeded in improving export dynamism. However, trade reforms during episodes of appreciating real exchange rates ended up, frequently, in an excessive destruction of tradable activities directed to domestic markets. Likewise, the export development has remained too concentrated in primary commodities with low value-added, which limits the transmission of export dynamism to the rest of the economy (see chapters IV and V).

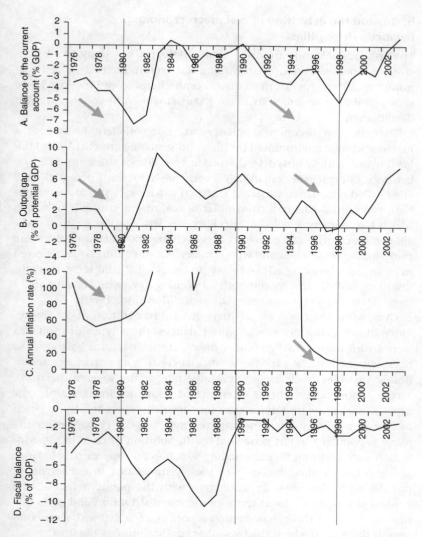

Figure II.1 Latin America (9): Macroeconomic balances, 1976–2003 (weighted averages)

Source: Author's calculations based on ECLAC data and Hofman and Tapia (2004). Includes Argentina, Bolivia, Brazil, Chile, Colombia, Costa Rica, México, Perú and Venezuela. Averages were weighted using GDP at 1980 constant prices.

b) Toward the definition of real macroeconomic balances: three pillars

The presence of significant disequilibria in the real economy, in a framework of repeated statements regarding the need to maintain macroeconomic equilibria, reveals inadequate comprehension of how to achieve those equilibria in order to make it sustainable and consistent with development.

Financial macroeconomic balances are not sufficient to achieve a macroeconomic environment for high and sustained growth. A third pillar must be added, linked to the productive side of the economy. The behavior of aggregate demand, at levels consistent with potential GDP (also called productive capacity, installed capacity or production frontier), is a crucial part of a third pillar of real macroeconomic balances, which has frequently failed in neo-liberal experiences. As well, are well-aligned macroprices, like interest and exchange rates. Frequently, these prices and aggregate demand were outliers (out-of-equilibria), as reflected in economies working either below potential GDP (the most frequent result) or, at full capacity but with a booming aggregate demand and a large external deficit (a more sporadic condition since 1980).

Thus, while there was increasingly general recognition of the importance of achieving macroeconomic balances, three types of problems were arising during the first half of the nineties. First, some balances had been obtained at the expense of imbalances in some other macroeconomic variables (such as the exchange rate or the external balance). Second, those achievements often meant a sacrifice in mesoeconomic aspects (neglecting important areas for competitiveness and equity, such as investment in infrastructure and teachers' wages). Third, despite the massive popular support generated by the solution of cases of hyperinflation and economic anarchy, failure to achieve an appropriate balance between the various objectives of society may cause broad sectors of population to feel great dissatisfaction with the public policies being applied and their results in terms of income distribution and participation. In our view, this dissatisfaction is partly connected with shortcomings in the way in which the two-pillar equilibrium was obtained.

While in the 1980s currency devaluations helped fuel inflation, in the 1990s, in contrast, the success achieved in reducing inflation was partly due, in a number of cases, to exchange-rate appreciations, the so-called *exchange rate anchor*. In fact, the vast majority of LACs revalued their currencies in real terms between 1990 and 1994, and again between 1995 and 1997. Renewed access to external finance in 1990–94 and 1996–97 made possible or actually encouraged successive real revaluations that acted as an anchor for the domestic prices of tradables. Furthermore, many countries that exhibited high rates of under-utilization of their productive capacity, with the renewed access to external finance and currency revaluations, were able to increase their rates of resource use while at the same time reducing inflation (see white arrows in panels A, B and C in figure II.1). Supply available in non–exports was able to respond fast to the increased aggregate demand, while relative consumers prices experienced a change in favor of non-tradables but with generally falling average rates of inflation.

Together with trade liberalization (see chapter IV; and ECLAC, 1998, chapter V), this caused the recovery in aggregate demand, both of individuals and of firms, to be increasingly intensive in imported goods. Imports thus went from a low level kept down by recession to an excessively high level, particularly in the case of consumer goods.

In the countries that appreciated most, with bigger and faster-growing external deficits, led by financial flows, price stabilization tended to be more rapid. They also became more vulnerable, however, as the gap between domestic spending and actual GDP (the external deficit) grew wider and external liabilities grew apace. As was to be expected, external creditors became increasingly sensitive to political and economic "bad news" that led to crises in the external sector.

Thus, some countries suffered traumatic setbacks in the fight against inflation in 1995 (Mexico, for example) or sank into recessions (Mexico, once again, and Argentina). When timely corrections were made, however, the necessary adjustments could be carried out without major upsets, to some extent like Brazil in 1995 and Chile in 1990–95. As documented in chapter IX, then Chile carried out *mini-adjustments* whenever detected starting imbalances in order to avoid subsequent *maxi-adjustments*.

After the 1995 crisis, the return of capital flows to Latin America in 1996–97 allowed, once again, a simultaneous improvement in economic activity and in price stability, but at the expense of a rise in external deficits. The result was an increase in the external debt, an acute exchange rate appreciation, and a subsequent penetration into *vulnerability zones*. In 1998, when the Asian crisis hits Latin America, there was a generalized downward adjustment in the region, especially in South America, with massive capital outflows and significant exchange rate depreciation. This time, however, inflationary processes did not take place. On the contrary, there appeared big output gaps as a result of contractive monetary policy, which gave priority to price stability over real stability (see panels A, B and C in figure II.1).

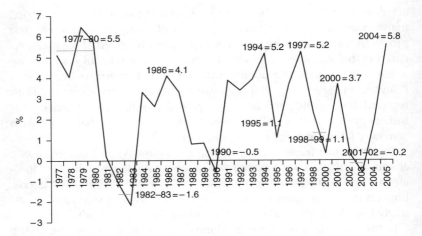

Figure II.2   Latin America: Swings in overall GDP growth, 1977–2004 (annual rates)
Source: Based on ECLAC data for 19 countries.

Behind the emergence of output gaps is the extreme instability in GDP growth rates. Figure II.2 shows how Latin America has faced volatile business cycles, with intense contractions and expansions. Evidently, the production frontier poses a limit to recoveries of actual GDP; only temporarily actual GDP can exceed potential GDP. While in recessive situations, actual GDP can be notably below potential GDP. The implication of this asymmetry is that average actual GDP, under real macroeconomic instability, is significantly lower than the average production frontier. This asymmetry, intrinsic to the economic reality, has significant implications for defining doses of objectives and policies, and for empirical research and econometrics (see chapter III, section 2).

During the emergency situations caused by the debt crisis, the Tequila crisis and the Asian crisis contagion, in many countries there were generalized cuts in public spending. These cuts not only affected redundant and bureaucratic expenses, but also areas where spending was already insufficient, thus slashing expenditure which was essential for changing production patterns with social equity. In such areas as infrastructure, education and labor training, investment – whether public or private – is often far below the appropriate levels for economies which are undergoing major processes of change (see Easterly and Servén, 2003).

Maintaining excessive expenditure cuts in these essential items for several years undermines the efforts to improve factor quality and poses obstacles to the full utilization of installed capacity; thus, lowering the efficiency of the changes in production which are under way in the region. As a consequence, economies operate with less dynamic production frontiers and in positions markedly below those frontiers. That is, their production capacity is under-utilized and tends to grow more slowly because of the lower level of investment, with consequent negative impacts on actual productivity, employment and profitability (see chapter III).

The negative effect of instability on *macrosocial* balances (including poverty and income distribution) has been well documented (see Lustig, 2000; Rodrik 2001a). It is known that the groups most affected by instability – periods of excessive growth of demand followed by usually lengthy periods of recessive adjustment in demand and output – are mid-and-low-income groups. During periods of expansion, the rate of inflation normally accelerates, and it is the poor who have problems protecting their assets and income against the "inflation tax". The period of downward adjustment tends to be accompanied by drops in wages and employment, and hence by a negative impact on consumption and wealth of low-income groups. These enjoy less fluid access to capital markets to palliate the negative impact on their spending capabilities. Recovery tends to take longer for people in lower income brackets than those in higher brackets. Thus, a pro-cyclical behavior of the share of lower-income groups in overall consumption, but with a downward bias, should be expected under instability (Morley, 1995).

c) Financial development, financierism and productivism

Financial development is a key ingredient for economic development. Channeling financial resources towards sectors of higher productivity improves overall efficiency in the economy and enhances economic growth. However, financial markets are imperfect. In a world of uncertainty, incomplete insurance markets, informational costs and contagious changes of mood, *ex ante* and *ex post* valuations of financial assets may be radically different. The time gap between a financial transaction and payment for it generates externalities in market transactions that can magnify and multiply errors in subjective valuations, to the point where finally the market corrections may be abrupt, overshooting and destabilizing (Stiglitz, 2000).

A distinctive feature of macroeconomic management in developed nations and in the most successful newly industrialized countries is the predominance of productive over financial dimensions. Development is led by the "real" side, with financial aspects at its disposal. It is a policy correlation contrary to the neo-liberal approach and the standard thesis of financial liberalization as a leading essential input for development.

The phenomenon of "financierism" – that is, the dominance of short-termist financial agents in the allocation of resources rather than real comparative costs or acquirable comparative advantage, because of incomplete markets or as a result of the influence of those agents in political decision-making – was particularly strong in the Latin American Southern Cone by the 1970s (Bacha and Díaz-Alejandro, 1983). The strength of the then new proposals was partly reinforced by pitfalls in policies in force. The deepening of inflationary trends, fueled by the 1973 oil crisis, worsened the negative effects of the prevailing "financial repression", which was reflected in frozen nominal interest rates whose real value rapidly became negative. The increased demand for loans widened the gap with the available supply of funds. These negative features encouraged naïve orthodoxy to speed up across-the-board financial liberalization, regardless of the economic conditions prevailing in each country.

As reviewed in chapter III, reforms undertaken, primarily in the Southern Cone, led to the establishment of banks without due guarantees, excessive self-loans by owners of financial companies, very short term maturities, and unstable interest rates, with substantial spreads between active (loan) and passive (deposit) rates. This resulted in short-term factors bearing more weight than long-term ones, which increased domestic instability, causing a negative effect on output and boom in credit for consumption (and for imported consumer goods in those countries that had liberalized imports). Thus, the naïve financial reform served to greatly increase consumer goods imports, with an increasing external deficit, but it also weakened the domestic productive apparatus (see Ffrench-Davis, 2002, chapter 5). The growing link with the international financial system facilitated the disassociation with the domestic productive system needs and encouraged capital flights during periods of domestic crises.

On the other hand, since the seventies, economic agents linked to the financial sphere gained greater overall influence in public and private enterprises, as well as in ministries and other governmental departments. This situation imposed the predominance at these levels of a short-termist bias over concerns for productivity and additions to productive capacity. A trend that was emphasized after the debt crisis, when foreign financial creditors and international financial institutions gained weight in the definition of domestic policies (see Devlin and Ffrench-Davis, 1995). In speculative markets, as Arrow (1974) pointed out, a considerable part of the efforts of economic agents focuses on acquiring information for personal benefit and leads to a zero sum or negative sum redistribution, owing to the use of real resources for these purposes. At a distributive level, indiscriminate deregulation also concentrates opportunities in favor of sectors with greater access to the financial system.

In short, total openness to the international market (such as those carried out in the nineties) can dismantle comprehensive efforts at domestic stabilization and encourage capital flight (Dornbusch, 1991). In fact, it could imply integration into more speculative segments of developed world markets (see chapters VI and VII). In contrast, insertion into the world economy should be aimed at promoting long-term capital inflows, accompanied by access to technology and export markets.

From the mid-nineties, campaigning and elected Latin American Presidents became usual visitors to Wall Street. International mass media, in turn, began to talk about the "market's candidate"; actually, just financial markets. The strengthening of this dimension has provoked a growing duality, worrisome for democracy, in the constituencies taken into account by authorities in EEs. The present features of globalization are raising the distance between decision-makers and financial agents *vis-à-vis* the domestic agents (workers, firms and tax proceeds) that are bearing the consequences. Thus, an outcome of the specific road taken by globalization has been that experts in financial intermediation – a microeconomic training – have become determinant, in too many cases, for the evolution of the domestic macroeconomic balances and their volatility (see chapter VIII).

Pressures from international financial markets has pushed some governments to offer guaranties for international investors as a mean to gain credibility away from what is consistent with growth and equity; even beyond what is necessary to achieve short run credibility with international financial markets. As shown by the Argentinean case, if public commitments are beyond the capacity that a democratic country can bear, the result may be praises in the short-term but a net loss in credibility in the medium and long term (see Neut and Velasco, 2003).

The case of Chile is an outstanding example of differences between the productivistic and the financieristic dimensions: while domestic and foreign financial media praised liberalizing policies during the military rule of Pinochet, Chile recorded the lowest investment ratio in the last half century. On the contrary, the reforms to the reforms in the nineties – including tax increases, labor reforms to strengthen workers bargaining power and significant increases in minimum wages – were received "with concern" by the large private entrepreneurs and the financial sector, while the investment ratio reached historical peaks (see chapter IX). Likewise, in Latin America support of political authorities to the "market economy" has never been as explicit and strong as since the nineties, just in the period with historical minimum levels in investment ratios. These cases show that enthusiastic praise from financial markets has, frequently, not been useful for productive development. One outstanding failure has been the incapability to progress from two-pillar macroeconomics to three-pillars real macroeconomic balances.

2. Real balances in Latin America: theoretical implications and actual results

a) Positioning on the production frontier: analytical and policy implications

One of the most fundamental macroeconomic balances (the third pillar) refers to the rate of utilization of productive capacity. In economies with inflexible price systems and *incomplete* factor markets, both positive and negative shocks provoke successive adjustments. The results are greater disparity between supply and aggregate demand, with a consequent gap between potential productive capacity and the use made of it. Unstable demand, in a stop-and-go setting, as shown inevitably means a lower average net use of productive capacity and a lower average actual productivity than those of a situation of stable proximity to the productive frontier.

The magnitude of the gap between effective demand and the production frontier has important static and dynamic effects. On the one hand, it affects the quality of project evaluation and the *ex post* productivity and profitability of the projects implemented. Indeed, higher rates of capital utilization mean that the average level of employment is higher and that the labor force combines with a larger stock of physical capital in actual use. While distribution of the fruits of higher productivity between labor and capital depends on diverse elements, higher actual productivity does mean that the potential welfare of labor and rentiers (wages and profits) can improve at present, with the higher average rate of use of capacity. If wages and profits grow, then fiscal revenues will grow as well. Then, workers, entrepreneurs and government will be able to sustain higher consumption and/or savings, with a net positive effect on overall economic welfare and on poverty reduction.

In the dynamic dimension, higher rates of utilization and the consequent increase in effective productivity tend to stimulate investment in new capacity (chapter III; and Schmidt-Hebbel, Servén and Solimano, 1996; Servén and Solimano, 1993). For the supply of investment to expand effectively, investors must perceive a real improvement in the short term and foresee that the reduction in the recessive output gap will be persistent and sustainable in the future. The dynamic effect will be all the more significant if solid expectations are generated, among the economic actors, regarding that public policies will keep effective demand close to the production frontier, and if, in addition, authorities undertake reforms to *complete* long-term capital markets, and enhance labor training and productive innovation (see chapter III).

Another dynamic consequence of a higher rate of utilization is a tendency towards greater equity. Indeed, low-income sectors, with less human capital, and small and medium-sized enterprises have less capacity to react to continuous unpredictable changes: they run more slowly when there are booms and have less chance to convert to other activities at times of recession. Instability is a significant source of inequity, and it rewards speculation at the expense of productive activities.[5]

The dynamic effects of the output gap vary according to the specific macroeconomic conjuncture. As we will see, the recent Latin American history shows that both the downturn and the overheating impose several challenges to economic authorities. In all the cases, the rate of utilization is closely linked to macroeconomic variables: "right" prices of foreign currency (the exchange-rate) and of capital (interest rates), predictability of aggregate and effective demand, and its composition (tradables versus non-tradables), and of capital flows.

b) Latin America in the eighties: the downturn

Latin America had reached an output peak around 1980–81. With the debt crisis, the rate of utilization of the available productive resources went down markedly. Investment was discouraged by the resulting output gap, the recessionary climate and the domestic adjustment policies adopted (based mainly on the restriction of aggregate demand and weak switching policies). As a result, capital formation experienced a significant drop all over the region in the 1980s and installed capacity became notoriously underutilized (see figure II.1, panel B).

This confirms the importance of price inflexibility, factor immobility, incomplete markets and flaws in information during adjustment processes in the real economy. They explain why adjustment usually proceeds significantly below the production frontier.

---

[5] See, for example, Rodrik (2001a); World Bank (2003).

In an "ideal" adjustment process, in a perfectly flexible and well-informed economy, with *complete* and homogeneous factor markets, excess aggregate demand is eliminated without any drop in production (or, more exactly, in the rate of use of capacity). On the other hand, in an economy that was underutilizing capacity in the tradable sector, an adjustment with a balanced mix of production and expenditure switching policies can raise output. Finally, in the typical setting of an economy with price inflexibility and imperfect factor mobility, the implementation of neutral demand-reducing policies usually leads to a significant drop in production, because such policies reduce demand for both tradables and non-tradables, thus giving rise to unemployment in the latter sector.

In fact, in the real world, in adjustment processes intensive in demand reduction, there tends to be a drop in production which gives rise to a lower rate of utilization of installed capacity, and discourages capital formation. The addition of switching policies, which act over the composition of output and expenditure, can cushion the reduction of economic activity. These policies are inherently selective, but they may be rather global – such as the exchange rate – or they may be more selective. The East Asian countries provide examples of success through extremely selective policies, and also of notably effective adjustment processes (Amsden, 2001; Bradford, 1992; Kaplan and Rodrik, 2001; Reisen, 1994). A mix of expenditure-reducing policies and switching policies should tend to make possible an outcome closer to a full utilization of potential GDP (Ffrench-Davis and Marfán, 1988).

c) Latin America in 1990–2004: from boom to bust and recovery

The revival of capital inflows to the region at the beginning of the 1990s provided the finance needed to take fuller advantage of the productive capacity available in most LACs at the end of the eighties. Then, the binding external constraint (BEC) – determinant leader of that macroeconomic conjuncture – was eased or eliminated, which freed governments from the pressures of the recurrent debt negotiations that had been diverting attention from the task of solving more basic, structural problems. At the same time, however, the new capital surge raised the challenge of ensuring the sustainability of macroeconomic balances.

The renewed inflow of capital had positive Keynesian-type effects: it eliminated the BEC, making possible a higher use of productive capacity for the whole region, and thus leading to a recovery in output (see figure II.1, panels A and B), income and employment (as well as investment, as shown in chapter III).

The increased availability of external savings made it possible to finance the larger imports associated with an increase in aggregate demand and in the utilization of existing productive capacity during the first quinquennium. The expansionary effect on economic activity was particularly marked in countries such as Argentina, Peru and Venezuela, which initially had significant output gaps (see chapter VII).

The degree to which inflows are reflected in GDP growth is strongly determined by (i) the initial gap between actual GDP and the production frontier; (ii) the nature of the domestic economic policies implemented, especially the macroeconomic ones; (iii) the expectations of economic agents; (iv) political events; and (v) external factors such as behavior of the terms of trade.

The speed with which capital inflows eliminated external constraints and generated a surplus of foreign currency led to a trend towards exchange-rate appreciation, rapid reduction of trade surpluses and an increase in the current account deficit (ECLAC, 1998, chapter XI); domestic spending rose faster than production and national income, and from 1992 onwards a trade deficit was registered at current prices, the first one in the region since 1981. Initially, these trends reflected the return to "normal" levels of aggregate demand, imports and the real exchange-rate, all of which have had to over adjust under the BEC during the eighties. However, the continued abundance of inflows prolonged these trends in time and tended to overshoot.

Most LACs opted for permissive policies towards the heavy capital inflows.[6] This tended to generate unsustainable imbalances, since there was excessive exchange rate appreciation and external deficits grew fast. National savings were crowded-out by external savings, as reflected in the fact that the increase of total investment was less than that of external savings. Actually, if the period 1983–91 is compared with 1991–98, while external savings utilized (net capital inflows less accumulation of international reserves) increased by 2.4 percentage points of GDP, the investment ratio grew merely 0.8 percentage points. Furthermore, the stock of short-term and liquid external liabilities also rose sharply.

---

[6] See chapter VI, and Calvo, Leiderman and Reinhart (1993) regarding the origin of the increased supply of funds to Latin America. Three papers in Ffrench-Davis and Griffith-Jones (1995) present an analysis on the main supplying markets: the United States, Europe and Japan.

The excess of expenditure over domestic production or income was concentrated in the private sector. In fact, while the external deficit worsened (rise in the deficit on the current account, financed with external savings), the public sector of many countries in the region registered a marked improvement between the decade of the eighties and in the nineties until the arrival of the contagion of the Asian crisis. Consequently, it was the rest of the economy, that is the domestic private sector, whose surpluses went down or their deficits widened. Consequently, the worsening of deficits on the current account was caused by the increased net expenditures of the private sector in the 1991–98 period. This outcome was the combined result of the large supply of foreign financing and the permissive domestic macroeconomic policies, usually praised by financial markets.

In the two sub-periods of economic recovery between 1990 and early 1998, macroeconomic policy management faced lighter demands than when the economy is already at its production frontier. In fact, a passive policy can give positive net results in such a situation. The capital inflow increases the domestic spending capacity: directly, in dollarized economies; through the monetization of such inflows in economies with a "dollar standard"; or through exchange-rate appreciation. Aggregate demand for domestic and imported goods expands in a context of improved expectations, fuelled by the access to foreign funds. The supply of domestic goods and services can respond to the greater demand thanks to the available installed capacity, while the resulting increased imports are covered by capital inflows.

When reactivation is completed and the production frontier is reached, any additional aggregate demand will require fresh productive capacity to satisfy it, and hence additional investment to generate a higher capacity. Consequently, even in order to sustain the modest growth rates registered by Latin America in the first half of the 1990s, much higher investment ratios were required[7] than the actual ones.

The other noteworthy point is that when actual output is reaching the production frontier, more active policies are needed to regulate the expansion of aggregate demand. Moreover, with a closing recessive output gap, the role of policies to enhance productive development (and increase potential output) becomes crucial. In fact, it is essential to keep

---

[7] After the sharp GDP declines in Argentina and Mexico in 1995, the gap between utilization and capacity grew wider, so that in 1996–97 a significant increase in actual GDP became feasible, until the margin of underutilization were to become again exhausted.

the rate of expansion of demand in line with the growth of productive capacity (and also with sustainable external financing). Otherwise, if passive macroeconomic policies are adopted in situations of positive external shocks (such as lower international interest rates, improved terms of trade or increased availability of capital) or of a domestic nature (a boom in the construction sector or in the demand for durable goods or stocks and bonds), then the economy will be subject to inflationary pressures and/or a growing gap between expenditure and output; in all events, a future adjustment in the opposite direction will usually be built up.

Indeed, if capital inflows stimulate processes of recovery in economies with unemployment of productive factors, actual productivity rises because of an increase in the rate of utilization of potential GDP. Then agents and authorities (and also academics, see chapter III) may confuse the jump in actual productivity that is based on the utilization of previously idle labor and capital, with a structural increase in the sustainable speed of productivity improvements. From the point of view of "rational" consumers, they tend to assume that there is an increase in their permanent income. Consequently, the market response would tend to be an intertemporal upward adjustment in consumption, with the external gap covered with capital inflows, as long as the supply of foreign savings is available. That implies a crowding-out of domestic savings that is based on biased information. The intertemporal adjustment ends being destabilizing.

Thus, as the production frontier is being neared, there is a growing need for more active and efficient macroeconomic policies. Indeed, it was the situation in 1994 in a growing number of LACs, but few of them took timely steps to adapt their policies to the new conjuncture. What initially, in 1990–92, had been equilibrating macroeconomic adjustments (in the current account, exchange rate, and aggregate demand), had become sources of vulnerability in 1994. For different reasons, Argentina and Mexico were especially vulnerable. Consequently, it is not surprising the explosion of the Mexican crisis in 1994 and its contagion to Argentina in 1995.

The Mexican crisis and its contagious effects in 1994–95 reopened the output gap in the affected countries. This gap was key to allow, in a context of low investment, the high regional growth rates in 1996–97, stimulated by the fast return of foreign capital (see chapters VI and VII). Then, the international crises that hit the region since 1998 on caused generalized recessive effects, mirrored in a high labor and capital unemployment. In some cases, the rate of underutilization was comparable to that of the eighties. Consequently, the investment rate reached a depressed average level, while poverty had risen and income distribution had worsened, and GDP growth was slower than the rise of population in 1998–2003.

Only in 2004, pulled-up by a strengthened world economic activity, a significant drop of the output gap took place. While potential GDP was expanding in the order of 3%, actual GDP rose 5.8% in that year (see chapter VII on the origin of this recovery, that differs from that of the two previous episodes).

In brief, it is necessary to further improve the capacity to implement real macroeconomic policies in order to reconcile the proximity of the economy to the production frontier with sustainability and price stability.

3. Domestic policies and macroeconomics for development

Domestic macroeconomic policies face the challenge of achieving an environment of reduced macroeconomic volatility, sustainable fiscal and external accounts and price stability. This task is complex since national authorities have lost several degrees of freedom as a result of liberalizing reforms in the last decades. As a consequence, the transmission of externally generated cycles has been exacerbated, especially from international capital markets.

When passive economic policies are applied in a context of *incomplete* markets and sticky prices, positive shocks translate into an increase in income and, hence, in domestic expenditure. It is possible to identify at least three sources of external shocks, in front of which economic activity can respond positively, insofar as installed capacity is available. First, an increase in export prices. Once the production frontier has been reached, however, if the shock still persists it will cause demand pressures that give rise to higher domestic prices and/or an increase in the external deficit. As swings in external prices are largely transitory, however, if the economy accommodates to that abundance, the subsequent adjustments will be traumatic.

A second source of external shocks are changes in international interest rates. These fluctuations affect domestic rates to some extent and their effects are thus transmitted through relative prices to aggregate demand; they influence the volume of net capital inflows, affect national income – since a rise (fall) in external interest rates reduces (increases) the national income of a net debtor country – and they affect the availability of foreign currency and hence the respective market.

A third source of external shocks, which has been the main determinant of macroeconomic instability of LACs since the 1970s, are the sharp fluctuations in capital flows, which will be analyzed in chapters VI to VIII. In this respect, private capital flows other than FDI are particularly noteworthy because of their volatility. The heavy short-term and liquid capital inflows recorded by a large number of LACs has led to underscore, in the recovery stages of the two cycles experienced since 1990, the weaknesses that persist in the real economy: the extreme structural heterogeneity in the access to financing, education and innovation. This extreme heterogeneity is at the core of underdevelopment and inequitable distribution of income, productivity and opportunities. The vigorous recovery at work in 2004–05 should not lead, again, to disregarding the negative implications that structural heterogeneity has for growth and equity under financial volatility. A reform correcting that negative feature demands a significant change in meso and micro reforms and policies, far away from the neo-liberal approach.

Now, back to macroeconomics, systematic efforts are needed to ensure that the funds received can be absorbed efficiently, that they are associated with investment in productive activities, and that a suitable proportion of that investment goes to the production of tradables. All this calls for active monetary, foreign exchange and fiscal policies, strict prudential regulation and supervision of the financial system, and regulations governing capital movements, especially of short-term and liquid flows.

a) Monetary policy

Monetary policy has increasingly taken the form of inflation targeting schemes (that is, a single anchoring approach) in EEs.[8] This trend has been, generally, accompanied by the adoption of flexible exchange rate regimes and an open capital account. The new policy mix imposes significant challenges to economic authorities, since it presents some crucial limitations regarding their counter-cyclical capabilities.

---

[8] The conditions that usually define an inflation targeting scheme are: (i) adoption of the inflation target as the economy's only (or dominant) nominal anchor, (ii) operational independence in the conduct of monetary policy committed to attain the inflation target, (iii) technical capability to forecast inflation and react accordingly, and (iv) high levels of policy transparency and accountability (see for example, Corbo et al., 2002). In Latin America, countries with inflation targeting schemes are Brazil, Chile, Colombia, Mexico and Peru. Argentina and Uruguay are converging towards that system. In East Asia, the list of inflation targeteers includes Indonesia, Korea, Philippines and Thailand.

Inflation targeting schemes in small open economies (like those of most EEs, particularly small as compared to the huge size of international financial markets), present significant pro-cyclical features. Indeed, given the importance of capital flows on business cycles in EEs, the turning point of the cycle will be probably featured, in its upper part, by the emergence of strong expectations of depreciation and downward pressures on aggregate demand and output and, in its lower part, by strong expectations of exchange rate appreciation and a recovery of aggregate demand and production. Given the fact that in more open economies, the weight of the exchange rate in the general price index is greater, the expectations of exchange rate depreciation (appreciation) will also be associated with expectations of upward (downward) inflationary trends. Consequently, the incentives of a Central Bank with a single nominal target will be biased towards implementing a contractionary policy just when the economy begins to experience the downward part of the cycle, and toward applying an expansive monetary policy during a recovery led by capital inflows; that is an straight pro-cyclical approach. Pro-cyclicality implies, given the asymmetries around potential GDP, an actual average of GDP below the average potential GDP.

Thus, a first challenge in the implementation of the monetary policy regime should be the elimination of this pro-cyclical bias. There are a number of possible solutions to deal with this issue. For example, the use of a domestic price index instead of a general price index in the definition of the inflation target (Parrado and Velasco, 2002) or the consideration of a long run inflation target to filter the transitory effects of exchange rate fluctuations and their impact on general CPI (Ball, 1999). Also, it is possible the inclusion of targets on external deficits (Marfán, 2005; Medina and Valdés, 2002) in order to deter the transmission of volatility from capital flows to domestic output, or the implementation (or strengthening) of real targets like the level of employment or the consistency of actual GDP with its potential level.[9]

As a matter of fact, Chile – frequently highlighted as a successful inflation targeteer during the nineties (Mishkin and Schmidt-Hebbel, 2002) – applied a pragmatic formula to reduce inflation, which was quite far from being solely based on the inflationary goal. Indeed, in addition to a formal inflation target (which aimed at a moderated rather

---

[9] Other point refers to the weight of every variable in the policy reaction function of the Central Bank. In this sense, it is important to recall that in recent years we are living an era of low or moderate inflation in developed nations, in Asia and Latin America. Under low or moderate rates of inflation, additional efforts to reduce it may have minor benefits and increasing costs.

than an abrupt reduction), used an informal target in the current account deficit (around 3% of GDP), and an exchange rate band to avoid excessive appreciation, in combination with a monitoring of the aggregate demand behavior (Ffrench-Davis and Tapia, 2001). This comprehensive counter-cyclical policy was quite systematic in the first half of the 1990s, and loosed coherency only gradually, during the rest of the decade.

However, even if the pro-cyclical bias is eliminated by adopting a set of goals (multi-anchoring), the problem of an insufficient power in monetary policy may remain. Indeed, a redefinition of the targets of monetary policy will be insufficient to develop a counter-cyclical policy if the Central Bank is unable to powerfully affect domestic expenditure in the short and medium term.

During a boom, if monetary policy is managed to regulate aggregate demand by raising interest rates, then residents will try to finance their investment projects with external credits, and short-term foreign investors will be attracted by a higher interest rate differential (frequently widened by expectations of exchange rate appreciation). As analyzed, capital flows may have a great stimulating effect in economies under significant output gaps and liquidity constraints (see Ffrench-Davis and Tapia, 2004). In this context, high real interest rates use to live together with a troubled tradable sector (because of RER appreciation) and a boom in aggregate demand and in non-tradable output, financed with external savings that typically crowd-out domestic savings. The policy failure shows up when actual GDP approaches the production frontier. The experience of LACs in the nineties, under a strong capital surge, was paradigmatic in this sense (ECLAC, 1998; Uthoff and Titelman, 1998).

During a bust, in turn, the capacity of monetary policy to face shocks is even more restricted, especially if the country is already in *vulnerability zones* (see chapter VII). Textbook theory states that a fall in the domestic interest rate, given the international rate, would cause capital outflows that will depreciate the exchange rate. Depreciation would favor the recovery in tradables output, stimulating overall GDP. In practice, however, in the short run the negative effects of depreciation on overall consumption and balance sheets are usually stronger than the positive pulls on tradables. If, on the contrary, monetary policy is used to stop the capital flight, the outcome is even more troublesome. In this context, the interest rate can be effective on the aggregate demand control (aggravating a recession), and ineffective on the capital flows under strong expectations of depreciation and contagion of pessimism. For instance, in order to compensate an expected devaluation of say 10% during one week it is needed a short-term interest rate exceeding an annual equivalent of well over 500%.

In summary, the effectiveness of counter-cyclical monetary policy in a context of open capital account and flexible exchange rates is much more limited than what is predicted by the standard static textbook model. Therefore, the main policy implication of our analysis is that it is crucial to regulate capital flows as a way of making room simultaneously for complementary counter-cyclical exchange rate and monetary policies.

b) Exchange rate regime

The exchange-rate regime has become an increasingly influential variable in EEs, both on trade and finance. It is subject to two conflicting demands, which reflect the more limited degrees of freedom that authorities face in a world of reduced policy effectiveness (see ECLAC, 2002b). The first demand comes from trade: with the dismantling of traditional trade policies (tariff and non-tariff restrictions), the real exchange rate has become a key determinant of international competitiveness and a crucial variable for an efficient allocation of resources into tradables. It is noteworthy how the two extreme proposals (corner solutions) disregard this fact. The second is from the capital account. Volatility in international financial markets generate a demand for flexible macroeconomic variables to absorb, in the short run, the positive and negative shocks generated during the cycle. Given the reduced effectiveness of monetary policy, the exchange rate can play an essential role in helping to absorb shocks. This objective cannot be easily reconciled with the trade-related goals of exchange rate policy; particularly, of a growth strategy based on export expansion and diversification (see Ffrench-Davis and Ocampo, 2001).

Intermediate regimes, of managed exchange-rate flexibility – such as crawling pegs and bands, and dirty floating – attempt to reconcile these conflicting demands (see Williamson, 2000). They are crucial for achieving sustainable real macroeconomic equilibria.

Completely rigid exchange rate systems tend to amplify external shocks, because they put too unrealistic requirements on domestic flexibility, in particular on wage and price flexibility in the face of negative shocks. Currency boards certainly introduce built-in institutional arrangements that provide for fiscal and monetary discipline, but they radically reduce any room for stabilizing monetary, credit and fiscal policies, which are all necessary to prevent crises during mid-term capital surges and to facilitate recovery in a post-crisis environment. Convertibility (á la Argentina in 1991–2001 and Chile 1979–82), allows the domestic transmission of external shocks, generating strong swings in economic activity and asset prices, with the corresponding domestic financial vulnerability. There is an amplification effect when agents consider that an external shock that is strong enough can induce authorities to modify exchange rate policy; this is particularly so when the rate appears to be an outlier price, too appreciated (see Ffrench-Davis and Larraín, 2003).

Notwithstanding the pitfalls of the family of nominal pegs, there are cases in which it can work efficiently. The currency board in Argentina, assisted by the capital surge to LACs since the early 1990s, was quite effective in contributing to defeat hyperinflation, evidently the more harmful problem of that economy in 1991. The most severe mistake of the Argentinean authorities – encouraged by the subsequent good ratings and appraisals received from IFIs – was not to use the opportunity provided by the international environment, in 1992 or 1993 and again in 1996–97, to flexibilize the exchange rate when inflation and the budget already were evidently under control, capital inflows were vigorous and spreads to EEs, quite explicitly including Argentina, were falling. It was an opportunity to shift to an intermediate regime and regain the exchange rate as a macro-policy tool.

On the other hand, the volatility characteristic of freely floating exchange rate regimes is not a problem when market fluctuations are short-lived; in such case they are easily faced with derivatives (see Dodd, 2003). But fluctuations become a major concern when there are longer waves, a longer-lasting process, as has been typical of the access of EEs to capital markets in recent decades. In this case, persistent appreciation of that macro-price during capital surges tends to generate perverse effects on resource allocation of irreversible capital formation. Moreover, under freely floating regimes with open capital accounts, counter-cyclical monetary policy exacerbates pro-cyclical exchange rate fluctuations, with significant costs derived from an inefficient resource allocation and losses in income and output.

The ability of a flexible exchange rate regime to smooth out the effects of externally-induced boom-bust cycles, thus depends on the capacity to effectively manage a counter-cyclical monetary policy without enhancing pro-cyclical exchange rate patterns. This is only possible under intermediate exchange rate regimes-cum-capital account regulations. That was, clearly, the case of Chile in the first half of the 1990s (see Ffrench-Davis, 2002, chapter 10; Le Fort and Lehmann, 2003).

In many cases bands did not behave well during the Asian crisis. That was partially induced by the actual management of the crawling band.

The huge increase in capital inflows to EEs, that took place between 1990 and 1997, did put severe upward pressure on exchange rates. The frequent response, in terms of expanding the size of the band or appreciating it, induced a credibility loss.[10] Subsequently, bands already with a too appreciated rate – and domestic economic structures growingly accommodated to that relative price change – had trouble in adapting to the sharp shift in the market mood brought by the Asian crisis, when capital inflows suddenly stopped. These facts induced a further credibility loss.

The major benefit of managed flexibility, including bands, arises in times without severe shocks. In that case, bands induce more real exchange rate stability, keeping the ability to partially absorb the effects of moderate shocks. Consequently, the exchange rate fulfils more efficiently its allocative role between tradables and non-tradables.

Obviously, intermediate regimes may also generate costs and shortcomings (see Ocampo, 2003). First, intermediate regimes are subject to speculative pressures if they do not achieve credibility in markets; in critical conjunctures, particularly after the rate has clearly become an outlier price, the costs of defending the exchange rate from pressures are very high. Then, it may be advisable to move, *temporarily*, to full flexibility. Second, sterilized reserve accumulation during long booms may also become financially costly. Lastly, the capital account regulations needed to manage intermediate regimes efficiently reduce those costs, but are only partially effective. However, all things considered, intermediate regimes offer a sound alternative to costly outlier macro-prices derived frequently from corner solutions and untamed volatility.

A policy suitable for a given macroeconomic environment may not be so in another. In this sense, one crucial element to bear in mind when adopting a given policy is how costly it may be to switch to an alternative policy (Ffrench-Davis and Larraín, 2003). As shown above, regarding the Argentinean case, credible pegged systems may be useful under a critical hyperinflation and plentiful supply of external funding. Floating systems are useful in times of financial distress, when authorities have doubts concerning the level of the real rate, or the nature of the shock they face; flotation allows them not to put in jeopardy their

---

[10] That policy reaction was, most probably, encouraged by the strong belief in fashion that financial crises were gone for long (or ever?). Recall, for instance, the proposal by the IMF, with the pressures from the Treasury of the United States and Wall Street, to change its articles of agreement in order to force member countries to across-the-board capital account opening (see a robust criticism in Bhagwati, 2004, pp. 204–5).

reputation defending a wrong price. Finally, bands or managed flexibility contribute to stabilize the real exchange rate. Stability in the real exchange rate has a positive upgrading and stimulating effect on exports and on growth (see chapter V; and ECLAC, 1998, chapter IV). But bands suffer a weakness if a "big shock" appears and *authorities fail to have avoided vulnerability zones during the previous boom*. In that case, they open the way to speculation, inducing significant financial instability, which can be faced, more efficiently, moving temporarily to a more flexible rate.

Corner solutions do not have symmetric consequences. With a capital surge, each policy will deliver different combinations of the evolution of the current account, of asset prices and of the real exchange rate. With a peg, capital surges create a demand boom, pulling-up asset prices, probably with a crowding-out of domestic savings and a worsening of the external balance (see Frenkel, 2004). Under a floating regime, a nominal appreciation will tend to take place making the process of real appreciation deeper (and henceforth potentially more disruptive) than with the peg. Pegs tend to work better in the upward phase of the cycle, but after the inflection point the float does it better in terms of the necessary expenditure switching. But, in this type of cycle there is the possibility of multiple equilibria based on self fulfilling beliefs: expectations of more inflows (outflows) may further appreciate (depreciate) an already appreciated (depreciated) currency.

Large deviations from equilibrium of the real exchange rate are costly for the real economy. Central Banks should be concerned with both the level and the stability of this macro price. In this sense, despite the road of full flexibility taken by several LACs since the Asian crisis, managed flexibility, with or without bands, is still a policy to be considered by policy makers. They need to be reticent with across-the-board liberalization of the capital account if the need for real macroeconomic balances is really a priority. Indeed, the actual behavior of capital flows tends to be inconsistent with real macroeconomic stability, particularly in terms of the sustainability of the exchange rate and economic activity. In this sense, authorities need to adopt flexible policy packages rather than single rigid policy tools (Ffrench-Davis and Larraín, 2003).

c) Fiscal policy

Fiscal policy should look at macroeconomic instability in two senses. On the one hand, since public revenues and expenditures are sensitive to business cycles, it is crucial to ensure a path of public expenditure consistent with the transitory needs that surge during the downturn (social subsidies) and with stable fulfillment of the permanent goals of the government (regular budget, including public investment). On the other hand, fiscal policy has also a macroeconomic role, in terms of the sustainability of public accounts and the regulation of aggregate demand. Fiscal policy has been at the core of the debate on adjustment programs in EEs. Both in East Asia and Latin America the more conventional recipes recommended achieving current or annual fiscal balances, under recessionary conjunctures that had depressed tax proceeds. That is a typically pro-cyclical behavior. In recession, usually fiscal policy has been directed towards keeping under control financial solvency, while during booms expenditure has frequently been expanded (Martner and Tromben, 2004). This pro-cyclical stance tends to restrict the room for social programs and the scope of public investment during recessive periods and, in doing so, strengthens the negative effects of volatility on living standards and future economic growth, respectively. In addition, a pro-cyclical fiscal policy has exacerbated the boom and deepened the bust in the private sector, increasing macroeconomic instability and complicating the functioning of monetary and exchange rate policies.

Development of counter-cyclical fiscal mechanisms in LDCs is especially relevant for three reasons. First, because domestic markets in developing countries tend to be much more volatile than in developed countries. This implies that the effect of the business cycle on the public accounts is stronger. Second, because in developing economies the size of automatic stabilizers tends to be smaller than in developed economies. Third, on the external side, the capacity to manage deficits is more limited, given the pro-cyclical character of international capital markets.

How to deal with these problems? As part of a counter-cyclical policy package, the concept of *structural fiscal balance* is the most outstanding fiscal component. There are different varieties, but the essential component is the measurement of the balance across the business cycle, estimating at each point of time what would be the public expenditure and income in a framework of sustainable full employment of human and physical capital. If the terms of trade fluctuations are relevant for fiscal proceeds – via profits of public or private exporters – the purchasing power of potential GDP should be estimated at the trend terms of trade. Given a tax burden, that trend must guide the evolution of public expenditure.

Developing countries typically concentrate their international trade on a few commodity exports, which are subject to highly volatile market prices. Especially, when a significant export – like copper in Chile, and oil in Colombia, Mexico or Venezuela – is public property, the establishment of a stabilization fund can contribute to both fiscal and overall macroeconomic sustainability. Also the coffee fund in Colombia has played, for long, a significant stabilizing macroeconomic role; since coffee is privately owned, the fund contributes directly to stabilize the current account and private domestic expenditure. Above the trend or "normal" public proceeds from that source are saved in these funds, so to finance public expenditure when proceeds are below "normal". It is highly recommended to initiate it in a scenario of high prices in comparison to trend prices, so that the fund could actually finance subsequent negative price scenarios.

All the mentioned measures help to develop a cyclically-neutral fiscal policy, where current expenditure is stabilized by linking it to its structural level. In persistent recessive situations, however, governments may decide to carry out expansive shocks of (transitory) expenditure increases and/or tax reductions, thus running contemporaneous structural deficits, in order to stimulate domestic demand.[11] Moving further, flexible tax rates have been proposed as an additional counter-cyclical device. For instance, it has been proposed to increase the VAT rate during booms and to compensate it with rate cuts during slack periods (Budnevich, 2003).

The fiscal instruments chosen to implement counter-cyclical policies must be pragmatically chosen (see Stiglitz, 2005). During booms, for example, a reduction in public expenditure will be probably insufficient to compensate an excess of expenditure of the private sector led by capital inflows. An increase in taxes, instead, can affect directly the agents with a higher propensity to spend. During an economic downturn, a tax relief may be ineffective under a depressed macroeconomic environment and a private sector reluctant to consume and invest. Public expenditures in non-tradables can, in this latter case, be a more effective instrument.

Fiscal policy ought to be part of the flexible policy package. Given that EEs are especially vulnerable to global economic downturns, over reliance on monetary policy may bring poorer macro results, as compared to a more balanced framework of counter-cyclical fiscal, exchange rate, and monetary policy, as well as prudential regulation of capital flows. The use of counter-cyclical fiscal policy requires as a precondition

---

[11] The case of Korea in 1998, when the fiscal deficit reached 4.2% of GDP, is useful to illustrate this approach. When the economy recovered, the fiscal balance returned to a surplus (Mahani et al., 2005).

to be on a path of solvent and sustainable fiscal accounts. Additionally, a more active role of counter-cyclical fiscal policy may emerge when transmission channels of monetary policy to the output gap are weak or show significant lags. Moreover, to spread the adjustment burden between fiscal, foreign exchange and monetary policies, may bring better macroeconomic results, with each macro-price (interest and exchange rates) closer to sustainable equilibria and an actual GDP close to its potential level.

d) Regulation of capital flows

Capital account regulations may perform as a prudential macroeconomic tool, working at the direct source of boom-bust cycles: that is, unstable capital flows. If effective, they provide room for action during periods of financial euphoria, through the adoption of a contractionary monetary policy and reduced appreciation pressures. If effective, they will also reduce or eliminate the usual quasi-fiscal costs of sterilized foreign exchange accumulation. What is extremely relevant, is that, in the other corner of the cycle, of binding external constraints, they may provide space for expansionary monetary and fiscal policies.[12]

Overall innovative experiences in the 1990s of across-the board price restrictions on liquid and short-term financial inflows, indicate that they can provide useful instruments, both in terms of improving debt profiles and facilitating the adoption of counter-cyclical macroeconomic policies. They are directed to provide a rather more stable macroeconomic environment during the boom and minimizing the costly adjustment during downturns from overheated disequilibria. They provide a more market-friendly environment for (i) irreversible investment decisions; (ii) avoiding significant output gaps between actual and potential GDP; (iii) avoiding outlier macro-prices (exchange and interest rates), and (iv) discourages outlier macro-ratios (deficit on current account/GDP; price/earnings ratios of equity stocks; net short-term and liquid external liabilities/international reserves).

The discussion on capital controls intensified with the well-known action of Malaysia, in 1998, imposing tough non-price regulations on outflows. Data supports the view that they were effective in contributing

---

[12] Ocampo (2003) emphasizes that capital account regulations also serve as a liability policy. The market rewards sound external debt structures, because, during times of uncertainty, the market responds to *gross* financing requirements, which means that the rollover of short-term liabilities is not financially neutral. This indicates that economic policy management during booms should seek to improve maturity structures, of both private and public sector liabilities.

to the sharp GDP recovery in 1999 (Kaplan and Rodrik, 2001). They were determinant in making feasible the active fiscal and monetary policies implemented by Malaysia.

But it is not enough to learn to get away from a crisis after suffering it. More important for significantly reducing the negative effects is to avoid the generation of external crises.[13] That is the role of regulations on inflows so to deter macro policies and ratios from penetrating into vulnerability zones. The positive "market-based" experience of Chile in the first half of the 1990s, *pari passu* with the gestation of the Mexican crisis, is presented in chapter VII (see also Agosin and Ffrench-Davis, 2001). On the other hand, traditional exchange controls, as in China and India (e.g., prohibitions on short-term financial borrowing) have worked quite efficiently for the objective of macroeconomic policy to significantly reduce the domestic macroeconomic sensitivity to international financial volatility.

e) Regulation and supervision of financial institutions

Finally, prudential regulation and supervision (PRS) that usually is designed under microeconomic concerns, also have macroeconomic implications. Consequently, PRS should take into account not only microeconomic risks, but also the macroeconomic risks associated to boom-bust cycles (Griffith-Jones, 2001; Ocampo, 2003). In particular, counter-cyclical devices should be introduced into prudential regulation and supervision. Aside the standard regulations on currency and maturity mismatches, they should involve a mix of: (i) forward-looking provisions for latent risks, on the basis of the credit risks that are expected throughout the full business cycle; (ii) more discretional counter-cyclical prudential provisions decreed by the authority on the basis of objective criteria (e.g., the rate of growth of credit as compared to GDP); (iii) counter-cyclical regulation on the prices used for assets given in guarantee, and (iv) capital adequacy requirements focused on long-term solvency criteria rather than on cyclical performance.

4. Concluding remarks

EEs are living a sharp paradox, with a consensus on the importance of macroeconomic balances, and a common situation in which the norm

---

[13] In 1997, the then Minister of Finance of Canada (today Prime Minister), Paul Martin, declared that "we have devoted almost all our time to make globalization happen and not to make it work right"; "we are spending energy in solving crises rather than avoiding them" (Martin, 1997).

have been costly disequilibria for large segments of the real economy, that is, of labor and physical capital. The sharp GDP recovery of 5.8% in 2004 is undoubtedly a positive fact, but took place after six years of a large disequilibria: the significant output gap in 1998–2003. This fact represents a costly failure of domestic macroeconomic policies by not keeping the economy on the production frontier. That failure was compounded by the pro-cyclical behavior of international trade and finance. It reveals the need of a radical reform in the way of conducting macroeconomic policies.

In order to deal with these inefficiencies, we need a *macroeconomics for sustainable growth* or *real macroeconomics*, focused not only on the stabilization of prices and on the control of fiscal deficits (as stated by the mainstream approach) but also on external balances (key in open economies) and real variables, which affect the nexus between present and future. The main real balance is the use of the productive capacity (i.e. the employment of productive factors, capital and labor, at their potential level), since it is crucial in the evolution of actual income, social equity, structural or "full employment" tax proceeds, capital formation and future growth.

The gap between the productive frontier and its rate of use implies a gross macroeconomic inefficiency, reflected in underutilized installed capacity in firms, unemployment of the labor force and reduced actual total factor productivity. A notorious effect of these recessive situations, usually, has been a subsequent sharp reduction in investment ratios, depreciation of labor skills and a rise in social inequality.

Real macroeconomic balances – including an aggregate demand consistent with productive capacity, sustainable (non-outlier) exchange rates and interest rates, fiscal responsibility and moderate inflation – are essential for growth and equity. Given the pro-cyclicality of financial flows, achieving those macroeconomic balances has as one requisite the comprehensive regulation of capital flows. The positive outcome is a macroeconomics for development. Naturally, when facing the need of regulating volatile financial globalization, developing nations must benefit from the availability of several alternatives, and choose a flexible set of policies, strongly counter-cyclical, that fit well with their economic structures, the degree of development of this market, and the democratic objectives of their respective society.

One notably relevant impact of real macroeconomic balances is on capital formation and its actual productivity. That is the issue tackled in the next chapter.

III

Growth, Productive Investment and the Macroeconomic Environment*

Introduction

One outstanding feature of Latin American economies in recent years has been the low rate of capital formation. In addition, the rate of utilization of the available productive capacity has been low and unstable, carrying with it a drop in *ex post* actual average productivity. These factors, which in fact bolster each other, account for the noticeable contrast between the slack economic growth since the 1980s and the dynamism exhibited by Latin American countries (LACs) in the three previous decades.

Between 1950 and 1980, Latin America achieved significant economic growth, with a 5.5% annual average rise in GDP. In spite of much evident inefficiency, high average growth was associated to sustained rising investment ratios and a relatively high utilization of installed capacity. This situation underwent a sudden reversal in the early 1980s; throughout the decade there was a sharp decline in public and private capital formation ratios. This was associated with the long recessive adjustment experienced by the region during the 1980s, under a binding external constraint (BEC), due both to the conditions prevailing in the world economy and to the specific domestic policies adopted. Most LACs suffered in the early 1980s severe financial shocks, which implied highly negative net transfers abroad coupled with a deterioration in the terms of trade (a trade shock). Generally, strong domestic demand-reducing policies and rather weak switching policies, were implemented in response to the external shocks, thus strengthening the natural recessive

* Sections 1 and 3 are partly based on "Capital formation and the macroeconomic framework: a neostructuralist approach," published in Sunkel (1993).

bias of the adjustment process associated to negative shocks. In the nineties investment rates experienced a minor recovery in the two cycles: 1990–94 and 1995–98, but with falls in 1995 and in 1999–2003; ups and downs were highly responsive to the volatile macroeconomic environment in the region, led by swings in financial flows.

This chapter analyzes the relationship between economic growth, productive investment, and the role of reforms and macroeconomic and microeconomic policies carried out in Latin America during the last quarter century. It focuses mainly on the analysis of the variables determining capital formation and capacity utilization. Both factors and their interrelations play a pivotal role in economic growth, owing to the direct impact of capital formation as well to the fact that it constitutes a channel for the incorporation of technological innovations and improved systemic productivity. It is stressed that the rate of use of potential GDP has a strong influence on capital formation ratios through four effects: (i) on actual productivity (an output gap implies a gap between actual and existing potential productivity); (ii) on actual profits and own financing sources; (iii) on access to capital markets; (iv) on the desirability of investment (if actual capacity is underutilized and expected to continue so for a while, it makes no sense for the prospective investor to expand capacity in more of the same, and investment in new activities is also discouraged by a depressed environment).

Section 1 summarizes the more relevant historical features concerning capital formation in Latin America, since the second half of the twentieth century. Section 2 reviews the economic performance of LACs after the liberalizing reforms associated with the "Washington Consensus," identifying the channels through which reforms affected potential growth. Section 3 focuses on the conditions required generating a "friendly" macroeconomic environment for capital formation; it includes a discussion on the economic reforms and their impact on prices that have macroeconomic implications (the so-called *macro prices*), such as the exchange rate and interest rates. Section 4 concludes.

1. Investment and growth in a historical perspective

a) The State-led growth model, 1950–80

Between 1950 and 1980 the economic growth of Latin America reached an average rate of 5.5% per annum (Ffrench-Davis, Muñoz and Palma, 1998). This rate exceeded the prevailing trend in other developing regions (with the exception of East Asia) and was well above the average for the industrialized nations (4.2%). This growth was associated with moderately higher investment ratios,[1] increased capacity utilization rates, and the expansion of sectors intensive in technological upgrading.

In the early 1950s Latin America faced bottlenecks linked to the shortage of external financing, as well as to the limited access to export markets and the supply of imported goods. Access to international capital and goods markets improved over the following two decades. The leading productive sector was that of manufacturing, which underwent a rapid growth that reached 7% annually in the 1960s, coupled with a significant incorporation of new technology. In the 1960s LACs enjoyed the greatest domestic and external stability of the post-war period, with comparatively minor crises in the balance of payments, and rising global productivity.

Nonetheless, as easy import substitution gradually became exhausted, it generated growing difficulties, involving increasingly limited investment opportunities for the domestic market and underutilization of the economies of scale. Producing for isolated domestic markets prevented an increasing number of manufacturing activities taking full advantage of economies of scale. In response to this, the region started to foster (though too mildly) its manufactured exports. Countries such as Brazil, Colombia and Chile implemented crawling-peg exchange rate policies (Williamson, 1981), and established other incentives to exports (including tariff exemptions for imported inputs), which contributed to its diversified expansion (Ffrench-Davis, Muñoz and Palma, 1998). Notwithstanding real exchange rate revaluations during the 1970s, Latin America achieved a significant 6% annual increase in the volume of exports during that decade.[2]

In addition, some countries (such as Brazil and Chile) put into effect financial reforms, several of which involved establishing price-indexing mechanisms to protect savings from inflation and prevent negative real interest rates. At the same time, the expansion of long-term loans by the World Bank and the newly created Inter-American Development Bank (IDB) contributed to the financing of public investment.

---

[1] The investment rate or ratio corresponds to the share of gross fixed capital formation (including machinery and equipment, and residential and non-residential construction) in GDP. In this chapter it is measured at 1995 constant prices. In order to estimate the net increase to the stock of capital, in economies like the LACs, about 7 to 11% of GDP must be deducted from the gross figure.

[2] A common mistake, that leads to the opposite assertion, is to look at figures for the entire region, including Venezuela. That shows an average annual growth of the quantum of exports of 2%. If Venezuela is excluded, the figure jumps to 6%. What happened is that Venezuela, a member of OPEC, reduced oil output sharply but reaped a significant increase in export proceeds (see ECLAC, 1998, table III.2).

Since the mid-1960s the capital formation ratio rose steadily, and accelerated further during the 1970s. This rise was associated with the fact that LACs had been operating for several years close to the production frontier as well as to changes in external funding opportunities, and the manner in which the countries in the region reacted to these options in the 1970s (Ffrench-Davis, 1983).

During the second half of the decade, most countries borrowed heavily in a supply-led process. The result was that most LACs, between the mid-1970s and early 1980s, accommodated to a large net transfer of funds from abroad. The foreign funding fostered a revaluation of real exchange rates. In parallel, some import liberalization was implemented in order to encourage the adjustment of domestic economies to the growing availability of foreign funds. Both factors induced the growing external deficit, which averaged 6% of GDP in 1981. The process was particularly intense in Argentina, Chile, Mexico and Venezuela; the two latter, oil-exporting countries, accommodated their economies both to the increase in foreign loans and to its remarkable expansion in export proceeds.

Investment ratios rose significantly during the period of increasing indebtedness, which suggests that external resources tended to complement national savings and contributed to the development of productive capacity of the region. Then, a significant share of inflows were tied to investment projects: IDB and World Bank development loans for public investment, official bilateral loans from developed economies for imports of capital goods, greenfield FDI. The common criticism that the first two were "tied" was compensated by the fact that they fulfilled the standard assumption that capital flows contribute to increasing investment.[3] With respect to the bulky bank loans, the composition of their use depended, to a large extent, on the domestic policies adopted by each country, as summarized below.

During 1970–82, gross fixed capital formation exceeded by 4 points the average ratio coefficient achieved in 1950–69 (table III.1). Nonetheless, the response of economic growth to the increase in the capital stock was proportionately lower. This was due to the fact that the large external funds promoted capital-intensive investment with long-term maturity periods, particularly in oil-producing countries. In some countries it also involved less rigorous (or a lack of) investment

---

[3] Recall that average annual growth was 5.5% in the 1970s, instead of 2.6% (the rate achieved in 1990–2004). It suggests that if policies were wrong, they were less wrong than since the 1990s.

Table III.1   Latin America (19): Fixed capital formation, 1950–2004 (as a share of GDP, scaled to prices of 1995)

	1950–69	1970–82	1983–91	1992–98	1999–2004
Argentina	18.2	22.5	15.6	19.0	15.6
Brazil	26.7	30.5	22.2	20.1	19.0
Chile	18.4	14.6	15.7	23.9	22.4
Colombia	22.0	19.7	18.9	20.9	14.4
Mexico	17.2	22.3	17.6	20.0	21.9
Peru	19.8	21.9	17.2	21.8	18.8
Uruguay	15.3	16.4	11.0	14.0	11.2
Venezuela	22.0	28.0	19.2	18.0	13.7
Latin America (19)	**21.5**	**25.8**	**19.2**	**20.0**	**19.0**

Source: ECLAC. Preliminary figure for 2004.

project evaluations, a trend spurred by the permissiveness of bank loans and the prevalence, during several years, of low or negative real interest rates in international markets (see Devlin and Ffrench-Davis, 1995). Consequently, there was a progressive erosion of the strategy of import substitution industrialization.

There were significant differences in performance between countries. For example, countries that liberalized across-the-board capital inflows, domestic financial markets and imports, in parallel, tended to show a lower investment ratio and reduced domestic savings. That is to say, external funds were directed at consumption, as in the case of Chile, and to capital flight, as in Argentina; in both cases, external savings crowded-out domestic savings. On the other hand, a better performance was obtained by countries, such as Brazil and Colombia, that implemented selective and moderate reforms in their trade and financial policies in the 1960s and 1970s, and encouraged the use of external debt to expand public and private investment (Ffrench-Davis, 1983; Wionczek, 1985; Griffith-Jones, 1988). Thus, it is clear that the greater capital formation in those countries was not a spontaneous phenomenon but, rather, a deliberate one. The negative experience in the 1990s reinforces this interpretation.

High effective demand and buoyant international commodities markets were macroeconomic factors that completed a virtuous circle for actual GDP growth. In fact, many LACs were able to sustain significant economic growth until the early 1980s. However, a growing current account deficit was incubated and external debt accumulated, while the abundance of funds led some countries to postpone necessary domestic reforms.

b) The debt crisis

In the 1980s Latin America faced a deep crisis arising from the large debt accumulated in the 1970s and a deterioration in the international capital and goods markets in which it operated. The abrupt reduction of bank loans, together with a deterioration in the terms of trade and a huge increase in international interest rates (for instance, the LIBOR rose from 2.5% in 1979 to 22% in 1981 in real terms), brought about an acute foreign exchange shortage, causing a severe recession in the domestic economies of the region. At the same time, the adjustment policies implemented, based primarily on strong demand-reducing and weak switching policies (Ffrench-Davis and Marfán, 1988), reinforced the output-reducing effect of shocks and discouraged investment. The setback in the region's output meant an underutilization of installed capacity. Investment underwent an even larger downturn as a result of uncertainty, the recessive domestic environment and the drying-up of external financing (see Devlin and Ffrench-Davis, 1995).

As analyzed in chapter II, in an economy with inflexible prices and *incomplete* and heterogeneous factor markets, "neutral" demand-reducing policies usually provoke a significant drop in actual production. This gives rise to a lower utilization rate of installed capacity, and subsequently a decrease in the capital formation ratio. In fact, per capita fixed capital formation declined by one-fourth between 1970–82 and 1983–91, with a resulting negative effect on the growth of productive capacity and employment generation.

During the 1980s, policy objectives were focused in dealing with the BEC (Fanelli and Frenkel, 1994). Achieving trade surpluses in order to serve debt became a priority, while concern for capital formation and the regulation of economic activity levels so as to maintain it close to the production frontier were neglected or turned non-feasible. This was partly the cause of the over 6 percentage points drop in capital formation and large capacity underutilization during the decade.

c) Ups and downs since the nineties

During the 1990s, renewed capital inflows, rather than contributing to increase productive capacity, helped most LACs mainly to recover from the deep recession that still prevailed in the late 1980s (see chapter II). During the first half of the nineties, investment recovered gradually; however, on average it grew much less than did capital inflows. In part, this was explained by the fact that most of the flows corresponded to short-term bond finance, secondary stock market trading and acquisition of privatized firms. Only about one-fourth of net flows were in the form of FDI and primary American Depository Receipts (ADRs) (ECLAC, 1998). Thus, most of the external flows were not directly linked with the domestic investment process, and rather financed increased private consumption, crowding-out domestic savings.

The relaxation of the BEC, brought about by renewed inflows in the early 1990s, allowed an increase in aggregate demand. Given improved expectations, this increase expressed itself in a recovery of economic activity. The then prevailing excessive installed capacity implied that domestic supply was able to respond to the enlarged demand for non tradables, while that for tradables now could be covered by increased imports financed with capital inflows.

Thanks to a higher rate of utilization of installed capacity, production increased beyond the expansion of output capacity, by about US$ 100 billion in 1994 in comparison with 1990 (at 1995 prices). That is, close to 40% of the 4.1% annual GDP growth in 1991–94 corresponded to a larger use of already installed capacity.

The story of recovery led by capital inflows was repeated after the Tequila crisis, especially in Argentina, Mexico and Uruguay (representing 37% of regional output), the countries that suffered more intensely the economic downturn in 1995. In 1997, the average growth in the region was 5.2%, with half of the countries growing above that rate. The investment ratio gradually recovered, but once again reached only a modest level, consistent with an annual expansion of potential output of just around 2.5 to 3%.

In brief, the increased availability of external financing was clearly beneficial during 1990–94 and 1996–97, inasmuch as it removed the BEC that was partly responsible for the low levels of investment and the severe economic recession during the 1980s. However, renewed access to external capital was not connected with a vigorous expansion of capital formation and productive capacity. In addition, it also posed challenges in regard to the sustainability of macroeconomic equilibria. Indeed, capital inflows had an adverse effect on the evolution of real exchange rates, contributed to domestic credit booms, and led to the accumulation of external liabilities (a large share of which had short-term maturities); thus, it made the economy more vulnerable to future negative external shocks, as witnessed by the Mexican crisis in late 1994, the Asian crisis in 1998, the Brazilian critical devaluation in 1999, the Argentinean crisis in 2001–02, and the recessive situation in most LACs in 1998–2003 (see chapter VII).

In 1998–2003, the region faced a new period of foreign financing shortage. The resulting balance of payments crises depressed aggregate demand and output (see chapters II and VII). The average annual GDP growth was only 1.2% (equivalent to an annual fall of 0.4% of per capita output). Since potential output was growing around 2%, the recessive output gap appeared again. The underutilization of productive capacity was determinant of a depressed investment ratio in 1998–2003. In 2004, most LACs showed a sharp recovery in economic activity, stimulated by an improvement in trade volume and prices. Regional GDP and capital formation grew 5.8 and 11%, respectively.

d) The role of FDI

Foreign direct investment (FDI) that comes to create new economic activities implies, usually, a one-to-one relation between inflows and capital formation. In that, tends to be quite different from short-term and liquid financial inflows (see chapter VI; and Ffrench-Davis and Reisen, 1998). There are several relevant empirical issues related to FDI; we have chosen two for a brief discussion here. One point is that, normally, FDI represents a minor part of capital formation in the world (about one tenth), as well as in Latin America or in Asia. Even in the most successful stage of development in Chile, in 1990–98, with record investment ratios, only 18% of gross fix investment corresponded to greenfield FDI.[4] FDI has, frequently, a high participation in exportable and technology-intensive sectors, where it can play a crucially positive role, but not in total capital formation. The second point is that the share of FDI in total flows increased considerably in the second half of the 1990s, especially following the contagion from the Asian crisis (see chapter VII). However, instead of being channeled into the direct creation of productive capacity, a high percentage of FDI flows were used to purchase existing assets. Hence, a paradoxical situation emerged, where very low rates of capital formation coincided with record high levels of FDI inflows.

Table III.2 shows the levels of FDI receipts of countries of the region. In 1998–2003, the average annual inflows of FDI more than doubled as compared with 1990–1997. However, the share of mergers and acquisitions (M&A) also grew considerably: from 41% to 52%. This high share of M&A not only implied a weaker link of FDI with gross capital formation, but also meant that inflows frequently turned into outflows by the residents who had sold off their assets. Nevertheless, it must be stressed

---

[4] Based on figures from the Central Bank of Chile and UNCTAD.

Table III.2 Latin America: FDI inflows and M&A, 1990–2003 (annual averages, US$ millions and percentages)

	1990–97		1998–2003	
	Gross inflows (US$ millions)	M&A (% of inflows)	Gross inflows (US$ millions)	M&A (% of inflows)
Argentina	4,607	56.9	7,521	97.9
Bolivia	278	91.2	815	10.4
Brazil	5,223	52.4	23,234	57.3
Chile	2,385	40.1	4,553	71.7
Colombia	1,717	48.5	2,189	35.9
Costa Rica	285	7.5	557	10.4
Ecuador	400	8.1	1,066	12.4
Mexico	8,139	26.3	15,738	35.1
Paraguay	119	3.0	120	19.8
Peru	1,522	49.6	1,512	26.4
Uruguay	95	8.3	238	11.6
Venezuela	1,694	42.3	3,262	31.4
Others (7)	823	15.9	2,593	38.8
Latin America (19)	27,286	41.1	63,398	52.1

Source: Based on UNCTAD figures.
FDI: foreign direct investment; M&A: cross-border mergers and acquisitions.

that the region's net greenfield FDI balance was positive during the period following the Asian crisis and served to offset the net outflows of financial capital.

2. Economic growth in Latin America in the age of the Washington Consensus

Economic growth in Latin America in the last few decades has been sluggish in every respect. Indeed, in 2004 per capita GDP in the region was similar to that in 1980. Viewed from a historical perspective, this period is the worst since the early part of the nineteenth century, which is associated with the independence processes (Maddison, 2001; Ocampo, 2004). If compared with the world performance, during the recent quarter of a century, it is seen that average per capita growth in the world was 1% per year, while in the United States was 2.2%, which reveals the huge divergence in the performance of Latin America in comparison with other EEs and developed economies in the same period.

Clearly, the debt crisis of the 1980s was a determining factor in the region's poor economic performance. It had a markedly negative impact: witness the average annual 0.7% decline in per capita GDP in 1981–89. The second part of the period, 1990–2004, is associated with the intensive economic reforms carried out within the framework of the Washington Consensus. The economies in the region moved toward a freer market situation in various areas, notably through trade liberalization (see chapters IV and V), opening up of capital markets (see chapters VI to VIII), privatization of public enterprises and the adoption of fiscal reforms (see Morley, Machado and Pettinato, 1999; Stallings and Peres, 2000). Although the growth outcome was much better than in the 1980s – the per capita average growth was 0.9% – they were still unsatisfactory as growth was still lower than world growth (1.2%), and growth in the developed world (United States: 1.7%), and was far below the 2.6% per year recorded by LACS in the period 1950–1980.

a)   Why has Latin American growth been so sluggish?

Why has growth been so disappointing, as John Williamson (2003b) puts it? This is a controversial point in regional discussions on economic policies. From the outset, some authors deny that Latin American growth has been disappointing (Easterly et al., 1997; Loayza et al., 2004). According to this interpretation, it was not reasonable to expect Latin American growth to be as high as in East Asia, the world's leading performance, rather than the world average, as the basis for comparison. However, the fact is that Latin American growth was not only much lower than that of the Asian countries; indeed, as shown above, it was below the world average.

Other fans of the Washington Consensus argue that reforms were too mild and/or were missing the second generation of reforms (such as legal and educational). With respect to the intensity of reforms, it is evident that the main ones had been notably intensive: import liberalization, liberalization of domestic capital markets and of capital accounts, privatization, and no money printing by Central Banks for the Treasuries. Actually IDB, World Bank and IMF were enthusiastic by 1997 of GDP growth (see for example, World Bank, 1997).

With respect to the second generation of reforms, there is no doubt that they are quite relevant. However, education is a valuable investment in the long-term future, with negligible impact on today's potential GDP. Legal reforms are also most relevant; for instance, for civilized, creative solutions of controversies, transparency of property rights, and expeditious creation of new productive activities. But we have shown that lack of growth is strongly associated to the macroeconomic policies, and trade and financial reforms implemented. There is need to *reform those reforms.*

The evident fact is that the reforms made, designed and praised by orthodoxy, have failed in bringing economic growth. The only period with which the 1990–2004 compares favorably in terms of regional growth is the 1980s. Given that the major policy change between the two periods is associated with the economic reforms introduced under the Washington Consensus, the contrast between the mediocre 1990s and the lost decade has been touted as proof of the positive effects of the economic reforms. According to Loayza et al. (2004) and Easterly et al. (1997), the effects of economic reforms on GDP growth have not been "disappointing" but significantly positive, raising the per capita growth rate in the region by close to 2 percentage points per year (actually a large figure if it were right). This, they assert, was reflected in an increase in the overall productivity of the economy.[5]

The foregoing assertion is based on two assumptions. First, that growth in the region was not greater because of external shocks. However, clearly, regional performance cannot be attributed to external trends alone. Whereas world growth was lower in recent decades, Latin America enjoyed favorable conditions during the 1990s: availability of external financing and significant growth in world trade (which increased by 5.5% in 1990–2004). Although there were disruptions due to external shocks, their impact on the economies of Latin America had an endogenous recessive component. In contrast, in 1990–97, Chile was able to achieve growth rates comparable to those of the Asian countries, by making the most of favorable conditions and applying comprehensive selective policies reducing its external vulnerability (see chapter IX). The second assumption is that GDP growth in Latin America cannot be explained by the accumulation of productive factors, but rather is determined by increases in total factor productivity (TFP); that is, increases in output would not be primarily explained by accumulation of physical capital, labor and human capital. They conclude that the TFP growth that they estimate is linked to the positive effects of the economic

---

[5] If econometric works find that economic reform and stabilization policies are responsible of a 2% additional annual growth in Latin America, while the region grows 1% per year, then other factors must be lowering economic dynamism. Easterly (2001), highlights this puzzle and states that possible candidates are a worsening in international conditions, miss-specification in regressions – that include non-stationary variables as regressors to explain a stationary variable (rate of growth) –, and the skill-biased technical change. None of those explanations take into account the way in which economic reforms were carried out and the associated economic effects: too much *market fundamentalism*, too simplistic technically.

reforms.[6] In what follows, this last assumption will be shown to be wrong.

b) Economic growth in Latin America: accumulation of factors or increases in productivity?

Several studies have found TFP explaining more than 50% of economic growth in Latin America. On this basis some authors assert that the accumulation of productive factors is unable to satisfactorily explain the different patterns of growth among countries; therefore, to them, "something else" – once again the TFP – should be the one driving economic performance.[7]

In recent years, several empirical works have highlighted that movements in TFP have been associated not only with economic reforms, but also with a number of additional determinants: education and human capital, institutional development, income distribution, etc. (see Barro and Sala-i-Martin, 2004). Most of those factors are positively linked to economic growth but it is not easy to quantify their effect or the channel through which they work. Therefore any interpretation of these results and their policy implications should be carried out carefully. First, all these works are not reciprocally consistent: if all of them were right, growth rates would be significantly higher. Second, most of them do not disaggregate the effect of changes in the rate of utilization of productive capacity.

Given the residual nature of TFP,[8] any error in the measurement of the rate of use and/or quality of factors, or of the factor shares will bias its calculation. In other words, TFP can capture much more effects that the

---

[6] "Loayza et al. (2004) state that changes in investment and saving do not help predict future changes in growth. ... Moreover, Solow-style growth-accounting exercises reveal that it is productivity growth and not capital accumulation what lies behind the major shifts in per capita output growth in the last decades in Latin America and the Caribbean. Specifically, the recovery in output growth experienced by the vast majority of countries in the region during the 1990s was driven in most cases by large increases in the growth of total factor productivity. This result suggests what regression analysis later confirms, that is, the growth recovery experienced by most countries in the region during the past decade was largely driven by structural and stabilization reforms that positively affected the economy's overall productivity."

[7] See Easterly and Levine (2002), Loayza et al. (2004).

[8] TFP is calculated by discounting the contributions of productive factors from GDP growth. Then TFP growth will be $d(tfp) = dy - \alpha \cdot dk - (1 - \alpha) \cdot dl$, where tfp, y, k y l represent logs of TFP, GDP, capital and labor, respectively. The parameter α is the capital share in GDP.

Table III.3 Latin America: Regressions of total factor productivity and output gap, 1950–2002

Dependent variable: Change in TFP	D(output gap)	t-Stat	R^2-Adjusted
Argentina	−1.003	−19.03	0.8784
Bolivia	−1.086	−8.300	0.5758
Brazil	−1.058	−14.55	0.8084
Chile	−0.846	−14.15	0.7993
Colombia	−0.950	−10.98	0.7012
Costa Rica	−1.078	−12.56	0.7656
Mexico	−0.742	−10.44	0.6837
Peru	−1.081	−13.71	0.7892
Venezuela	−0.881	−11.13	0.7110

Source: Author's estimates based on TFP and output gaps calculated by Hofman (2000) and Hofman and Tapia (2004). Constant not reported. The output gap is the difference between actual and potential GDP as a share of the potential GDP.

simple "technical progress," which is the standard interpretation in many empirical studies and textbooks.[9] In that sense, TFP is frequently interpreted as a "measurement of our ignorance" (Griliches and Jorgenson, 1967).

Since, in general, there are not good estimates of the utilization of capital, conventional calculations of the TFP use the total stock of capital, what implies that the actual use of that factor is not duly taken into account, which introduces an upward bias in the incidence of TFP. Evidently, the size of the bias will depend on the degree of underutilization of capital. Since developing economies are significantly more volatile than developed economies (a feature that has intensified in the last quarter of century, with a real instability notably higher than in the three previous decades),[10] the relationship between actual and potential GDP has been more fluctuating. Consequently, the bias of underutilization in estimates of TFP has tended to be more intense.

Table III.3 shows simple regressions of the change in TFP in response to variations in the output gap for nine LACs. It is evident that in all these countries, the evolution of TFP can be explained by changes in the rate of use of productive resources in percentages ranging from 57% to 88%. This highlights that any empirical research on determinants of TFP

[9] See, for example, Barro and Sala-i-Martin (2004). The seminal paper of Solow (1957) interprets movements in TFP as "technical change."
[10] See Ffrench-Davis and Tapia (2004), and Hnatkovska and Loayza (2003).

that does not correct for changes in the use of capital, will be accounting essentially for variations in the output gap instead of reflecting permanent changes in the production function or "technical progress." In that case, changes in the macroeconomic environment will be wrongly interpreted as structural changes in productivity. That leads to a notably, misleading, policy recipe: "don't bother to understand why capital formation has been so low, because it is not so relevant for growth." Moreover, if a transitory change in TFP is understood as a permanent rise in the rate of GDP growth, economic agents may assume an increase in permanent income and run a costly *destabilizing intertemporal adjustment* in the allocation of resources (see chapter II).

In short, while TFP is a valuable concept for measuring technological change, estimates tend to be biased in a context of changes in the degree of use of productive factors, particularly physical capital, such as occurred to a very great extent in Latin America in recent decades. As a result, it is plainly wrong to draw policy lessons from this type of research. In fact, the studies that do not take into account changes in the utilization rate are severely biased and erroneous in their repeated conclusions, which can bring costly consequences for both components of growth with equity.

Once adjustments are made for the rate of use, capital stock reappears as the main productive factor in most LACs. In particular, in developing economies, capital is the limiting factor for growth on account of its relative scarcity and, thus, it is the dominant variable in the definition of the production frontier. This does not mean that changes in productivity – as well as in employment and job quality – are not very important factors. Actually, they really are. Our view is that convergence with developed economies needs the contribution of all the factors in the aggregate production function, in diverse proportions depending on the level of development.

But it is most relevant that they also are complementary among them in a broad spectrum. Productivity increase brought by technological change is, undoubtedly, an outstanding component of economic development. Nevertheless, technology frequently needs to be embodied in factors of production (physical and human capital) in order to be part of the production function. Even intangible technology associated with the organization and generation of institutions usually requires investment in equipment and infrastructure, and depends on a more highly-skilled labor force. Additionally, a high investment ratio tends to be associated with high or rising employment rates (i.e., East Asian economies, Brazil and Mexico in their decades of vigorous growth, Chile in 1990–98). The accumulation of factors is essential.

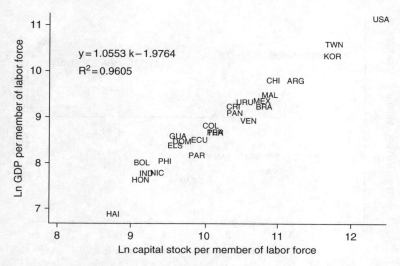

Figure III.1 EEs and USA: Capital stock and GDP, 2004 (capital stock and GDP per member of labor force, natural log)

Source: Author's calculation.

Both capital and GDP are measured in 1995 prices. Capital stock was calculated through the perpetual inventory method assuming an average working life for capital of 30 years.

Figure III.1 shows the relationship between the stock of capital and GDP (both variables measured per member of the labor force) for 26 economies, including 19 LACs, six East Asian countries and the United States. The year 2004 was chosen for the comparison, as it was a relatively buoyant period globally and, therefore, actual and potential GDP were relatively closer. The positive relationship is very strong, which reinforces the idea that the capital stock is a determining variable behind the level of per capita GDP.

Figure III.2 uses the same sample of countries to determine whether GDP growth is associated with growth in capital stock. For this purpose, average annual GDP growth and capital stock growth (net fix investment) were considered (both variables measured per member of the labor force) between 1980, another year of comparatively high utilization of the factors of production, and 2004.[11] Once again, it is clear that

[11] We are assuming that all the countries had the similar high rates of utilization of factors in 1980 and 2004. That was not probably the case in countries that suffered GDP drops in one of the two years: Bolivia, El Salvador, Venezuela, the United States and Korea in 1980 and Haiti in 2004.

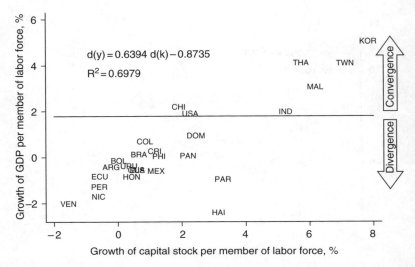

Figure III.2   EEs and USA: Capital stock and GDP growth, 1981–2004 (annual average growth per member of the labor force)

Source: Author's calculation.

Both capital and GDP are measured in 1995 prices. Capital stock was calculated for both 1980 and 2004 through the perpetual inventory method assuming an average working life for capital of 30 years. The horizontal line indicates the US average rate of growth.

the increase in capital stock accounts for much of the increase in GDP. The exceptions are Haiti, a country in turmoil as a result of internal conflicts that have conspired against the use of its productive capacity, and Paraguay, where the capital stock series are biased by the construction of huge dams, whose effect on production tends to be lagged over time. Barring these two cases, the explanatory power of the regression increases from 70% to 90%. Moreover, it is clear that most of the differences in growth between Latin America and the more dynamic countries of East Asia are attributable to the rapid growth in capital stock. In other words, the behavior of the variable which accounts for 70% to 90% of the production trend, i.e., capital formation, is well understood and its impact is evident, as shown. Capital accumulation continues to be a robust determinant of potential GDP. Evidently, other variables are relevant, such as the increase in labor participation (occupied people as share of the labor force or of the working age population), human capital, technology and social capital, but changes in capital formation have been intensive, and carry along with them changes in incorporation of technology and labor. Capital formation has been performing as a leading variable of the evolution of potential GDP.

Figure III.2 also illustrates, again, the "disappointing" non-convergence of the region with respect to the USA. The United States and East Asian economies have been growing more rapidly than almost all LACs (where only Chile converges in the 1990s).

c) Economic reforms and growth

It is crucial to understand the transmission mechanisms of the effects of economic reforms or policies. While TFP and capital formation can stimulate each other, there are significant differences regarding the size of their fluctuations and their interpretation. In general, biased estimates of TFP will embed transitory variations in the rate of use of potential GDP, while the dynamics of capital formation will be linked to permanent changes in the economy, that is to say, the potential output.

Indeed, short-term macroeconomic balances affect long-term economic performance (Ffrench-Davis and Tapia, 2004). But, a policy that increases the rate of use of productive factors will contribute to long-term growth only if its positive effects are permanent, raising the production frontier. If, on the contrary, economic activity is stimulated at the expense of an imbalance in another variable (such as the external accounts), then the positive effect will be counterbalanced as soon as a new adjustment (such as a balance of payment crisis) takes place, opening again the gap between actual and potential output and discouraging capital formation and innovation. This outcome was common under interventionist policies, but intensified under neo-liberalism. We need to suppress both.

LACs economic reforms in the 1990s (trade and financial liberalization, large privatization processes, fiscal reforms), in a context of renewed access to international capital markets, may have contributed to a recovery in actual GDP, but it was coupled only by a temporary and slight rise in capital formation. Thus, economic reforms would have helped to use the idle capacity existing after the debt crisis of the eighties, but that effect is mistakenly captured in biased TFP estimates, while indeed corresponds to changes in the rate of use of productive factors (see table III.3). However, there is no need to make structural reforms for using already existing capacity, since that is the role of a reform on macroeconomic policies, in a move toward a macroeconomics for development. What we need are structural *reforms to the reforms* that have been made under the aegis of the Washington Consensus, in order to increase that capacity, including meso and microeconomic issues.

LACs were over-adjusted in the eighties (as well as in 1995 and in 2003); consequently, an intense recovery in economic activity was feasible with a relief in the binding external restriction (see chapter II). That happened due to exogenous shocks, both in 1990–94, in 1996–97 and 2004 (see chapter VII). However, in the two first cases, economic recovery was achieved at the expense of imbalances in the external sector and, therefore "gains" from higher use of potential GDP were, to a great extent, just transitory. As a matter of fact, in 2002–03 the rate of underutilization climbed to the average level of the eighties (see figure III.3, below) and capital formation was depressed. Behind this return to a recessive conjuncture are the pitfalls in macroeconomic policies reviewed in section 3 and chapter II. In 2004, there was a new intense recovery in GDP growth, similar to those of 1994 and 1997 (all three exhibited GDP rises between 5 and 6%). That jump in GDP has tended to be interpreted, by naïve econometrics, as a sudden increase in productivity of capital, labor and government (TFP) of LACs; but down-to-earth pragmatic econometrics reveals that it is an increase in the rate of use of potential GDP; a drop in the output gap. That positive improvement in the use of resources implies that there was an inefficient use before. That inefficiency is a failure of neoliberal macroeconomics. Once again, this recovery relied on external positive shocks; this time, improved terms of trade and export volume.

To sum up, the bulk of the effect of economic reforms on long-term growth should be analyzed through the impact on potential output. According to Hofman and Tapia (2004), the potential GDP per capita grew, on average, only 0.5% between the eighties and nineties, 2 points below the growth rate of 1950–80. In the next section we explore the main factors behind that weak expansion of productive capacity. There is need for reforms to the reforms, including a move to a macroeconomics for development, to make this recovery in 2004, the prelude of sustained development.

3. Real macroeconomic balances and productive investment

The international and domestic macroeconomic environment in which specific productive development policies are implemented has a decisive impact on (i) the behavior of investment and savings, (ii) the rate of utilization of resources, and (iii) the attitudes and skills that are promoted within a country. Given the high macroeconomic instability experienced by LACs in the last quarter of a century, policies that may appear to be very efficient in a microeconomic sense (e.g., in enterprises that survive a given recessive adjustment process), turn out to be inefficient at a macroeconomic or global level. The latter is required for an accountability that considers the effective productivity of all available resources and the evolution of the stock of resources.

The swings in economic activity have frequently taken place under an automatic adjustment approach. This is characterized by amplifying the effects of the external shocks at the domestic level; given a drop in national income, originating in a deterioration of the terms of trade or a worsened access to financial markets, the "automatic adjustment" adds a further deterioration by lowering domestic output. The automatic adjustment is undoubtedly very effective in reducing the external gap, but severely inefficient at the overall macroeconomic level.

Rather than automatic adjustment, for preventing this destructive multiplication of external shocks, real macroeconomic balances require active monetary, credit, fiscal and foreign exchange policies, as well as a productive development policy. Policies regulating aggregate demand – implying the management of the capital account – must be complemented with switching policies in both supply and demand. This essentially involves a balanced set of short-run policies and coordination with the productive development program, in order to promote a change in the structure of expenditure and output so as to maintain a greater rate of utilization and expansion of productive capacity.

a) Macroeconomic environment and investment ratio

Enhanced real macroeconomic stability tends to provide an incentive to capital formation: that is, a more favorable environment for improvements in productivity rather than speculative dealings, greater emphasis on increased capacity instead of expansion of conglomerates or economic groups through acquisitions and mergers, and greater effective productivity thanks to a larger rate of utilization of the existing capacity of capital and labor. This can contribute to creating a virtuous circle, that encourages capital formation and increases in productivity. If, instead, high real instability provokes a reduction in the rate of use of productive factors, investment losses dynamism because of a series of negative effects: lower actual productivity, a reduced return to capital and falling savings, and worsened expectations about the future. Likewise, innovative efforts (normally of long maturing periods) depend significantly upon the existence of real macroeconomic tranquility.

Figure III.3 shows the relationship between the rate of underutilization of productive capacity (the output gap) and the investment ratio for

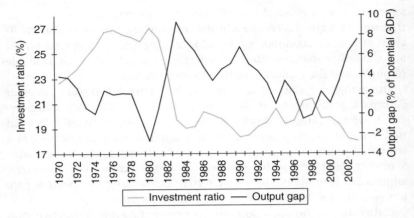

Figure III.3 Latin America (9): Output gap and investment ratio, 1970–2003 (prices of 1995)

Source: ECLAC and Hofman and Tapia (2004).
Averages for Argentina, Bolivia, Brazil, Chile, Colombia, Costa Rica, Mexico, Peru and Venezuela. The investment ratio measures the ratio between the fixed capital formation and the GDP. The output gap measures the difference between potential and actual GDP as a share of potential GDP.

LACs during the last three decades. It is a robust interpretation that, to a significant extent, investment performance responds to the rate of use of existing resources. This has been a dominant feature in LACs, given the intense real instability during these decades. Real macroeconomic instability has overwhelmed the incidence of structural variables and crowded-out their contribution to development. When real macroeconomic balances are achieved, then the incidence of structural variables – microeconomic and mesoeconomic – on capital formation and its quality emerge clearer.

As discussed in chapter II, sustained real macroeconomic balances can be achieved by using a comprehensive set of coordinated macroeconomic policies. Balances include an effective demand close to potential GDP, and exchange and interest rates that reflect mid-term trends in their respective markets.

b) Structural reforms, macro prices and capital formation

Latin America needs to significantly increase capital formation in order to sustain a growth rate of 5 or 6% per year. Therefore, fostering investment must be given priority in the policy agenda. Previous sections highlight that after the implementation of liberalizing reforms in LACs, economic growth has been disappointing and investment rates have reached historical minimum levels. Even in the three peak years of 1994, 1997 and 2004, productive investment was notably low as compared to ratios in East Asia, and Chile (in 1992–98). It is noteworthy that, in the 1970s and 1980s, investment ratios in Chile were also depressed as in LACs in the 1990s. They share a neoliberal approach, that tends to be *unfriendly* with capital formation and productive development.

In fact, paradoxically, economic reforms aimed to make room for private agents in a market economy (that is, supposedly to be market-friendly) have ended up damaging the environment for investment, challenging the long-term development of the private sector.

Given the reduction in public investment in most LACs (Easterly and Servén, 2003), at present productive investment depends more heavily on market expectations of profitability. In particular, not only the unstable behavior of aggregate demand has been discouraging for capital formation, but also key *macro prices* have shown "wrong" levels, inconsistent with a sustained and dynamic productive development. Additionally, meso and microeconomic productive development policies were weak or plainly absent (Williamson, 2003a). In brief, economic reforms have been market *unfriendly*.

Here we examine, briefly, how reforms have strengthened the allocative role of macroprices while they have made them quite volatile.

i) Capital account liberalization and foreign exchange policy

The exchange rate has a strong impact on the allocation of resources between tradables and non-tradables. This role was strengthened by the sharp reduction of protectionism in EEs. On the other hand, in a framework of open capital accounts, the short-term segment of capital markets has a heavy weight in the foreign exchange rate dynamics (see chapter VII). Due to its nature, foreign currency lends itself to speculative operations and bubbles more than other items, since it serves as an instrument for capital flight and a medium of exchange and hoarding (see Lessard and Williamson, 1987; Dornbusch, 1989). Consequently, the working of the foreign exchange market (implying both access to foreign exchange and the exchange rate adjustment) has significant macroeconomic effects, unlike many other goods or assets with purely micro implications.

The set of conditions reflecting the reality of most LACs in recent years (variable and inertial inflation, fluctuating terms of trade, inflexible productive structure and need to transform this structure, and abrupt changes in external supply of financing and its terms), render the two traditional extreme formulas of free and fixed nominal exchange rates inconvenient.[12] The alternative *vis-à-vis* the problems that arise from these two extreme options consists of what is called "intermediate regimes," with both foreign exchange rates and capital account managed by the Central Bank (see chapter II, and Williamson, 2000).

Exchange rate instability tends to reduce the capacity to identify comparative advantages, a trend that undermines capital formation. It often has a negative and stronger impact on new exports, on those undertaken by companies with less diversified markets, and on those with more limited access to capital markets. Consequently, exchange rate instability, although affecting all exports, is biased against non-traditional products (Díaz-Alejandro, 1975; Caballero and Corbo, 1990; ECLAC, 1998, chapter IV). The bias also affects nationally owned enterprises as compared to diversified transnational corporations.

The existence of instability, given imperfect capital markets and binding external restrictions, also involves a relation between foreign exchange policy and the average level of effective demand. Instability usually reduces the average rate of use of resources and biases the market toward the short-term and rent-seeking. This is a strong reason for avoiding an exchange rate that closely follows short-run fluctuations of international prices and capital flows. A policy that avoids extreme ups-and-downs allows for a sustainable higher average level of effective demand and economic activity.[13] Therefore it tends to allow for a greater utilization of capacity and to encourage investment.

In fact, with the mix of effects that are generated, there tends to prevail a positive income effect (due to the higher rates of use and the corresponding encouragement to investment) over the price effect of the exchange rate on imports of capital goods; thus, it tends to lead toward a higher absorptive capacity and faster growth. A more "sustainable" level of the exchange rate also reduces the energy spent by governments in facing balance of payments crises.

---

[12] The mainstream vision has changed over the time. A free exchange rate was advocated by closed economy monetarism. Open economy monetarism (the monetary approach to the balance of payments) advocated a fixed exchange rate, as that applied between 1979 and 1982 in the monetarist experiment in Chile, and in Argentina in 1991–2001. After the Argentinean crisis (in 2002), the approach in fashion is that of a fully floating exchange rate regime but with an ambiguous tolerance to interventions under "exceptional" circumstances.

[13] It tends to have a greater inflationary impact, which can be compensated for by policies that favor social concertation related to the level of prices and income. In its absence, economic policy is forced to overly depend on restricting aggregate demand below the production frontier.

In short, it is essential, for the exchange rate to be guided by the trend shown by balance of payments projections (at full employment), seeking to attenuate the transmission of short-term fluctuations of the terms of trade or capital flows into the domestic economy. Regulation of the capital account and of the access to the foreign exchange market are crucial to moderate destabilizing capital flows (see chapters II and VII).

ii) Financial reforms and interest rates

The interest rate is another key macroeconomic and allocative variable. The more naïve orthodox proposal is to leave it fully free. According to this approach, in "small countries" the liberalization of interest rates would imply (adjusted by sovereign risk) the parity with the international rate. Actually, the parity does not prevail even between most developed countries (for instance, between the USA and the European Union, with or without control for expectations about exchange rates). There are several alternatives for reforming interest rate policy. Liberalization can be complete, as in the case of full peg to the dollar in Argentina 1991 or Chile 1979. Also, policy may include indirect regulation via operations of the Central Bank with short term papers, avoiding affecting purposely the yield curve, or intending to affect it through the terms of the papers it operates with the market.

Liberalization experiences have shown that external and domestic rates do not converge rapidly to a unique level; in EEs, liberalized domestic interest rates have been unstable and much higher than international ones; and with spreads markedly higher for long periods (ECLAC, 1998; Ffrench-Davis, 2002, chapter 5). This, naturally, is a strong signal against productive investment.

Proposals for financial liberalization were encouraged by the previous unsatisfactory experience with increasingly interventionist policies and heavily subsidized interest rates. The latter occurred particularly in countries with high inflation. In response to this, countries such as Brazil and Colombia, that succeeded in increasing investment ratios during the 1970s, undertook heterodox financial reforms: capital movements and domestic loans were regulated, orienting them toward productive investment; positive and active but moderate real interest rates were established by the central banks; and long-term financing channels were created.

During the 1980s and 1990s there was an upsurge of financial reforms, both relating to domestic capital markets and the capital account. The predominant pattern followed the more naive orthodoxy, repeating to a large degree the 1970s inefficient reform experience of the Southern

Cone. The reform consisted of the extensive and abrupt liberalization of interest rates, maturity terms and credit allocation, and the relaxation of prudential regulations and supervision on financial institutions. There was widespread disregard for the high risk of generating speculative bubbles, adverse selection, and moral hazard as Chile had misdone in the 1970s. It is interesting to note that "financierism" assigned a strategic role to the sector's liberalization, without considering in the design of reforms the characteristics of the "product" in question (see chapter VI, and Díaz-Alejandro, 1985; Stiglitz, 1994). The general outcome was a large rise in financial savings in the short-run segment of the capital market, a weakened long-term segment, without an increase in national savings. For rather long periods, the markets exhibited highly fluctuating interest rates, increased spreads and weak prudential supervision. As a consequence, Latin America suffered several banking crises during the nineties replicating that of Chile in 1983 (Stallings and Studart, 2005).

There is no doubt that the financial system should play a crucial role in attracting and allocating savings. In this respect, financial reforms were needed in LACs. Consequently, the issue is how to implement reforms that contribute to productive development and macroeconomic stability, rather than the reverse. Across-the-board financial liberalization has proven inefficient on both counts, particularly during the adjustment process (Díaz-Alejandro, 1985; Held, 1994; Zahler, 1998; Stiglitz, 2000). It is important to take care that financial reforms do not generate a diversion of savings toward consumption, speculation, and the concentration of wealth, rather than toward productive investment. The outcome is closely dependent on the nature and sequence of financial reforms.

The reorganization of the financial system should aim at harnessing resources toward savings and investment, in direct connection with the productive apparatus. Reforms in pension systems – and the subsequent emergence of privately managed funds – have generated significant and increasing potential sources of long-term financing. The neoliberal approach has pressured to achieve liberalization in the regulations affecting the management of those resources, specially pressing for liberalizing investment abroad. The size of those funds gives them a crucial role in a reform to the initial reform to ensure that those resources can be (i) a factor of real macroeconomic stability (see Zahler, 2005) and (ii) a factor of gradual restructuring in the domestic capital market to enhance capital formation and productive development.

A new approach should grant priority to linking the financial system to the domestic investment process rather to the external financial markets, to contribute to greater economic stability (which implies keeping non-outlier real exchange rates and regulating interest rates so as to avoid very abrupt fluctuations, and negative or exorbitantly high real interest rates) and better distribution of economic opportunities.

These objectives require a more complete capital market, rather than the standard outcome of neoliberal reforms biased toward the short term. What is needed is an institutionality that encompasses a vigorous long-term segment of the financial market, in order to finance productive investment. Greater access is also needed by small and medium firms and people with low and medium income levels, who typically suffer the social segmentation of the capital market. They need this market to deal with contingencies, to invest in education and labor training, and to promote the development of productive activities and their modernization. Specialized credit entities and guarantee mechanisms are required in order to do what the market has been unable to do spontaneously. The priority in this field should be to favor access to financing at "normal" rates, as well as access to the resources that low and medium-income sectors do not possess: technology, some inputs and services, marketing channels, long-term financing, and infrastructure.

iii) Foreign trade policy and macroeconomic effects

Here we would like to highlight three macroeconomic effects of trade policy. First, excessive protectionism restricts investment and its productivity, by enclosing production within the limited domestic frontiers. This was the growingly prevailing keynote in Latin America since the crisis of the 1930s.[14] In the other extreme, indiscriminate liberalization of imports, within the framework traditionally prevalent in Latin America, changes relative market prices and the availability and diversity of goods in favor of consumption. Coupled with the new consumption credit facilities in a liberalized financial market, market incentives shift from savings to imported consumption goods. In fact, owing to the financial reforms implemented during the 1970s in the Southern Cone, or later in the 1990s in the rest of Latin America, the financial market tapped a markedly greater proportion of total savings, and then reallocated a significant portion of these funds to consumption, which reduced actual domestic savings (Zahler, 1988).

---

[14] See the normally ignored, critical views, of Prebisch (1963; 1981), arguing in favor of export promotion, principally through regional integration. See, also, Fajnzylber (1990); Ffrench-Davis (1979, chapter VIII); Ocampo (1993).

Consequently, it is advisable to use a gradual sequence of policies involving net positive pulls: for example, a stronger export-promoting inducement on the demand for resources, rather than the abrupt negative pulls of import de-substitution, supported with a financial system geared to productive development. What is ultimately intended is to foster the efficient production of both exportables and import substitutes, amidst a dynamic investment process. The relative strength of positive and negative pulls determines whether adjustment is made below or along the production frontier or transformation curve, and how fast this frontier is shifted upward (see chapter IV).

Second, across-the-board import liberalization in sectors where output differentiation is important, contributes to segmenting domestic demand in different varieties and hampering the operation of local producers. This is important in sectors such as durable consumer goods and their parts and components, in which there are economies of scale and specialization. Therefore, trade policy should reconcile external competition with local utilization of these economies of scale and specialization. A transition with predominant export promotion, gradual import liberalization, comprehensive macroeconomic equilibria, and effective mesoeconomic policies contributes to a positive hysteresis, as shown by several East Asian economies.

Finally, in a world of "limited information" (Arrow, 1974), an attribute of selective tariffs and export incentives is that they contribute to enhancing in the market the presence of sectors in which there are investment opportunities. Improved visibility mobilizes savings and capital formation. In other words, the efficient (which obviously implies moderate) use of tariffs and export incentives not only enables the reallocation of given resources, but may also contribute to an expansion of the production frontier. The dominant trend since the 1990s, toward free trade in EEs has limited the role that tariffs (and other trade policies) have played in successful EEs; the features of the Uruguay Round and several free trade agreements did reinforce that trend. In this context, other alternative developmental policies – such as those aimed to *complete* domestic factor markets and to channel capital flows to productive investment – have gained more responsibility in the task of enhancing productive development.

Latin America needs to be actively and selectively linked with the world economy. Naturally, the exchange rate plays a key role in a process of trade integration. The task of acquiring new comparative advantages plays a crucial role in promoting domestic productive development, by creating new investment opportunities in the market and enhancing productive innovation.

4. Concluding remarks

GDP growth has generally been disappointing in the decade and half of intensive reforms under the rule of the Washington Consensus. One strong variable underlying these unsatisfactory results is the poor behavior of the investment ratio. Gross capital formation recovered only slightly up to 1998, from the very depressed levels of the 1980s. After the Asian crises, the investment ratio declined to historical minimum levels.

It is not feasible to attain a sustained high economic growth rate with a low investment ratio. Frequent statements highlighting that TFP is the leader factor in economic growth, over investment, are based on biased calculations that, preponderantly, actually capture changes in GDP resulting from changes in the rate of use of productive factors. It is possible to increase growth rates transitorily without additional investment by using idle capacity, but only as long as there remains an output gap.

Permanent gains in productivity can be a very significant source of growth, but they take time in being achieved. Moreover, improvements in productivity usually must be associated with a strong pull to investment. Therefore, accumulation of both human and physical capital is a necessary condition for economic growth.

In view of the disparity between aims and actual achievements, reformers may argue that the effects of the reforms are only slow to work out, at least as regards the recovery of gross capital formation and growth. Why should this be so? One possible answer is that the outcome of reforms naturally takes time. However, that time is a valuable commodity in economics. Thus, the present value of the series of effects of any economic policy is highly important, and not just the flows achieved at the end of the adjustment process. An alternative answer is that the reforms have been very simplistic, against a background of segmented and incomplete markets. Our own reading is that both interpretations are correct, and that the over-simplicity helped to enlarge the initial costs and to make the lag in the positive effects of the reforms greater. An eloquent example was the long adjustment process in Chile, with low average investment ratios between 1974 and 1988, and average GDP growth of less than 3%. However, in Chile reforms to the reforms in the early 1990s were crucial to allow a high and sustained increase in investment in that decade (see chapter IX).

The weak recovery of gross capital formation in most of the countries of the region is dependent on the macroeconomic environment and on the availability of factors of production. With respect to the macroeconomic environment, first, the strongest variable has been the size and expected evolution of the gap between actual GDP and the productive frontier. This is a function of the quality of macroeconomic management.

Second, the poor performance of capital formation is due to "wrong" macroeconomic prices, which are also a function of the quality of the policies in question and the development of the domestic capital and foreign exchange markets. The exchange rate, which is an effective incentive for the production of exportables, began to appreciate markedly in the early 1990s. Investors noted that as the economy came closer to the productive frontier, the exchange rate lagged behind, and in several countries an undesirable inconsistency occurred: against all pragmatic recommendations, rapid liberalization of imports had to coexist with exchange-rate appreciation. Generally speaking, exchange-rate appreciation discourages the production of tradables, particularly in a situation of trade liberalization thus worsening the balance of positive/negative pulls on gross capital formation.

The other main macroeconomic price – interest rates – has also behaved in a way that discourages capital formation. Although in many cases these rates were not as high as during the debt crisis of the 1980s, very high real rates have still prevailed. This is not an intrinsic result of the market, but rather of the way the financial reforms have been carried out. High real interest rates, a financial market oriented toward short-term operations, and the limited access that small and medium-sized enterprises have to that market, form a tough obstacle to productive development. This indicates that the financial reforms have been very deficient, leaning toward high-risk portfolios and "outlier" interest rates. A serious effort needs to be made to *reform the reforms* in order to create, replicate or simulate financial markets for long-term operations, small and medium-sized enterprises, technology and human capital.

Indiscriminate opening of the capital account can do great harm to productive development and the well-being of the bulk of population. Foreign exchange and macroeconomic instability, which is usually associated with across-the-board opening, is always very costly for productive sectors and equity. We have seen, however, that effective and efficient regulation is perfectly possible, as Chile, China, Colombia, India, Malaysia and Taiwan have shown in recent years (see chapters VII and IX). Active foreign exchange, fiscal and monetary policies are an essential step, but insufficient on their own. In order to achieve real macroeconomic balances they must be accompanied by efficient regulation of capital flows and stabilizing management of aggregate demand.

Part Two
Trade for Development

IV
Trade Liberalization Strategies and Growth*

Introduction

In recent years, many Latin American countries (LACs) embarked upon trade liberalization drives. The earlier sustained process of import liberalization was launched in Chile in the mid-1970s; by the end of that decade, its economy had become one of the most open in the world.

By the mid-1980s, after more than half a century of protectionism, a radical change in the development strategies of several LACs was becoming evident. As early as 1983 Costa Rica set out on a gradual transition from the import-substitution model, which it had been implementing at the national and Central American levels, to a model oriented towards forging a more dynamic position in the international economy. Then, in 1985, Bolivia and Mexico started up relatively fast-paced liberalization programs.

In the early 1990s, several other LACs joined in this movement, including Argentina, Brazil, Peru and Venezuela. Even Colombia, which had undertaken a gradual program in 1990 to open up its economy over a four-year time span, decided to step up the pace of its liberalization effort in 1991 so that it could be completed in 1992. Thus, although several LACs were moving forward at different speeds, it was clear that the region had reached a major turning point. Moreover, it should be noted that many LACs were non-members of GATT/WTO. Since 1986, fifteen

* Revised and updated version of a paper co-authored with Manuel Agosin, published in *CEPAL Review* No. 50, Santiago, August 1993. The useful comments of Oscar Altimir, Renato Baumann, Robert Devlin, Winston Fritsch, Jorge Katz, Bernardo Kosacoff, Carlos Massad, Joseph Ramos, Jaime Ros and Gert Rosenthal are highly appreciated.

of them (including Mexico and Venezuela) have become members of that organization (Bouzas and Keifman, 2003).

In this chapter we focus on import liberalization processes, the context in which they were carried out and their direct effects. In chapter V we review the export performance and its links with economic growth.[1] Section 1 presents some introductory considerations regarding the state-led industrialization or import substitution strategy. Then, it analyzes the conditions that trade opening should meet in order to contribute to economic development. Section 2 summarizes the main liberalizing trade reforms performed in LACs, concluding with an analysis of reforms in Chile and Mexico. Section 3 reviews part of the voluminous literature on East Asian export-oriented economies (the Republic of Korea, Taiwan and, more recently, Indonesia, Malaysia and Thailand) so that LACs' more recent experiences can be compared with other cases of a longer standing and quite different character. Section 4 presents an analytical framework, stylizing the different paths followed by LACs and East Asian countries. Then some of the key elements of trade reforms are examined, in the light of the conditions required to open up an economy in a way that will stimulate its long-term development.

The greatest differences between the liberalization efforts of LACs and the way in which Asian countries have opened up their economies are that most Latin American liberalization programs have been carried out rapidly and the state has played a passive role, whereas the opening of East Asian economies has rather been a long, state-led process, involving the construction of a production apparatus oriented towards international markets. When imports were liberalized in Asia, the economy's structural transformation had already been advancing and manufactured exports had been on the rise for a long time. These conditions were buttressed, in most cases, by real macroeconomic equilibria and high investment ratios. In contrast, the drastic import liberalization carried out in LACs were launched during the initial stage of their internationalization strategies, and often coincided with recessive stabilization processes and low rates of capital formation.

1. From import substitution to import liberalization

In the world of today, systemic competitiveness and a more dynamic position in world markets must be attained in order to achieve sustained

---

[1] Interesting studies on the effect of trade liberalizations on growth can be found in Rodrik and Rodríguez (2001), and in Winters (2004).

development. Therefore, high and cumbersome restrictions on imports must be reduced.

The basic problem with the protectionist policies of the past was that, in the final analysis, they were usually so arbitrary that policy-makers did not know what they were promoting and why (Ffrench-Davis, 2002, chapter III; Fritsch and Franco, 1993, p. 32). The protectionist policies of the past, both in Latin America and in other regions, were often exploited by private concerns seeking economic rents. In many cases no social benefits were evident, and the resulting industrial structures tended not to be competitive on the international market and to continue being dependent on government protection indefinitely. It should be recognized, however, that these schemes permitted the establishment of industrial sectors that subsequently served as the basis for a development more strongly oriented towards international competitiveness. Additionally, it must be recalled that GDP growth and living standards improved quite fast in the import substituting industrialization (ISI) period, particularly between 1950 and 1980 (Ffrench-Davis, Muñoz and Palma, 1998). However, by the 1970s, ISI was becoming exhausted as a source of sustained development. Undoubtedly, a reshuffle was needed.

In order for trade reforms to be successful, the value added by the creation of new activities must exceed the value subtracted by the destruction of existing activities. This tends to be associated with an increase in exports greater than the decrease in import substitutes;[2] such export activity must have positive spillover effects on the rest of the economy, which will depend upon the degree of diversification and of value-added they contain; and that international competitiveness must be attained through a continuing increase in productivity rather than by means of low wages and of rising subsidies or tax exemptions.

This is why it is essential to open up an economy in a way that will not entail the indiscriminate destruction of existing installed capacity and making feasible an effective switching of resources among productive activities. A crucial condition is the graduality of the process,

---

[2] This does not mean that the option of import substitution should be discarded. The larger the domestic market in question, the greater the potential scope of import substitution. This is attested to by the fact that the exports of countries such as the US and Japan represent only about 10% of their GDP. What is more relevant about the new development strategy is the idea that firms producing goods and services, whether for the domestic or international market, must become increasingly competitive during the learning period. This is achieved, in part, through exposure to outside competition and with a vigorous domestic policy for productive development.

associated with the capacity of the various economic agents to adapt to the policy-induced market changes. This process needs to be coupled with a sustained, credible change in relative prices favorable to the production of exportables and with the completion or creation of the markets and institutions essential to a steady increase in productivity. That should include – with a bias favoring small and medium enterprises (SMEs) – labor training, improvements in infrastructure, incentives for technological innovation, the development of long-term segments of capital markets, and an increased ability to negotiate access to external markets.

This focus has not, generally speaking, been the one chosen by LACs launching trade liberalization initiatives (Bouzas and Keifman, 2003). The specific approaches adopted tended to be abrupt and to suffer from serious shortcomings in three crucial areas. First, unilateral bids to open up an economy would make sense in an open, dynamic, competitive world economy, but are less advisable in an international economy where protectionism is still a very real factor, and a strong trend toward the formation of regional trade blocs and trade agreements is observed (ECLAC, 1998, chapter II). Second, this process is based on static comparative advantages and short-term gains in resource allocation, but benefits fade-out if it is concentrated in areas of activity whose world markets are more sluggish and/or less intensive in technological innovation. Third, the recent move towards capital markets deregulation has hampered the reallocation of resources which was supposed to be brought about by trade liberalization because, under the conditions prevailing in the 1990s, it has been conducive to sharp exchange-rate appreciation, high real interest rates and weak supply of long-term funding. These factors discourage the productive investment needed to bring about structural change, and cause resources to move away from the production of tradables and to concentrate more in purely financial investment (see chapter VII).

2. Trade liberalization in Latin America

Many countries in the region have undertaken deep trade liberalization reforms since the debt crisis. Eight of the nine countries shown in table IV.1 – all but Costa Rica – introduced reforms that could be described as drastic and abrupt. Moreover, generally, import liberalization was carried out within a short period (1989–90 to 1992–93). Argentina implemented the bulk of its liberalization program in April 1991. In Chile – with a starting point extremely protectionist in 1973 – the process ended

Table IV.1 Latin America (9 countries): Summary of import liberalization processes

Country	Program starting date	Maximum tariff — Initial	Maximum tariff — Year-end 1993	Number of tariff rates — Initial	Number of tariff rates — Year-end 1993	Average tariff — Initial	Average tariff — Year-end 1993	Mid-1996 — Maximum tariff	Mid-1996 — Number of tariff rates	Mid-1996 — Average tariff	Real exchange rate change[a]
Argentina[b]	1989	65	30		3	39[c]	15[c]	33	21	14	-41
Bolivia	1985	150	10		2	12[d]	7[d]	10	2	10	98
Brazil[b]	1988	105	35	29	7	51[e]	14[e]	35[g]	29	13	-35
Colombia[b]	1990	100	20	14	4	44[d]	12[d]	20[h]	8	11	-20
Costa Rica	1986	150	20		4	53[e]	12[e]	20	4	9	5
Chile[f]	1973	220	10	57	1	94[e]	10[e]	11	1	11	-36
Mexico	1985	100	20	10	5	35[e]	11[e]	11	1	11	28
Peru[b]	1990	108	25	56	2	66[c]	13[c]	35[i]	24	14	-32·
Venezuela	1989	135	20	41	4	35[d]	10[d]	20[j]	8	16	-40

Source: ECLAC, on the basis of national figures and information provided by LAIA's Secretariat (LAIA = the Latin American Integration Association). Data exclude preferential tariffs.

[a] From the average of the triennium around the initiation of the liberalization program up to the average of the 1994-96 triennium for all countries, except those more hit by the Tequila Effect, for which the 1992–94 average was used; the exchange-rate for exports has been used. [b] Tariffs include surcharges. [c] Weighted by domestic production. [d] Weighted by imports [e] Simple average of tariff items [f] Chile's first trade liberalization program was started in 1973 and completed in 1979. The 10% uniform tariff remained in force until 1982. Therefore, the information given in the first row corresponds to that period (1973–82). The second row contains information on the reduction of import duties on a second process starting in 1985; after being raised to 35% in 1984, the uniform tariff was successively reduced to 20% (1985), 15% (1988) and 11% (1991). [g] There are 49 rates (out of 11 800) which exceed that level: 12 at 40%; 23 at 65% and 14 at 70%. [h] There are 46 rates (out of 7 200) which exceed such level: 45 at 35% and 1 at 40%. [i] There are 66 rates (out of 9 700) which exceed such level: 16 between 40% and 45%; 12 between 45% and 70%; 19 between 70% and 200%; and 19 between 200% and 260%. [j] There are 13 rates (out of 6 600) at a 35% level.

Non-tariff barriers by mid-1996:

Argentina: In 1989–91 most non-tariff restrictions were abolished. By mid-1996, prior-licensing requirements and import bans for a total of 88 vulnerable products were still in force. Bolivia: Almost all non-tariff restrictions have been abolished, with the exception of only 12 restrictions related to vulnerable products. Brazil: In 1990, the list of banned imports and prior-licensing requirements were eliminated. However, 101 import restrictions, which concentrate on vulnerable products, authorizations, and domestic content or domestic purchase requirements, were maintained. Colombia: Nearly all restrictions concerning the prior-licensing requirement were lifted in late 1990. There remain 27 restrictions to vulnerable products, 10 specifications of domestic purchase and with relation to production characteristics. Costa Rica: Most import permits and other restrictions have been eliminated. Chile: Applies price bands to 3 agricultural products, plus a total of 41 restrictions to vulnerable products. Mexico: Has eliminated prior-licenses and applies restrictions only to 10 vulnerable products. Peru: Applies import restrictions to 22 vulnerable products. Venezuela: Import restrictions are applied to 41 vulnerable products.

by mid-1979. Even Colombia, a country with a traditional gradualist approach, accelerated its program of gradual trade openness and reduced drastically its tariffs in 1990–92.

The experiences of the East Asian economies as well as of Colombia since the mid-1960s (Ocampo and Villar, 1992) and of Costa Rica between 1983 and 1990 (Herrera, 1992) support the choice of a gradual approach that permits the reconversion of existing industries rather than destroying a large percentage of a country's installed capacity, as inevitably occurs during a rapidly-applied import liberalization, particularly if the exchange-rate appreciates.

In Colombia, the transition made in the mid-1960s from an import-substitution model to a pragmatic model that placed priority on both import substitution and export promotion, played a pivotal role in steering the manufacturing sector towards an increasingly external orientation, while avoiding the trauma associated with drastic liberalization drives such as that of Chile in the 1970s. In Costa Rica, tariff reduction was also a gradual process and was coupled with export incentives and drawback mechanisms; Chile moved in this direction again only by the mid-1980s. The expansion of non-traditional exports – the most salient feature of Costa Rican development in the 1980s – was in large part generated by firms established during the earlier import-substitution phase. In addition, a deliberate effort was made in the nineties to promote foreign investment in the production of exportable textiles and electronics.

In most LACs, after the initial impulse from late-1980s and mid-1990s, trade openness tended to stabilize. In fact, some countries such as Argentina, Costa Rica, Ecuador, Mexico, Paraguay and Uruguay adjusted somewhat their policies in the opposite direction in order to face the balance of payments problems derived from the Asian crisis and its effects in Latin America from 1998 on. Figure IV.1 shows the rapid evolution of import liberalization in the region as a whole between 1987 and 1994, the slower advance up to 1998 and the subsequent slight reversal. However, as reviewed in chapter V, the reciprocated trade openness, based on Free Trade Agreements, became very significant in recent years.

In all cases, albeit to varying extents, quantitative restrictions were dismantled and tariffs lowered significantly. In general, the amount of tariff protection provided differs considerably from its pre-reform levels, and the spread of rates of effective protection has diminished substantially. No country has yet adopted a tariff rate of zero, however, and most have a schedule of tariff rates with ceilings ranging from 10 to 35%, and simple averages of between 9% and 16% (see table IV.1).

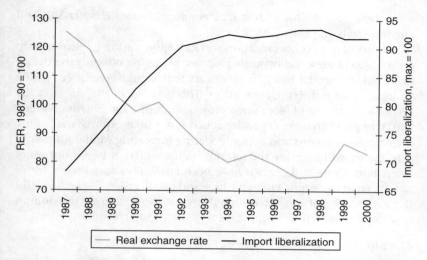

Figure IV.1 Latin America: Import liberalization and real exchange rate, 1987–2000 (indices)

Source: Authors' calculations for 16 countries, based on table VII.2; Morley, Machado and Pettinato (1999) and database of Economic Development Division, ECLAC.

These regional trends in trade policy have been complemented by bilateral or multilateral free trade agreements covering a wide spectrum of items (see chapter V). Intra-regional agreements have given reciprocal preferential access to regional partners, through tariff reductions. With the exception of Cuba, all LACs have opened their markets in this way; in 2003 one fifth of their trade was intra-regional (see table V.3). On the other hand, Chile and Mexico have made significant moves toward extra-regional integration, by signing agreements with the European Union, the United States and Asia. In the case of Chile, the actual tariff paid is lower than 2%, while the uniform rate with non-associated countries is 6%.

In a number of countries, trade liberalization measures were accompanied by the liberalization of the capital account. Under the capital surges prevailing from the early nineties to 1998, the liberalization of the capital account prompted considerable exchange-rate appreciation (see figure V.1) just when trade reforms urgently required the opposite: a compensatory depreciation. Some countries (Chile and Colombia) were more successful than others in countering this pressure on their currencies; in order to do so they resorted to foreign exchange controls and other heterodox forms of financial engineering (see chapter VII, and Ffrench-Davis and Villar, 2005).

The mix of import liberalization and RER appreciation implied a sharp destruction of import substituting sectors, including not only inefficient firms over-protected but also producers that would be efficient under "normal" (not-outlier) relative prices. This was one of the causes of the increase in the rate of labor unemployment during the nineties (Weller, 2001). Imports, in turn, expanded much faster than exports, weakening the external accounts and accommodating increasing capital inflows.[3]

Below we will examine the reforms implemented in two countries of the region. Chile and Mexico have been chosen because their reforms have been in place long enough (three and two decades, respectively) for the effects to be reflected in economic performance, thereby providing a basis for an evaluation of impacts on growth and investment.

a) Chile

Chile's trade liberalization scheme is the oldest and the longest continuously-applied program in the region. In late 1973, before the introduction of reforms, Chilean foreign trade was subject to a great deal of government control: nominal tariffs averaged 94% and ranged from 0% to 750%; countless non-tariff barriers were in place, including the requirement of large prior deposits for 60% of all imports, the Central Bank's discretionary authorization of exemptions to that restriction, and a cumbersome multiple exchange-rate system involving eight different official rates, with a 1000% difference between the lowest and the highest (Ffrench-Davis, 2002, chapter 3; Meller, 1994).[4]

i) The sweeping reforms of the 1970s

As part of a far-reaching scheme for handing over the vast majority of economic decisions to market forces, in 1973 trade reforms were launched which covered the elimination of all non-tariff trade barriers, a sharp process of reduction of tariff levels, and the establishment of a single exchange-rate. Although it was not one of the programmer's initial goals, by June 1979 a uniform tariff of 10% had also been established.

[3] According to Santos-Paulino and Thirwall (2004), the generation of external imbalances is an empirical regularity in trade liberalization experiences in developing countries.

[4] Notice that this was the situation in 1973. However, in the second half of the 1960s, there was a reform in process that included the gradual rationalization of the import regime and the improvement of export promotion mechanisms.

Table IV.2 Chile: Average tariff and real exchange rate, 1973–2004 (annual averages)

Year	Average tariff[a] (percentages)	Average tariff collected[b] (percentages)	Real exchange rate[c] (1986 = 100)
1973	94.0[d]		65.1[d]
1974–79	35.3		73.2
1980–82	10.1	10.1	57.6
1983–85	22.7	22.7	79.1
1986–89	17.6	17.6	106.6
1990–95	11.9	10.5	99.5
1996–98	11.0	8.5	80.3
1999–2001	9.0	6.4	88.0
2002–2004	6.3	3.2	100.2

Sources: Ffrench-Davis (2002, table 8.1), Central Bank of Chile and Chilean Custom Service.

[a] Simple average. [b] Weighted average of actually paid tariffs, including the effect of exemptions and preferential arrangements negotiated with trade partners. [c] The nominal exchange-rate was deflated by the Chilean Consumer Price Index (CPI; duly corrected for 1973–78) and inflated by an external price index. [d] December 1973.

During the first two years of trade liberalization, real devaluations of the government-controlled crawling exchange rate offset the reduction in the average nominal level of protection (table IV.2). This gave a strong boost to exports other than copper and afforded some protection for the more efficient import-substituting activities. In 1976, however, the real exchange rate began to appreciate. One main reason for this was that exchange-rate policy gradually shifted away from support for the opening-up of the economy and towards inflation control. This trend reached its height in 1979, when the nominal exchange rate was pegged to the dollar, in line with the monetary approach to the balance of payments, then in fashion, in an effort to anchor domestic inflation to the international rate. The liberalization of the capital account, in combination with the high level of liquidity in international capital markets, made possible and encouraged the currency appreciation (Ffrench-Davis, 2002, chapters 4 and 5).

Interestingly enough, in 1979, when trade liberalization had been completed and a uniform 10% tariff was established, the real exchange rate was at almost the same level as it had been at the start of the liberalization process in 1974. Although there was a great deal of water in the average nominal tariff (94%) existing at the start of the liberalization process, the fact remains that there had been a sharp reduction in effective tariffs. Basic trade policy theory would have indicated a need for a compensatory devaluation; policy-makers initially asserted the same, but in the end they actually did just the opposite. In the three years following the completion of the import liberalization program, appreciation accelerated, and this had a severe dampening effect on the production of tradables. Imports expanded at a notably faster speed than exports and crowded-out domestic output which, with more normal macro prices (non-outlier interest and exchange rates), would have remained more competitive.

ii) Rectifying reforms in the 1980s

The domestic and balance-of-payments crises that hit Chile in 1982 as a result of a combination of errors in economic management and three severe external shocks (an increase in interest rates, a drop in copper prices and then the sudden stops of external credit) caused aggregate demand to fall 30% and GDP to shrink 16% between 1981 and 1983. In an effort to cope with the crisis, a number of discrete devaluations were applied by mid-1982 and, later on, a crawling peg was reintroduced. Between 1982 and 1988, the real exchange rate depreciated 130%. At the same time, the uniform tariff was raised in stages up to 35% in September 1984. Starting in March 1985, as the severe shortage of foreign exchange eased, the tariff was gradually lowered again, reaching 15% by 1988.

Following the crisis, trade policy became more pragmatic in several respects. The government began to make active use of anti-dumping measures to protect the economy from unfair trade practices. To this end, the total tariff (the normal plus compensatory surcharges) was raised up to a maximum of 35% – the level to which Chile had committed itself with GATT in 1979 – on imports that Chile could prove were being dumped. In addition, price bands, allegedly consistent with international price medium-term trends, were set for three main agricultural products (wheat, sugar and oilseeds); this departure from the uniform tariff made a significant contribution to agriculture recovery in the mid-1980s. With regard to exports, the drawback was revised and a simplified system was adopted for non-traditional exports; under this system, such exports became eligible for a refund of up to 10% of their value so long as total exports of the corresponding item did not exceed a given annual maximum.

iii) Contrasts between the two reforms

In summary, Chile carried out two very different trade reforms: a radical reform in 1974–79 and a moderate reform package, with a mix of restriction and liberalization with selective intervention, in 1983–89. While it is true that the basic characteristics of the country's trade policy – in terms of deleting non-tariff barriers and the adoption of a uniform tariff – have not changed since 1979, the tariff had once again become relatively high by 1984 and was, in addition, accompanied by export subsidies, anti-dumping measures and price bands. In fact, the tariff level averaged 20% in 1983–89, which doubled the 10% for 1979–82. The greatest difference, however, was that during the first liberalization drive the exchange-rate had appreciated steadily in the second half of the 1970s, and in the early 1980s. During the second reform, on the other hand, the tariff reduction from its peak of 35% in September 1984 to 15% in 1988 was accompanied by a sharp real depreciation (associated with or pressed by the debt crisis). This sent out positive signals to exporters and producers of importables. As discussed below, during the second trade reforms the production of exportables grew more steadily. Unlike the first liberalization effort, it was also coupled with a strong upturn in the production of import substitutes since 1984.

In the 1990s, Chile had to cope with another external capital surge. However, whereas a prolonged exchange rate appreciation was allowed during the first trade liberalization – in keeping with the country's increasingly passive policy regarding private capital surges – in the first half of the nineties, a successful effort was mounted to curb the peso's appreciation in order to safeguard the competitivity of producers of tradables. To this end, policy systematically shifted away from unrestricted entry for capital inflows, by discouraging arbitrage of short-term and liquid capital flows. The Central Bank used a crawling peg whose point of reference became a basket of currencies. The exchange rate was allowed to fluctuate within a band, but subject to intra-margin intervention (dirty floating). As regards capital flows, foreign loans and deposits and portfolio investment were subject to an unremunerated reserve requirement (that had to be deposited at the Central Bank for one year), which particularly discouraged volatile short-term funding. These and other policies curbed, during the first half of the 1990s, the real upward trend in the currency, which began early in 1988, with a notably high copper price, and, then, the return of private foreign capital (see Agosin and Ffrench-Davis, 2001).

Undoubtedly, the second reform yielded better results than the first. The first was begun during a deep depression (1974–75) and ended in another (1982). Both crises were associated with severe external shocks whose domestic effects were exacerbated by the naive dogmatism with which the liberalization of the external sector was implemented and by the confusion that dominated with respect to the policies required to achieve a creative rather destructive adjustment.

During the first trade reform, sharp tariff reductions and the dismantling of quantitative controls appear to have had a greater positive impact on export growth than the tariff policy of the second reform; in the first case, in the starting point the large majority of domestic prices of current (consumer and intermediate) importables were not tied to international prices;[5] consequently, there was enormous room to reduce costs through substituting imported inputs for domestic ones, and broad opportunities for bringing about changes in relative profitability. The fact remains, however, that because of the recessionary situation in which the import liberalization was implemented in the seventies, the abruptness, and market unfriendly trends exhibited by the exchange rate and interest rates, the strong export performance was achieved at an extremely high cost in the rest of the economy, where the export dynamism was felt too weakly; indeed, per capita GDP (as measured by comparing its 1973 and 1981 peaks) grew less than 1% per year, fixed investment was far below its historical levels, and the economy exhibited a sharp de-industrialization, as evidenced by a five percentage points drop in the share of manufacturing in GDP. Many potentially strong manufacturing enterprises went bankrupt as a consequence of the particular combination of trade, exchange rate and interest-rate policies during that period (see chapter IX).

In 1984 the Chilean economy began to recover and, since the nineties, it went on to achieve sustained growth based on an expansion of exportable supply. The primary reason for the strong performance turned in by non-traditional exports was not the reduction of the country's tariffs, however, since tariffs were lowered from 35% to 15% between 1984 and 1988, but the rate had been 10% in 1979–82.

During the second reform, the depreciation of the currency was the main variable underlying Chile's export success; as said, the real exchange-rate more than doubled between 1981 and 1988; in the case of non-traditional exports, the exchange-rate pull was strengthened by the 10% drawback. Two aspects that must be taken into consideration when evaluating Chile's two trade reform programs are their impacts on capital formation and the manufacturing sector. Although gross capital formation had increased since the end of the recession of the early 1980s, only by the end of that decade the investment ratio had recovered the levels recorded in the sixties. The inability to surpass that investment ratio prevented it

---

[5] Most capital goods imports were subject to a wide range of tariff exemptions.

from achieving significant growth in the period 1974–89; indeed, the average cumulative growth rate for that period was under 3% per year.

Notwithstanding the better performance of trade and manufacturing in the second reform, the de-industrialization process set in motion by the first programme was not reversed, and exports continued concentrated in natural resource-intensive products. However, the share of products with higher value-added (mainly non-traditional exports) expanded from their low base, the investment ratio rose, and the creation of new productive capacity by the early 1990s began to increase at a sustainable pace, faster than the rate recorded for the 1960s. A 2.9% average GDP growth in 1974–89, was followed by a 5.2% in 1990–2004.

b) Mexico

Mexico launched in mid-1985 a drastic import liberalization program and a gradual dismantling of its traditional industrial policy. It is important to note that, in contrast to the Chilean experiment of the 1970s, Mexico's liberalization effort was implemented in parallel with a steep real depreciation of the currency (in 1982–83 and in 1986–87), which gave the manufacturing sector a large cushion for its adjustment (Ten Kate, 1998; Ros, 1993). These large devaluations were necessary in order to cope with the balance-of-payments and fiscal crises sparked by the drying of inflows (in 1982) and the drop in oil prices (in 1986–87).[6]

Before embarking upon trade liberalization, Mexico had used a wide variety of policies to control imports, stimulate industrial output and steer the manufacturing sector towards external markets. In addition to a widely dispersed tariff structure, having a ceiling rate of 100%, Mexican producers were protected by a system of licenses applying to 92% of imports and by the use of official prices for customs valuations which, in one-fifth of cases, were higher than actual import prices. Exporters of non-traditional products were given large tax breaks to offset the anti-export bias of trade policy. Furthermore, for quite some time Mexico had successfully been using industrial promotion programs supporting import substitution in "strategic sectors" (in some cases, together with export promotion). These programs, which provided firms with protection in the domestic market and with tax incentives in exchange for the achievement of increasingly higher local integration or

---

[6] In Mexico, as in Chile, Colombia, Ecuador and Venezuela, devaluations contribute to improve fiscal accounts, since the earnings from its main export are a major source of revenue and have converted the public sector into a net supplier of foreign exchange.

export targets, had become the country's main industrial policy tool during the "difficult stage" of import substitution (Ros, 1993). Overall, GDP growth of Mexico had been high in 1950–80, reaching 6.6% per year, collapsing to 1.9% in 1981–85.

i) The reform launched in 1985

The trade liberalization program began in July 1985 with the elimination of quantitative controls on a large number of tariff positions. Primarily affected were intermediate and capital goods, but the changes also applied to some consumer goods. Tariff rates were set high initially so as to compensate the elimination of direct controls. Then, in 1986, Mexico joined GATT, and its entry fee was a commitment to continue to substitute tariffs for direct controls and, later on, to reduce tariff rates. At the same time, an anti-dumping system was set up but it did not play a major role until the mid-1990s. Together with the introduction of what was called the Economic Solidarity Pact, trade reforms were intensified in 1987–88: a large part of prior permits for consumer goods was discontinued; the remaining official prices were eliminated; and the tariff structure was simplified to involve only five rates, ranging from 0 to 20%, with a production-weighted average of 10% and an import-weighted average of 6% (see table IV.3).

Mexico's trade reform encompassed exports as well, with many export permit requirements being eliminated. Those quantitative export restrictions that continued in effect were made necessary by the existence of price controls (on some agricultural products) or by bilateral or international agreements (regarding coffee, sugar, steel and textiles, which together still represented one-quarter of non-oil exports, including the value added by the maquila industry). The traditional export subsidies were eliminated, in part as a consequence of bilateral agreements with the US. The main export incentives in use by 1994 were programs allowing duty-free entry for temporary imports and exemptions for inputs imported by export firms.

The use of industrial promotion policies was also reduced substantially, although they continued to exert significant effects on exports. The remaining programs, which continued to place quantitative restrictions on imports, primarily applied to the automobile, microcomputer and pharmaceutical industries. However, with the entrance of Mexico to NAFTA, these programs were destined to gradually disappear.

The thick exchange rate cushion created by the real devaluations of 1986 and 1987 enabled the government to launch its Economic Solidarity Pact, which included a freeze on the exchange rate and wage

Table IV.3 Mexico: Trade policy indicators and real exchange rate, 1981–96 (percentages)

Year	Domestic production protected by import permits[a,b]	Domestic production protected by official prices[a,b]	Average tariff [a,b]	Number of tariff levels	Maximum tariff	Real exchange rate[c] (1985 = 100)
1981	64.0	13.4	22.8	n.a.	n.a.	72
1984	92.2	18.7	23.5	10	n.a.	115
1985	47.1	25.4	28.5	10	100	100
1986	39.8	18.7	24.5	11	50	139
1987	25.4	0.6	11.8	11	40	145
1988	21.3	0.0	10.2	5	20	118
1989	19.8	0.0	12.5	5	20	110
1990	17.9	0.0	12.4	5	20	108
1991	17.0	0.0	12.5	5	20	98
1992	16.5	0.0	12.5	5	20	91
1993	16.5	0.0	12.5	5	20	85
1994	n.a.	0.0	12.5	5	20	87
1995	n.a.	0.0	12.5	5	20	129
1996	n.a.	0.0	14.0	24	35	112

Sources: Banco de México; ECLAC (1998); Ros (1993); Ten Kate (1998).

[a] The figures shown for 1985–90 refer to December of each year; the figures for 1981 correspond to April 1980 and those for 1984 correspond to June 1985.
[b] Weighted by output.
[c] Exchange-rate applying to exports.

restraint. In fact, the exchange rate began to be used as an anchor for controlling inflation. During 1988 the nominal exchange rate was frozen. Then, the real rate steadily appreciated until 1995 when there was a sharp depreciation associated with the peso crisis of December 1994.

The Economic Solidarity Pact was highly successful in curbing inflation sharply. Along with the privatization of the banking system and some other public enterprises, the liberalization of FDI and portfolio inflows, and the participation in the Brady Plan (see Devlin and Ffrench-Davis, 1995), it helped to change expectations regarding the future of the Mexican economy. This change, in turn, attracted large volumes of foreign capital and repatriation of flight capital that had left the country at the time of the debt crisis (see chapter VI for the contribution of changes in world financial markets). This capital inflow that lasted up to 1994 sustained the fast pace of revaluation, and a huge current account deficit in 1992–94. All ended up in the severe crisis of late-1994. Like Chile after the debt crisis of 1982, Mexico reestablished some trade protection after 1994.

ii) GDP and export performance

Exports of manufactures have achieved high growth rates and the manufacturing sector's share of GDP has expanded slightly, but the Mexican economy's overall post-reform growth rates have been quite modest and the deficit on current account was growing and achieving extremely high levels. Indeed, between 1985 and 1996, per capita GDP did not increase at all.

Supporters of across-the-board trade liberalization contend that import liberalization is what has made the boom in non-oil exports possible, by giving producers of exportables access to high-quality inputs at international prices and by making it less profitable to produce for the domestic market (thereby indirectly encouraging an export-oriented reallocation of resources). All pro-exports changes. However, the sharp increase in exports, mainly non-oil, had begun in 1983, before the introduction of trade reforms, and it is therefore difficult to attribute the expansion entirely to those reforms. Ros (1993) has estimated that nearly one half of the increase in non-oil exports during the period 1982–88 was accounted for by three sectors (the automobile, computer and maquila industries, partly controlled by FDI)[7] which did not benefit from the measures adopted in order to open up the economy, either because their imports of inputs were already duty-free (the maquiladoras) or because the imports that were competitive with their output remained subject to restrictions under industrial development programs (automobiles and personal computers).

One hypothesis which fits in better with actual trends in the Mexican economy in the 1980s and early 1990s is that the non-oil export boom had more to do first with the steep real depreciations recorded in 1982–83 and 1986–87 and with the depression that hit domestic markets, which encouraged producers to look for markets abroad, especially in the US. Import liberalization may have played a more secondary role for export promotion, especially during the first post-liberalization decade. It must be stressed that during this first decade, imports expanded to a notably larger degree, with a rising deficit on current account (see table VII.3), that exploded in the Tequila crisis. As in the debt crisis, with the Tequila crisis there was a sharp depreciation, a 39% contraction in imports of consumer and capital goods, and an abrupt decline in GDP.

Hence, Mexico's successful bid to expand its exports initially was largely made possible by its earlier import substitution effort and the

---

[7] In this estimate, only the value-added by the maquila sector was classified under non-oil exports.

development programs implemented in strategic sectors (Ros, 1993). This was reinforced and expanded by a more depreciated exchange rate, first as a result of the debt crisis, with a real devaluation of 60% between 1981 and 1983, and then as a result of the trade reform in 1986–87 (see table IV.3). With both exchange-rate adjustments the real exchange rate doubled between 1981 and 1987 (this great adjustment is similar to that of Chile). However, this effect was gradually eroded, due to the appreciation in the nineties that ended up in the 1994 crisis. Then with the entrance to NAFTA (and to other trade agreements) and as time went by, new export activities have been developed, especially those directed to the NAFTA markets. The traditional concentration of the destination of the Mexican exports to the US was intensified after signing the NAFTA. The share on total Mexican sales rose from 83% in 1993 to 89% in 2004. As said, however, GDP growth has been quite low, averaging 2.6% in the two decades (1985–2004) since these reforms were launched. Notice the sharp contrast with 1950–80.

3. Lessons from East Asian dynamic economies

Despite their great diversity, the manufactures-exporting economies of Asia have some characteristics in common with regard to their development strategies and policies (and their results). This fact makes a comparison between them and Latin America particularly instructive. The analysis to be undertaken in this section will be based on the experiences of the Republic of Korea and Taiwan, which have been engaged in an outward-looking industrialization process for several decades. Since the late 1970s, other Asian economies (Indonesia, Malaysia and Thailand) have been implementing rather similar policies and they, as well, have succeeded in achieving growth led by exports of manufactures. In all these economies, the industrialization process started out with an import-substitution model. Without exception, these economies made the transition to an outward-oriented industrialization model based, in large part, on the industrial skills and capacities they had developed earlier. There was not a start from scratch.

In general, the strategy used was to provide relatively equal incentives for exports and for production for the domestic market within any given industry, but to offer quite differentiated incentives (and changing over time) to industries or sectors. In formal terms, the effective exchange-rate (EER), which incorporates the effects of all the various incentives (tariffs, subsidies, etc.), for exports was more or less equal to the effective exchange-rate for import-substitution activities in a given industry$_i$, but differed substantially between industry$_i$ and industry$_j$: $EER(X_i) \approx EER(M_i)$; $EER_i \neq EER_j$.

Although the level of protection in Korea and Taiwan decreased considerably in the past decades and is now approaching levels characteristic of developed countries, these economies began their outward-oriented industrialization processes with high protective barriers that were not dismantled for the sake of reorienting the economy towards exports, as it happened in LACs.[8] One facet of this process, which an observer of the rapidly-growing economies of Asia cannot help but notice, is the state's ability to provide incentives and then to take them away. In other words, the state has demonstrated a striking ability to apply temporary promotion policies. Furthermore, such incentives have traditionally been granted in exchange for the achievement of specific performance targets, usually in the area of exports.

Another highly significant aspect of these experiences was the authorities' success in forestalling a major revaluation and preventing the real exchange rate from experiencing sharp fluctuations such as those usually seen in the LACs.[9] The anti-export bias of tariffs and other substantial trade barriers was in most cases offset by various sorts of export subsidies. In order to manage their exchange rate, most of these economies exercised effective control over foreign capital flows and achieved a significant degree of real macroeconomic stability.

The Asian experiences document that across-the-board trade liberalization is neither a necessary ingredient of dynamic exports nor of export-led growth. In fact, most of these economies were able to maintain relatively protectionist policies and to grow outward, at the same time, with a significant expansion of non-traditional exports. Two factors played a fundamental part in accounting for this phenomenon, which contradicts conventional trade policy recipes. First, in all the successful cases, the authorities made heavy use of various export subsidies to offset the anti-export bias implicit in the protection of importables; each one of the Asian economies examined has had drawback

---

[8] For example, in 1976, more than a decade after its industrialization process was launched, the Republic of Korea had tariffs ranging from 0% to 150%, and for nearly 1,000 tariff items (approximately 40% of all items), the rates were between 30% and 60%. Non-tariff mechanisms and exemptions were also used heavily (Balassa, 1981, chapter 16; Bhagwati, 1978).

[9] Up to the early 1990s. In chapter VII is discussed the Latinamericanization of several East Asian countries, and the subsequent crisis in 1997 (including Korea but excepting Taiwan).

mechanisms for tariffs and indirect taxes paid by exporters,[10] and sizable credit facilities. The second factor is that incentives were provided in exchange for the achievement of specific performance targets and for limited periods of time.

Although all of Asia's fast-growing economies have certain characteristics in common, there are also some significant differences among them that are of interest to Latin America. One of the most interesting aspect of Korea's experience was the different ways in which mature and infant industries were treated (Amsdem, 2001; Westphal, 1992).

In fact, the provision of incentives (which were tied to export targets) for government-promoted infant industries was much more aggressive. The main tool for this purpose was the award of temporary monopolies to selected firms, in the branches of industry that the Government wished to promote, in exchange for the achievement of specific export targets. This meant that, in practice, the promotion of import substitution worked also as an export-promotion mechanism (Krugman, 1990b). These firms soon became exporters, since they were able to subsidize their external sales with the substantial profits they realized in the domestic market. Perhaps the crucial factor in arriving at this result was that the way incentives were managed by authorities prompted these firms to attain international competitiveness from the very outset. This emphasis enabled them to rapidly take advantage of economies of scale and "learning-by-doing."

Another important element was the preferential access to short- and long-term credit, which was provided to firms in the selected sectors. This form of "financial repression" has been justified in the literature, because of market failures associated with asymmetric information, which is a feature especially intense in capital markets (see Stiglitz, 1994; 1998), and market incompleteness that is typical of developing economies. Actually, by choosing certain sectors, the government was favoring specific conglomerates whose creation it had encouraged. This stimulus for the emergence of agents of production in state-promoted sectors, in conjunction with ample access to credit at subsidized interest rates for these activities, was the State's (successful) way of making up for the capital markets' shortcomings (Amsden, 2001). The industrial policy was a sequential one: in the 1960s priority was placed on investment in cement, fertilizers and oil refineries; in the late 1960s and early 1970s, the emphasis was on steel and petrochemicals; in the 1970s, it was

[10] Incentives were intended to reach both direct and indirect exporters, the latter being producers that sell inputs to exporters.

placed on shipyards, capital goods and consumer durables (including motor vehicles); and in the 1980s, the focus was on electronics, telecommunications and informatics.

The industrial and trade policies applied in the Taiwanese economy have in some ways been similar, particularly as regards the sequencing of state support for specific firms and sectors: special assistance was given to the textile, glass, plastics, cement and consumer electronics industries in the 1950s; synthetic textiles and steel in the 1960s; motor vehicles in the 1970s; and informatics since the late 1970s (Wade, 1990, chapter 4). These industries were expected to become internationally competitive, an expectation that was fulfilled in most cases.

Some of the promotion mechanisms were similar to those used in Korea, including the protection of the domestic market, subsidized long-term credit, and tax exemptions. One different facet of the Taiwanese experiment, however, was the active use of state enterprises and investment and the promotion of foreign investment (usually in partnership with national capital) in the selected sectors. In general, Taiwan development was intensive in small and medium firms while that of Korea was intensive in economic groups (*chaebols*).

As time has passed, the state's leadership role in implementing this industrial strategy was tempered and took on a less interventionist cast in both Taiwan and Korea. As the state withdraws from its leadership role in industry, protection was gradually taking on the same role that it performs in industrialized countries, (i.e., that of defending the most backward sectors, especially agriculture). However, these liberalizing trends took office after more than two decades of extraordinary productive development and economic growth, which averaged around 7% per year.

The Latin American liberalization efforts and the longer-lived Asian programs yield lessons that may have an important bearing on economic policy management in Latin America. These findings can help to adjust reforms now under way, so that they will contribute to reach (though quite late) the goals initially sought by trade reforms: improving production patterns, in terms of efficiency and equity, and speeding up growth.

4. The framework for an analysis of trade strategies

Trade reforms in LACs were usually undertaken as part of a broad-ranging process of change, in which international competitiveness and exports played a leading role. The main instrument of reform was an indiscriminate and rapid liberalization of imports. The aim was to expose producers of importables, which often received a high level of protection, to international competition. It was expected that this would result in higher productivity, with the absorption of new technologies and increased specialization. Producers not adapting to competition would be crowded out of the market, and the resources freed up would be swiftly absorbed by other activities, primarily in the production of exportables. The underlying assumption was that this process would take place under a context of full employment of productive factors (labor and capital). Any underutilization of factors would be the result of either obsolescence or a distorting public intervention.

Exports are encouraged, indirectly, (i) by the reduced cost and wider range of importable inputs, which become available with the reform, and (ii) by the exchange-rate depreciation, which the liberalization of imports would supposedly tend to prompt in the foreign exchange market.

In the real world, the reaction of import-substituting activities will depend on how much relative prices change, how swift the change is, and how well the relevant producers are able to adjust. It is more effective if producers can be given the time they need to restructure, but no more than is strictly necessary, so that they will actually be prodded to change. For example, if a tariff is redundant, all the water can be eliminated abruptly; similarly, quotas and other non-tariff barriers can be translated into tariffs. However, the reduction of utilized effective protection should be paced to allow producers to introduce innovations, increase their level of specialization and reallocate their resources. The pace of the adjustment will depend on the credibility of the timetable for change, on the macroeconomic environment (consistency between actual aggregate demand and potential GDP, right macroprices: exchange and interest rates), and on the access producers have to the set of resources they will need in order to restructure. These resources – particularly important for small and medium size enterprises – are, among others: a vigorous long-term capital market, a qualified labor supply, available new technologies, access to external markets, and the provision of adequate infrastructure. They will determine whether exposure to competition will be a net creative or net destructive process. Therefore, it is not surprising the poor performance of neoliberal reforms, since they did not take into account the relevance of these factors as a key ingredient of the process.

The reaction of exports will depend on how much use they make of importables and on how such goods were dealt with in the pre-reform trade system. Often, imports of inputs and capital goods by exporters have benefited from tariff exemptions, but in several cases exports have been discouraged by arbitrary trade restrictions.

The real exchange rate will be a decisive factor in determining the response of output (both of exportables and importables). In order for a trade reform to be successful, the net effect of the changes must be to boost the net production of tradables. The ability to restructure will also depend on the overall dynamism of investment, which is linked to the mentioned set of factors. Naturally, a higher investment rate makes feasible a more constructive adjustment, with more winners and less losers, closer to full employment.

To sum up, the combination of changes in relative prices, in their credibility and graduality, and in the macro- and meso-economic context in which reforms are implemented, will determine whether their effects on resource allocation will be predominantly positive or negative.

a) Two trade reform styles

There are two broad competing alternatives for the sequencing of reform and the resulting output or production frontier path: the restructuring process can start out with an expansion of the production frontier – as did occur in the newly industrializing economies of East Asia – or it can begin with a drop in economic activity and form part of an adjustment process that, for a significant time, takes place below the production frontier. Both cases are depicted in figure IV.2.

In figure IV.2, the X axis represents the value added in the production of exportables and the R axis represents the rest of GDP (the sum of importables and non-tradables). R_0X_0 is the initial frontier and P_0 is the starting point of actual production, below the frontier, which entails a low export coefficient and some degree of inefficiency in resource allocation. Within the framework of a dynamic expansion of the production frontier, the reforms should bring effective production closer to that frontier (that is, actual GDP must grow faster than potential GDP) and should shift the output mix towards a larger share of exportables.

In an export-led strategy, in which the liberalization of imports plays a lagged secondary supporting role (as in the case of the dynamic economies of East Asia), the adjustment process of GDP will tend to follow a path such as that described by the curve P_0P_e. This curve denotes a more than proportional increase in X together with a moderate growth rate for R, within the context of an expanding production frontier and a gradual increase in the efficiency of existing firms. Thus the economy is positioned on, or near, a steadily expanding production frontier.

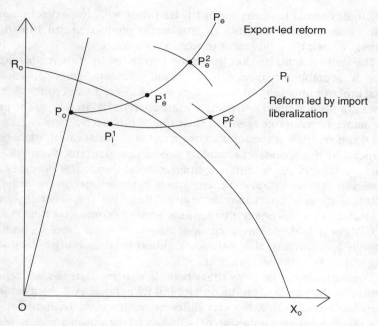

Figure IV.2   East Asia and Latin America: Two differing trade reform strategies

The curve P_oP_i denotes a different strategy, similar to that used in neoliberal reforms, under the Washington Consensus, in LACs; this approach is led by import liberalization and has involved the bankruptcy or down-sizing of a significant share of import-substituting firms, together with a gradual increase in exports. These "desubstitution" pressures dominate adjustment during the early stages of the process, and the economy will therefore be positioned below the production frontier. This fact tends to discourage investment, which will, moreover, force the frontier to remain stationary during the initial years of the reform (see chapter III).

Under this second strategy, the firms who survive will tend to be, on average, stronger and more dynamic than in the first case. During the early years of adjustment in the second case, however, the volume of productive resources available and their rate of use will be lower, owing to the higher rate of bankruptcies and downscaling of activity; the underutilization of resources will thus be greater, and the stimulus for total investment will be weaker. Therefore, a higher degree of microeconomic efficiency will tend to be combined with a lower degree of macroeconomic efficiency. The hysteresis of the process dictates its end result, since what happens during the transition will have a determinant effect upon the level of wellbeing, and on the production structure, that emerges when the adjustment process is completed.

The well-known assertion that trade reform led by import liberalization is favorable for consumers as a result of cheaper imports, ignores that broke or unemployed consumers are net losers. In an economy that does not depend upon rents, any welfare analysis has to rely on the performance of economic agents in their role as producers.

Of course, there is room for a large number of variations in these two options in the process of changing production patterns. Even within each product category, different intertemporal trends will probably be observed. There will also be crossovers between categories: import-substituting enterprises may be converted, in part or in whole, into importers, or – in response to reforms – may become exporters (Katz, 2001). For the sake of this discussion, however, we have focused on two sharply differentiated alternatives in an effort to characterize two opposing styles of internationalization.

The final destinations of these two alternative strategies are represented by the points of production P_i^2 and P_e^2 in figure IV.2. Both exhibit vigorous increases in X but very different results for R. The point P_e^2 is associated with economies such as those of Japan, Korea and Taiwan, whose GDP did show strong growth over an extended period of time, with an X-led economic growth, but significant rises in R as well. During the 1960s and 1970s, Brazil's growth curve was also characterized by a more even rate of expansion in X and R (in the vicinity of the prolongation of OP_o). Chile's situation in its first reform, on the other hand, is depicted more accurately by P_i^2, with a steep increase in X but the stagnation of R as compared to output in P_o; (actually R decreased in per capita terms). That explains why GDP grew less than 3% per year in that period. However, in the nineties, the performance of the Chilean economy – in terms of export dynamism and its composition – was closer to that of East Asia. Indeed, in 1990–98 overall GDP grew 7.1% per year, while X rose 9.9%, and R increased at a vigorous annual rate of 6.5%.

b) The role of the exchange rate

The way the exchange rate is managed will undoubtedly play a decisive role in determining the outcome. Averting an (outlier) exchange-rate appreciation would seem to be crucial to the success of any trade reform whatsoever. As shown above, the Chilean experiment of 1976–81 (as well as that of other Southern Cone countries during the 1970s) document just how harmful the combination of a real appreciation and a drastic import liberalization can be. In contrast, the new adjustment undertaken by Chile since 1983 was more successful and sustainable than the programme implemented in the 1970s, because a reform was coupled with a steep real devaluation and direct incentives to exports.

More recent liberalization programs in Latin America, particularly the most abrupt ones, such as in Argentina and Peru, were implemented in the presence of sharp real appreciation. The experiences of diverse LACs show that except in the short term, when it is used as a means of changing expectations, the exchange-rate anchor for domestic prices has proven to be extremely flimsy, particularly in high-inflation countries (see chapter II). Evidently a policy tool is lost, the exchange rate being a crucial policy tool for changing production patterns while maintaining external equilibrium. This is one of the strong messages of the East Asian success experiences until the mid-1990s.

In the 1950s and 1960s appreciation became, sometimes, feasible because it was compensated for by increased import restrictions. In the 1990s, in the face of import liberalization, appreciation can be feasible given the terms of trade only under two situations. First, with fast rising exports, in response to high productivity gains; it is a case of sustainable productivity-led appreciation (Balassa, 1964). But, in general, trade reforms in the 1990s resulted in imports rising faster than exports, which prove that appreciation was stronger than the productivity change. Second, appreciation becomes feasible with large capital inflows, as in the 1990s, while expectations of creditors/investors remain positive.

Under conditions such as those prevailing during the second half of the 1970s or most of the 1990s, external financial liberalization made the management of the real exchange rate more difficult (Williamson, 2000). Short-term capital flows generated by the expectation of turning a speculative profit from the differential between international and domestic interest rates may cause the real exchange-rate to become highly unstable, and may thus hinder the management of this variable, which is an economic policy tool of crucial importance in any attempt to change production patterns. Moreover, instability in exchange and interest rates tends to encourage a rent-seeking (capital gains) attitude, which predominates over productivity-led profits, and tends to provide confusing signals to resource allocation. Consequently, for consistency an export-led development strategy should regulate capital flows.

c) Incentives: selectivity versus neutrality

Past experience and the cases discussed here contradict the hypothesis that, once a country has made its incentives neutral by dismantling protection and discontinuing subsidies, resources will be reallocated spontaneously and costlessly to the sectors in which that country has comparative advantages. Chile's experience in the 1970s attests to the high costs of a radical liberalization drive, which did away with selectivity. It is unlikely that the present value of costs of transition will be compensated, for the majority of workers and entrepreneurs, by the more rapid growth after adjustment has been completed. Nonetheless, even if there were full compensation, the Asian experiences suggest that more selective and gradual policies of liberalizating imports, together with stronger support for non-traditional exports, are required to enable the economy to turn in a stronger overall performance.

If the aim is to change production patterns efficiently, in a way that will make the economy more open to trade (of imports as well as exports) and carve out an upgraded position in international markets, then the negative pulls generated by liberalization will not suffice; policies that create positive pulls will also be needed. Obviously, this does not imply a return to the high, indiscriminate protective barriers of the past. In fact, it can be argued that import substitution policies erred by being too indiscriminate rather than too selective. What is needed is a much greater degree of selectivity, but ensuring that deviations from neutrality are few and well chosen (see chapter V).

There are no compelling theoretical reasons for choosing absolute uniformity in the case of tariffs, in the case of a second-best world. If most industrial activities are subject to dynamic economies of scale of a more or less diffuse nature, then it can be argued (as it is by Rodrik, 1992) that it is best to benefit some broad categories of activities rather than getting embroiled in trying to pick winners by favoring specific industries. Moderation in the number of tariff levels or brackets will help to curb abuses and rent-seeking activism. Furthermore, any high tariff in excess of the base level should be temporary in nature.

Export subsidies are necessary to promote an efficient form of industrialization in the presence of import duties, avoiding the anti-export bias of the past. One mechanism to avert an anti-export bias is the establishment of drawbacks on inputs used in the production of exportables. Indeed, cases can be found in both Latin America (e.g., Colombia, Costa Rica and Brazil) and Asia where subsidies for non-traditional exports have yielded positive results. In order to minimize the possibility that such subsidies may be misused, subsidies should decrease as exports increase based on a pre-established, publicly-announced timetable that is not subject to renegotiation.

Policy-makers should bear in mind that the international situation has changed substantially since the burgeoning economies of East Asia embarked upon their export-based industrialization processes in the 1960s and 1970s. Today, it would be much more difficult to offer incentives of the magnitude that were granted at that time by the East Asian economies, both because of the more protectionist environment that now exists in the international economy (which now makes it more likely, for example, that developed importing countries would protect themselves against export subsidies by levying countervailing duties) and because international trade rules and standards are much stricter after the Uruguay Round than they used to be.

There is one very important policy area in which there is a natural symmetry of positive and negative pulls or $EER_{xi} \approx EER_{mi}$. In the case of countries in a process leading to a free trade area or a custom union, it implies encouragement for intra-regional imports *pari passu* with intra-regional exports. The proliferation of regional integration agreements in the 1990s has tended to soften the impact of unilateral import liberalization and to provide a significant incentive to exports of manufactures. Regional integration processes, under the cover of relatively low external tariffs, have been named open regionalism (see chapter V).

d) The relationship between import liberalization and export promotion

Experience has demonstrated that it is more efficient to make deep import liberalization (the stage beyond eliminating water in protection) only once a sustained increase in exports and a dynamic transformation of production have been achieved. The cases of the East Asian countries bear witness to this fact (Sachs, 1987). This is the first of the options set forth in the analytical scheme presented above (figure IV.2). Although this course of action is no longer a feasible option for many LACs after the Uruguay Round, the Asian experiences demonstrate the need to take direct steps to boost exports rather than waiting for import liberalization alone to indirectly have the stimulating effect on export performance.

In the majority of the liberalization programs being pursued in Latin America, the option of promoting exports first and liberalizing imports later has already been explicitly ruled out; a liberalization program has already been carried out, and it was done in a context where the creation of productive capacity in these countries was far from being dynamic. Imports have been liberalized without providing any significant incentives for exports other than reducing restrictions on imported inputs and the assumption of spontaneous depreciation of the currency. Moreover, many countries that have undertaken sweeping reforms have proceeded to dismantle or cut back export promotion schemes, whether they had been successful or not in the past. This explains why negative pulls have been stronger than positive pulls; hence, the high costs of these liberalization programs in terms of growth while the transition is being made to a new equilibrium. One constructive question that might be posed at this point is, given the constraints imposed by the path already chosen, how can the overall efficiency of the reforms be enhanced? The suggestions that follow in chapter V are directed primarily to answer that question.

V
Export Dynamism in Latin America: Why has it been Insufficient for GDP Dynamism?

Introduction

Since the mid-eighties, Latin America recorded significant export dynamism. This was associated, first, with depreciation of local currencies as a result of the debt crisis, and secondly, with a generalized process of trade liberalization. Indeed, regional exports grew over 7% in 1990–2004. However, despite the export success, the overall economic performance was rather poor, with an annual growth rate of GDP of 2.6% for the region as a whole. Why were the high rates of export growth in the nineties not associated with a vigorous GDP growth in Latin America as did happen, for instance, in the East-Asian Economies?

The answer is not simple. On the one hand, trade reforms in LACs implied net negative pulls on import substitutes (see chapter IV), which contributed to costly external imbalances that evolved into crises during this decade and a half (see chapter VII). On the other hand, the intensity and quality of export dynamism and its linkages with the rest of the domestic economy have exhibited notorious differences with those of East Asia. LACs still export principally low value-added commodities.

After a first phase of unilateral trade liberalization, the region witnessed a new trend of intra-regional integration, characterized by the signature of numerous bilateral and multilateral intra-regional preferential regional trade agreements (PRAs). The new strategy – the so-called *open regionalism* – improved the balance of trade opening of Latin American nations because of its reciprocal effects in terms of wider markets for participants. In turn, the increased regional trade stimulated a change in the export basket, favoring a higher share for non-traditional sectors, particularly manufactured goods. However, large potential benefits from PRAs remain underexploited because the process is still incipient and vulnerable to the regional instability, as proved by the set-back after 1998.

This chapter summarizes the export evolution since the early nineties in Latin America, and its links with economic development. Section 1 analyzes the relationship between export dynamism and economic growth. Section 2 reviews the experience of open regionalism in Latin America, highlighting the main features of the PRAs in the region and their consequences on export quality. Finally, section 3 discusses a set of export enhancing policies contributing to sustained economic development.

1. Exports and development

Exports must be a leading sector of economic growth. Accordingly, Latin American exports must continue to grow faster than GDP. The success in the export target and the failure in generating high GDP growth and convergence with developed economies reveals that dynamic export expansion is not a sufficient condition for vigorous economic growth. To understand this result it is necessary to analyze the channels through which exports can affect economic development and the regional performance in this respect.

a) The role of exports

There are different channels by which exports can boost a country's rate of economic growth: by (i) generating the foreign exchange which will enable it to purchase the imports required for its economic expansion, at a lower real cost than that of producing import substitutes; that increases the average productivity of the domestic economy, and of the world; (ii) exploiting economies of scale and specialization, directed to the broader external markets; (iii) giving rise to positive effects or linkages with other local activities, which make it possible to harness underutilized capital and human resources or stimulate new investments; (iv) bringing greater contact with the international best practices, exposing export activities and their suppliers to the demands of competitiveness, and (v) exports can also play a macroeconomic role. In economies under a binding external constraint (BEC), increased exports contribute to raise the rate of use of resources. For instance, the significant recovery of actual GDP in 2004 was generated by the direct increase in the quantum of exports, a multiplier pull of that quantum on aggregate demand, and a pull from terms of trade improvement. This macroeconomic welfare enhancing effect of exports came to fill the empty space left by a poor real macroeconomic policy prevailing in 1998–2003 (see chapters II and VII).

From the standpoint of generating foreign exchange it is important not only the volume of exports but also the return obtained from them. Thus, it is crucial to promote exports of goods and services with a growing and vigorous external demand over time. One of the pitfalls of a strong concentration of traditional exports in natural resource-based products is that their long-term world demand grows slowly. In addition, many developing countries put pressure on the supply, causing a fall in international prices. In order to sustain a high growth of export quantum – for example, between 8 and 12% per annum – without a worsening in terms of trade, it is necessary to diversify the export basket towards products with more dynamic demand.

As regard the spillover effects from trade on the rest of the economy, the larger the number of firms and productive sectors associated with exports the greater the impact on the production structure. Similarly, this impact increases along with the national capacity to absorb the knowledge acquired by export firms. This is why it is important to deepen the linkages between export activity and the rest of the productive system and to improve domestic mechanisms for the transfer and dissemination of technology, as well as human resources training.

Thus, public policies to support exports are key ingredients to enhance development. A strategy of international insertion must give priority to growth and diversification of exports as a long-term goal. But, at the same time, the strategy has to strengthen the linkages of exports with the rest of the economy, by coordinating export promoting policies with a set of mesoeconomic policies including measures to promote productive development, via technological innovation and labor training. All in a context of consistent exchange rate, fiscal and financial policies (see chapter II; and Bouzas and Keifman, 2003).

b) Export performance since the nineties and its effects on growth

When comparing export performance and economic growth in the few last decades, two contrasting empirical relations emerge in Latin America. First, cross section analyses reveal that there is a positive relationship between exports and economic growth: over the last three decades, countries with a higher export growth have tended to experience a higher GDP growth (ECLAC, 1998, chapter III; Macario, 2000). Since the eighties, exports have grown faster than non-exported GDP, becoming one of the most dynamic components of the regional economy.

This first fact appears to support the idea that export promotion should be the pillar of development policies.

Second, the positive correlation between export performance and economic growth does not hold in a time series analysis in Latin America. Indeed, during the period of the highest economic growth in the Latin American history (1950–80) exports did not show an impressive dynamism; in contrast, in the nineties a mediocre GDP growth was accompanied by a strong expansion of exports. This disconnection is due, on the one hand, to the fact that GDP does not depend exclusively upon exports: non-exported GDP accounts for the vast majority of economic activity. In a long-term view, export growth rates in the nineties are the highest in the recent history. Given a slow economic growth, the share of gross exports in GDP grew from just 11% in the 1970s to 22% in 2000–04 (in current prices; see table V.1). On the other hand, the indirect effects of exports on growth have been weak. This second empirical fact highlights that export development must be consistent with a comprehensive framework of systemic competitivity for export dynamism to result associated with vigorous GDP growth.

Table V.1   Latin America: Trade and economic growth, 1950–2004 (annual average growth and shares in GDP, %)

	1950s	1960s	1970s	1980s	1990s	2000–04[d]
Latin America (19)						
Growth of GDP	4.9	5.7	5.7	1.8	2.8	2.1
Growth of exports[a]	4.2	4.5	2.4	4.8	8.1	5.7
Growth of imports[a]	3.2	3.5	7.6	−0.1	10.6	4.1
Exports/GDP[b]	12.4	12.1	10.8	14.9	15.6	22.6
Imports/GDP[b]	12.0	11.6	11.7	13.1	16.6	22.5
Latin America (18, Venezuela excluded)						
Growth of GDP	4.7	5.7	6.0	2.0	2.8	2.2
Growth of exports[a]	3.5	4.9	5.5	5.6	8.4	6.0
Growth of imports[a]	2.0	5.0	7.2	0.6	11.0	4.2
Memo: World						
Growth of GDP	4.4	5.5	4.2	3.0	3.1	3.7
Growth of exports[c]	7.1	9.0	5.9	3.7	5.8	4.9

Sources: ECLAC, IMF and WTO.

[a] Goods and services, based on national accounts data at constant prices.
[b] Exports and imports of goods and services from the Balance of Payments in current US dollars. Nominal GDP from national accounts.
[c] Exports of goods.
[d] Preliminary figures for 2004.

In the 1980s, LACs made strenuous efforts to generate foreign exchange to meet their external liabilities. In this sense, export development was not, in many cases, the result of deliberated export-enhancing policies but the consequence of significant exchange rate devaluations, derived from the binding external constraint and the depressed domestic environment. In fact, LACs achieved sizable trade surpluses to finance net financial transfers abroad. This conjuncture of external restriction strengthened the positive effects of exports. As a result, countries that reached higher rates of export growth were, on average, those that also were able to recover economic activity more rapidly in that period. However, since at the same time, the rest of the economy still suffered a severe recessive adjustment, good export performances in terms of volume and trade diversification (see ECLAC, 2002, chapter 6) were not accompanied by a high GDP growth.

In the 1990s, in the context of the reforms being implemented in their economies, most LACs placed considerable emphasis on openness to international goods and capital markets as the leader of the development process. Nonetheless, while there was an improvement in output growth compared to the lost decade, the economic performance was still disappointing. Table V.2 shows that in 1990–2004, export rose on average 7.3% per annum, well over the world merchandise trade growth of 5.5%. Regional GDP growth, instead, was only 2.6%, below the world average.[1]

During the period of economic recovery in 1990–97, exports grew 8.3%, close to 40% faster than international trade. Undoubtedly, this was a noticeable achievement. As reviewed in section 2, the boom in intra-regional trade played a key role, but exports to extra-regional markets also grew at a fast pace. This was the so-called open regionalism.

However, while exports expanded 8.3% yearly, GDP grew only 3.2% per annum. Why export dynamism was not accompanied by a better economic performance? First, the share of net exports in GDP was still modest in LACs during the nineties. This implied that the direct effects of increased exports were limited; exports contributed directly only 1 percentage point to GDP increase. Second, positive macroeconomic externalities from exports to the rest of the economy were weaker than in the eighties: this time, the economies were not facing a binding external constraint (on the contrary there was an excess of foreign currency)

---

[1] Per capita average GDP growth in 1990–2004 was 0.9% in Latin America, 1.2% in the world and 1.7% in the United States.

Table V.2   Latin America and the world: Growth of exports and non-exported GDP, 1990–2004 (annual average rates of growth, %)

	Latin America (19) Gross Domestic Product			World	
	Total	Non-exported value-added	Exported value-added	Exports	GDP
1990–97	3.2	2.5	8.3	6.1	3.1
		(2.2)	(1.0)		
1998–2003	1.3	0.5	5.4	4.5	3.4
		(0.4)	(0.9)		
2004	5.8	4.8	10.8	6.9	4.6
		(4.0)	(1.8)		
1990–2004	2.6	1.8	7.3	5.5	3.3
		(1.6)	(1.0)		

Source: Latin America: based on official figures from ECLAC for 19 countries. World: based on IMF and WTO. Figures into brackets are estimates of points of GDP growth contributed by exports and non-exports, respectively. Export value-added was estimated by discounting the imported content in exports from gross exports of good and services. The imported content was assumed to be equal to the share of non-consumer imports of goods in total GDP; for Mexican maquila, we used actual figures of value-added.

and, therefore, there was not a Keynesian like contribution of exports. Third, the export basket implied low productive externalities, since it remained concentrated on goods with low technological content and low labor-intensity. Moreover, trade liberalization processes had positive effects on exports but at the same time had negative effects on import-substitutes (see chapter IV). Thus, there was a poor expansion of the rest of the economy, which grew only 2.5% per year.

Chile was an exception in this regard among LACs. During the same period 1990–97, exports rose 10.6% per year, while GDP grew 7.6% thanks to a dynamic 6.9% expansion of the rest of the economy. The same pattern can be seen in East Asia; for instance, in 1990–97, East Asia recorded an average GDP growth of 7%, accompanied by great dynamism in non-exported output that expanded around 6% per year. This performance mirrors a framework of systemic competitiveness and high investment, not only in exportables but also in non-tradables and in import-substitutes.

Starting in 1998, the impact of the Asian crisis and the subsequent slowdown in growth in developed economies dragged down the prices of exports and eroded the terms of trade of the non-oil-producing countries of the region. In 2001–03, terms of trade were 10% lower than in 1997. A sharp drop in intra-regional trade, especially in South America, followed the contagion of the shock from Asian markets. Consequently, the export drive in the region as a whole lost momentum, declining to a quantum expansion of 5.4% a year in the period 1998–2003.

The East Asian crisis was also felt through financial channels. There were sizable outflows of short-term and liquid capital. Both trade and financial shocks, in a context of domestic vulnerability (see chapter VII), provoked a persistent economic depression in 1998–2003. Domestic markets experienced the worst effects, as shown in table V.2. A moderated export growth of 5.4% per year was associated to a low expansion of the whole economy of 1.3%, given that the non-exported GDP (then accounting for 84% of total output in LACs) grew only 0.5%. The last two figures become negative when measured in per capita terms, since population rose annually 1.6%. Thus, there was a lost sexennium that resembles the "lost decade" of the eighties.

In 2004, a sharp improvement in external conditions took place. The world economy grew 4.6% and overall trade expanded 6.9% (see table V.2). The rise in world demand meant an increase in export prices for LACs. One of the causes of this booming scenario is the increasing importance of China – whose economy has expanded 10% per year in the last decade – in global trends. The dynamic Chinese economy has eased an export-led recovery in the case of commodity producers among LACs (for example Argentina, Brazil, Chile and Peru) that have significantly increased their exports to China. On the other hand, however, Chinese development has challenged manufacturing exports from some LACs with a similar specialization pattern. This is the case of Mexico and Central America, that now face a stronger competition both in international goods markets (especially in the USA) and in the attraction of greenfield FDI.

Therefore, the significant recovery of GDP in 2004, with a 5.8% rise, was led by increased exports. However, over two-thirds were achieved by an increase in the output of non-exports, as shown in table V.2. Correspondingly, the output gap was reduced but not exhausted.

2. Open regionalism

During the nineties, together with the trend of unilateral trade liberalization (see chapter IV), several integration agreements were signed among different combinations of LACs. They contributed to a significant rise of intra-regional trade. This model of rather open economies with a growing interdependence among regional markets is known as *open regionalism*.[2]

a) An analytical basis for preferential regional trade agreements (PRAs)

The conventional literature on the benefits and costs of economic integration focuses on tariff preferences in a framework of optimal competitive equilibrium. Equilibrium is assumed to be disturbed only by the existence of import restrictions. In this framework, integration is beneficial only if it implies a net move toward free trade. That is, if the effects of trade creation (shift toward cheaper sources of supply) are larger than those of trade diversion (shift toward more costly sources of supply). The crucial issue, however, is how costs are measured and how they evolve; in the standard approach, it is at actual market prices net of tariffs, assuming away transitional costs and *incomplete* markets, as well as ignoring the role of acquirable competitivity. The assumptions lead to the obvious conclusion that overall unilateral liberalization is the optimal national policy and, consequently, superior to PRAs.

Why, then, do so many nations want to be involved in integration processes, even in these times of fashionable free trade? Regional integration builds on strategic considerations arising from imperfect and *incomplete* markets at home and abroad, which handicap the spread of efficiency gains in certain sectors and the development of new productive patterns with progressively higher degrees of value added. The five issues that follow are related to trade in goods and services, and provide analytical bases to support regional integration arrangements with preferential import regimes. One crucial assumption we adopt is that regional integration takes place in a framework of open regionalism, with "moderate" external tariffs.

(i) First, world markets are not widely open and stable. Nonetheless, they are broad, have grown about 50% faster than GDP in the last half century, and have reached one-fifth of world GDP. However, LACs

---

[2] See Devlin and Giordano (2004). Up until June 1990, the predominant view in the region was that integration accords should be of a partial, very limited scope, along the lines of the LAIA agreement in force at the time. The mainstream economic view was that trade blocs were inefficient and hindered world trade. It is interesting that President Bush's Initiative for the Americas, launched in 1990, changed or overshadowed that view, and, subsequently, concerns about trade diversion appeared to have been disregarded by authorities.

exports are concentrated in natural resource-based primary and semi-manufactured commodities. Thus, with or without participation in PRAs, world markets have been and will continue to be crucial for traditional exports of LACs; instability actually prevails in those markets, but it refers more to prices rather than to access (or volume). However, for many non-traditional products (including non-traditional natural resources), access to markets is more limited and unstable. It is for these types of products that PRAs become relevant to foster a diversifying growth of exports.

(ii) Second, given those distortions in world markets, economies of scale and specialization are more difficult to secure for an emerging country. To lock in improved access to regional foreign markets helps to make use of those economies, and in fact this achievement has been a leading target of policy-makers and a force encouraging regional integration. As a consequence, in face of economies of scale, what otherwise would be a costly trade diversion can become a cost-reducing and welfare-enhancing trade diversion.[3]

(iii) Third, domestic factors markets are *incomplete* or distorted. Labor training, technology and long-term capital are scarce, with non-existent or infant markets in LACs. These market failures are more significant for non-traditional exports of differentiated products, whether of natural resources, manufactures or exportable services. If access to external markets is improved for these exportables, it can strengthen the effectiveness of efforts to complete markets and dilute segmentation.

(iv) Fourth, infrastructure, trade financing and knowledge of markets (marketing channels, organized transportation, standards, etc.) are often biased against intra-regional trade in LACs. All these special "factors" of trade have been traditionally more developed for deals with the "center" while they are non-existent or more rudimentary for trade among LACs neighbors. This is a significant variable explaining why intra-regional trade has been lower among LACs than what the gravity of geography suggests.

(v) Fifth, in economies reforming trade policies, sliding away from excessive and arbitrary protection for import substitutes and inputs of exportables, there tend to emerge significant transition costs. These are enhanced if the exchange rate happens to appreciate, as it was the case in most LACs in the 1990s.

East Asian nations minimized transition costs in the 1960s and 1970s with an export-led strategy for opening to the world economy (see

---

[3] The geometry of economies of scale and their implications for the net effect of trade diversion on welfare is analyzed in Corden (1972) and extended in Ffrench-Davis (1980). Winters (1998) presents a recent survey on the assessment of PRAs.

chapter IV). That is, in their opening processes, nations like Japan, Korea and Taiwan put stronger emphasis in export promotion than import liberalization; thus, in the transition period they provided a net positive balance of pulls for the domestic output of tradables (encouraging use of capacity, and investment to increase that capacity). Given the LACs option for an import-led reform, a parallel process of regional PRAs becomes more attractive, in order to increase the efficiency of the productive transformation (ECLAC, 1998). In fact, PRAs add a compensatory ingredient to unilateral import liberalization: they foster reciprocal exports in tandem with reciprocal imports. Hence, the doses of positive and negative pulls to economic activity and investment are more balanced under PRAs, than is the case in pure unilateral import liberalization.

All these five points represent significant restrictions on the expansion of production and trade in goods and services relatively intensive in knowledge and longer learning curves, elements that are now recognized as key components of the growth process. Regional integration can be a strategic tool to partially overcome these obstacles, thus allowing countries to make a better globalization (Devlin and Ffrench-Davis, 1998) by:

- expanding market size to facilitate greater specialization and industrialization through economies of scale and possibilities to exploit economies associated with the agglomeration of production activities.
- enhancing the forces of competition, enlarging a market with preferential reciprocal access, and intensifying the specificity of information flows, all of which in turn should induce new domestic investment and provide better conditions to attract efficient FDI.
- PRAs contribute to accelerate the emergence of new producers and traders of non-traditional exports. In effect, the learning curve associated with subregional export experience can serve as a platform for new international exports; history has shown that developing countries must achieve new dynamic comparative advantage on the road of their long-term convergence with industrialized countries, preparing EEs better for further advances in multilateral liberalization. Fulfillment of commitments and achievement of real macroeconomic balances are determinant of the results to be gotten.

b) Intra-regional trade and enhanced export quality

The strategic dimension of regional integration requires that the profile of intra- and extra-regional exports from Latin America display marked differences, in terms of their product structure and technological content, with manufactures accounting for a much larger share of intra-regional trade, as shown in table V.4 below.

i) Ups and downs in intra-regional trade

Intra-regional trade expanded at a fast pace since 1990. Total intra-regional exports more than tripled between 1990 and 1997. Initially it was principally a recovery from the sharp drop of the 1980s. However, given a notably rapid growth, shortly the prior peaks were reached. Subsequently, the Tequila crisis reduced the share of intra-regional exports, particularly those to Argentinean and Mexican markets. The recovery in those markets in 1996–97 meant also a rebound in regional trade. In particular, MERCOSUR showed a persistently rising share of reciprocal trade; it jumped from 9% of their total exports in 1990 to 25% in 1997 (table V.3).

It is interesting to compare GDP growth, total exports and intra-regional exports (all in real terms).[4] Latin American GDP grew 22% between 1990 and 1997, while total exports rose 77%. Within these, intra-regional exports expanded 175%, while to extra-regional markets they rose 59%. That is, faster than world trade (that rose 53%), with a gross extra-regional export/GDP elasticity over 2. These data support the hypothesis of open regionalism, with trade growing fast with all markets, but with a rising share to partner's destinations. Nonetheless, the direct impact of this trend in intra-regional trade on economic growth was bounded since reciprocal exports represented only 3.5% of regional GDP.

Since 1998, intra-regional trade suffered an abrupt setback. First, the Asian crisis and then the Argentinean crisis and Brazilian adjustment severely hit most South American economies. Indeed, LACs depreciated their currencies and adjusted their imports to face balance of payments problems. As a result, the contraction of intra-regional exports was particularly sizable in MERCOSUR and in the Andean Community, with annual average nominal drops of 8% and 2% in 1998–2003, respectively. This was another dimension of the so-called lost sexennium in Latin America.

ii) The composition of reciprocal trade and technological intensity

Development based on a growing and sustained systemic competitiveness is boosted by the dynamic effects derived from technological

---

[4] Given the lack of price indexes by destination, we deflated current figures by the general export price index. Consequently, figures are in "real terms" instead of quantum levels.

Table V.3 Latin America and the Caribbean: Intra-regional trade, 1990–2003 (US$ millions, percentage shares and annual growth rates)

	1990	%	1994	%	1997	%	2003
Andean Community[a]							
1 Total exports	31,751	1.5	33,706	11.4	46,609	2.7	54,716
2 Intra-regional exports	1,312	30.1	3,752	14.5	5,628	−2.3	4,900
3 Share of intra-regional exports (2:1) (%)	4.1		11.1		12.1		9.0
MERCOSUR[b]							
1 Total exports	46,403	7.5	61,890	10.1	82,596	4.4	106,674
2 Intra-regional exports	4,127	30.7	12,049	19.5	20,546	−7.7	12,695
3 Share of intra-regional exports (2:1) (%)	8.9		19.5		24.9		11.9
CACM[c]							
1 Total exports	3,907	8.9	5,496	19.1	9,275	6.3	11,146
2 Intra-regional exports	624	20.7	1,326	5.5	1,559	25.5	3,082
3 Share of intra-regional exports (2:1) (%)	16.0		24.1		16.8		27.7
CARICOM[d]							
1 Total exports	4,118	2.1	4,471	9.4	5,861	3.3	6,466
2 Intra-regional exports	509	6.9	666	13.6	976	12.1	1,377
3 Share of intra-regional exports (2:1) (%)	12.4		14.9		16.7		21.3
Latin America and the Caribbean[e]							
1 Total exports	116,341	8.6	161,718	13.8	238,467	7.8	298,735
2 Intra-regional exports	18,727	18.2	36,552	17.8	59,731	0.2	60,018
3 Share of intra-regional exports (2:1) (%)	16.1		22.6		25.0		20.1

Source: ECLAC. Growth rates of exports are annual averages in 1991–94, 1995–97 and 1998–2003, in current prices.

[a] Andean Community (Bolivia, Colombia, Ecuador, Peru, Venezuela).
[b] MERCOSUR (Argentina, Brazil, Paraguay, Uruguay).
[c] CACM (Costa Rica, EL Salvador, Guatemala, Honduras, Nicaragua).
[d] CARICOM (Bahamas, Barbados, Belize, Guyana, Haiti, Jamaica, Suriname, Trinidad and Tabago, Anguila, Antigua and Barbuda, Dominica, Granada, Monserrat, Saint Kitts and Nevis, San Vicente and Granadinas, Santa Lucia).
[e] Latin America (37 countries, excludes Mexican Maquila).

apprenticeship. The strategies to improve international linkages, based on productive development, emphasize the role played by trade in stimulating the development of activities, which make intensive use of knowledge and technology, and generate externalities.

In this sense, trade among LDCs is supposed to be characterized by goods that are more technology-intensive than exports to industrial

Table V.4 Latin America and the Caribbean: Geographical and specialization export patterns, 1990–2002 (shares)

Type of Product	In total exports	By type of product and region					
		Latin America	United States	European Union	Asia	Others	World
1990							
Primary	49.8	12.0	33.6	30.0	9.1	15.3	100
Industrialized based on NR	24.5	16.2	26.3	29.9	15.3	12.3	100
Industrialized non-based on NR	24.5	27.6	29.8	19.3	13.1	10.2	100
Rest	1.3	13.3	21.4	16.3	3.7	45.2	100
Total	**100.0**	**16.9**	**30.7**	**27.2**	**11.5**	**13.7**	**100**
1997							
Primary	41.7	16.0	29.3	28.4	13.5	12.8	100
Industrialized based on NR	26.5	28.8	24.5	18.4	15.7	12.7	100
Industrialized non-based on NR	27.3	53.5	22.7	11.4	7.1	5.3	100
Rest	4.5	6.4	11.2	8.3	0.5	73.5	100
Total	**100.0**	**29.2**	**25.4**	**20.2**	**11.8**	**13.4**	**100**
2002							
Primary	43.9	16.8	30.6	23.9	13.7	15.1	100
Industrialized based on NR	24.2	26.3	25.3	21.1	12.9	14.3	100
Industrialized non-based on NR	29.0	40.7	32.6	12.3	7.7	6.6	100
Rest	3.0	10.3	15.9	24.9	0.7	48.2	100
Total	**100.0**	**25.8**	**29.5**	**19.9**	**11.4**	**13.4**	**100**

Source: ECLAC. NR: Natural resources.

Includes 32 countries (excluding Mexico), which explains differences with table V.3.

countries.[5] Table V.4 presents data for LACs confirming the validity of that assumption. Actually, the profile of intra-regional trade has contributed to improve the composition of LACs exports: the predominance of primary exports was partially replaced by manufactures, which

[5] Another way of putting that feature is that intra-LDCs trade tends to be capital intensive as opposed to trade with industrial nations, which tend to be labor-intensive. This line of thought, in a static approach, assumes that trade with rich countries is more convenient for LDCs. However, in those markets LACs have to compete with suppliers with notably lower wages, such as China and India.

in 1997 accounted for over one-half of intra-trade, and were rising 18% per year (in current dollars). This notable increase in manufactured exports corresponded especially to new industries, including both labor-intensive and capital-intensive activities. This was a rather widespread phenomena, since the region provided dynamic markets for the sales of manufactures for several LACs (ECLAC, 1998, chapter III; 2004a; Bouzas and Keifman, 2003). It is highly relevant to notice that border trade (with neighbor countries) represents the bulk of intra-regional trade for most LACs, a new proof that geography matters.

Table V.4 also shows the sharp sensitivity of reciprocal trade to the macroeconomic environment. Compare the 54% share of manufactures based on non-natural resources in 1997 with the 41% in 2002. That drop reflected the impact of the prevailing recessive environment, particularly in MERCOSUR, in 1998–2003.

Products which encounter a relatively high share of their demand in regional markets exhibit more advanced technological characteristics than exports channeled towards extra-regional markets. Thus they tend to contribute with larger externalities to the domestic economies. Usually, they correspond to sectors in which international demand tends to be more dynamic. Their price trends are more stable and their factorial terms of trade evolve more positively over the long term than those of traditional exports (Ocampo and Parra, 2003).

To sum up, intra-regional trade, because of its characteristics, associated with both vicinity and similarity of development levels, improves the quality of LACs linkages with the global economy and provide a dynamic context of technological apprenticeship, leading to greater international competitiveness and a more diversified, balanced pattern of specialization.

Additionally, given the macroeconomic juncture by the early 1990s, reciprocal trade also made a rather neo-keynesian contribution to the LACs', economies. Indeed, the encouragement to intra-regional exports increased the demand for domestic resources and for investment; this is positive for growth and efficiency in a framework of economies operating below the production frontier and conducting import liberalization. Tariff preferences, removal of reciprocal import restrictions and creation of additional outlets for domestic output (with harmonization of standards, transportation, improved infrastructure, marketing channels, reciprocal investment, etc.) contributed to increase the rate of use of resources and to encourage some productive investment. Contrariwise, the recessive macroeconomic environment, in 1998–2003, worked in the opposite direction. This is one more strong reason for moving toward a macroeconomics for development.

iii) Challenges to intra-regional trade

Regional economic integration yields significant benefits not only in economic terms but also in the political, social and cultural spheres. However, the transition toward comprehensive real integration can be a source of instability and imply allocative costs. During the early nineties, transition was easy. The integration process took place during years of booming economic activity after a recessive over-adjustment of intra-regional imports. Therefore, there was large room for growth of reciprocal trade, even though now under rather moderate tariff preferences. Latin America took advantage of that opportunity.

However, the region suffered, once again, severe adjustments in 1995 and since 1998, which meant the emergence of tensions in the integration process. This is another consequence of real macroeconomic instability in LACs. Indeed, as regional integration becomes more intense, economic interdependence increases and so do risks of macroeconomic contagion. In this context, it is crucial to harmonize several dozens of partial agreements, to have more effective dispute settlement mechanisms and to make stronger efforts for macroeconomic coordination.

But one extremely unexpected challenge was the emergence in the early 1990s of the alternative of trade agreements between developed economies and EEs, with a wide diversity of levels of development.[6] This innovative but risky trend was opened by the US/Mexico/Canada NAFTA free trade agreement, followed by more ambitious comprehensive agreements of the European Union (EU) with Mexico and Chile (Leiva, 2004). Two demanding challenges emerge. One is that 50 highly integrated states (the US) move toward free trade of goods and finance with weaker LACs' economies, which maintain diverse barriers among themselves. Trade and finance integration takes place without explicit and powerful support for leveling development among members, as the US and the EU had in their respective processes of internal convergence. The agreements with the EU have included cooperation and support in some relevant areas; instead, agreements with the US (for instance that with Chile) have posed obstacles for convergence, like limits for prudential macroeconomic regulations of capital flows.[7]

The second challenge is associated to the trade/development link. As Rodrik (2001b) has put it, trade is not the target; it is an input. There is

[6] See an interesting collection of essays on the proposal of a Free Trade Area of the Americas in Estevadeordal et al. (2004).
[7] See the solid criticisms to those pro-cyclical clauses in Bhagwati (2004), Stiglitz (2002), and Williamson (2003b).

need for making trade agreements as if "development really mattered". Particularly with productive development policies that generate systemic competitivity, especially enhancing the position of SMEs. The Uruguay Round imposed too many identical rules for countries at highly different levels of development. A risky application of "one-size-fits-all".

These trends could make more difficult the management of an efficient process of Latin American integration; but, it can also provide a stimulus to define horizons for the necessary convergence and coordination of policies within the region.

c) Export processing zones

Several Latin American and Caribbean countries have accorded differential treatment to export processing units on quite a large scale as a way of boosting their exports and, in addition, of heightening labor absorption and the internationalization of technical progress (see Buitelaar, et al., 1999). Export processing zones (EPZs or maquila producers) are physical and economic enclaves where free trade and export-promotion policies can be applied without altering the trade regime in the rest of the country.[8] These zones are areas placed outside the jurisdiction of the country's custom authority. Generally speaking, EPZs encompass labor-intensive activities. This model has gained great importance in Mexico and several Central American and Caribbean economies in recent years (where maquila represents about one half of total exports).

EPZs have significantly contributed to generate productive employment and increase the figures on export's technological content in some LACs. However, the level of net exports from EPZs is considerably lower than their gross exports owing to their high content of imported inputs. For example, the value-added by EPZs in Mexico represents just 30% of the gross value of their exports (Kuwayama and Durán, 2003). Consequently, one of the shortcomings of EPZs is their weak linkage with the rest of the economy. That is mirrored by intense growth in their exports in parallel with a minor effect on GDP. The infrastructure required for the establishment and operation of EPZs, if granted by the host country, may considerably raise the cost of the significant number of jobs created. Additionally, in some cases, the concessions and incentives granted to firms located in EPZs have crowded-out local producers

---

[8] The definition of EPZs as physical enclaves is not entirely accurate in all cases. In a number of countries, some export-processing plants enjoy differential treatment with respect to fiscal and foreign exchange matters even though they are located within the custom authority jurisdiction.

whose facilities were placed outside the zone. Recently, the higher relative labor cost in Latin America as compared to that of some new suppliers of manufactures has led to some transnational corporations to move their productive units from LACs to Asia, where wages are significantly lower. That has implied a negative shock to economies like Mexico and Dominican Republic.

3. Export enhancing policies

a) Stability of the productive environment and role of the exchange rate policy

While exports compete in external markets, macroeconomic conditions in local markets play a significant role in their development and in the interrelationship with the rest of GDP. Exporter firms depend heavily upon a friendly domestic environment, with interest rates and exchange rates at levels consistent with competitive rates of return and *complete* factor markets. A framework with too high interest rates and an over-appreciated and volatile real exchange rate is a severe obstacle for an intense export development, based on high value-added products with dynamic comparative advantages. Unfriendly market conditions also impose a bias against domestic firms (especially SMEs and firms intensive in domestic inputs), since foreign-owned exporters can contract debt at international interest rates and, given their diversification, are naturally hedged against exchange rate risks.

Nowadays, most policy-makers and academics agree that a "competitive" and stable RER is an input for a sound trade development.[9] A depreciated real exchange rate improves export competitiveness, and its stability favors productive investment in tradable sectors and higher value-added activities.[10] However, in the last decades, short-term macroeconomic management and the reform agenda have been inconsistent with those goals linked to long-term development. In fact, in a number of countries, trade liberalization measures were accompanied by the liberalization of the

---

[9] These goals are also present in the "Washington Consensus" decalogue, published by Williamson (1990).

[10] Studies by Caballero and Corbo (1990) and ECLAC (1998, chapter IV) have proved the validity of this principle. For exports intensive in imported inputs there is a natural matching between revenues and costs in foreign currency. In the case of exports based on natural resources, static comparative advantages (economic rents) are stronger enough to resist exchange rate swings. In contrast, for high value-added exports (for example, for those labor-intensive), the exchange rate is key in defining their competitiveness.

capital account, which during the 1990s prompted considerable exchange-rate appreciation (see chapter VII, and ECLAC, 1998, chapter XI) just when trade reforms urgently required a depreciation.

On the other hand, since the Asian crisis, several LACs have adopted flexible exchange rate regimes, which has implied strong exchange rate volatility. In many of those cases, the Central Bank has adopted an inflation-targeting scheme. In this context, the management of the exchange rate as a key macro price to support the transformation of the productive apparatus has been fading.

b) Other horizontal policies

There is a wide range of horizontal policies that can contribute to increase systemic competitiveness in developing economies, featured by *incomplete* or nonexistent markets. Among them, one most important is the improvement of educational standards and reducing its unequal distribution. But that is not enough. The vast majority of the labor force of the next decade already left the formal educational system, and therefore, it will not be affected by its reform. Labor training is the public policy required for gradually improving the quality of the existing labor force in the medium term. In economic terms, this is the way of flexibilizing the labor supply instead of advancing exclusively in flexibilizing labor demand. These policies not only have a direct effect on labor productivity but also they contribute to improve income distribution. Indeed, there is a strong tendency to intergenerational reproduction of poverty, where a child that was born in a poor household is most likely to remain poor as a result of the low-quality education. Actions in this area have *high* social returns in terms of productive development and higher social integration.

On the other hand, between two thirds and three quarters of Latin American workers are employed by SMEs, which face many obstacles for improving their productivity because of financing and technological constraints, worsened by real macroeconomic instability. Indeed, there are differences between large and SMEs in access to highly-qualified labor, financial markets and risk capital, and technology. As a result, SMEs present the highest potential for productivity improvements. Improving their access to long-term financing and new technologies contributes to reduce the productivity gap between large and small and medium firms, which increases overall efficiency.

c) Selective policies

Experience suggests that, together with a rationalization of trade incentives, some degree of selectivity must be exercised with respect to productive development policy. This is what was done in the fastest-growing economies of East Asia.

The promotion of non-traditional exports appears to be a particularly appropriate sphere for selective trade policies. The main reasons for implementing such measures are offsetting the anti-export bias inherent in tariffs; the shortcomings in capital markets for financing exports; and the economies of scale and positive externalities associated with learning opportunities that exporting provides. Without an active export-promotion policy, exports will tend to be concentrated in a few enterprises and on traditional products for which demand is less dynamic and which are more vulnerable in global markets.

One basic prerequisite for promoting the competitiveness of export firms is to guarantee them access to inputs on competitive terms. These firms should have access to flexible mechanisms for importing inputs on a temporary basis to produce exportables. Other alternatives are tariff exemptions or drawbacks, with a minimum of red tape. Such mechanisms could also be applied to indirect exporters (domestic producers of inputs for exporters).

Pioneer export firms could be supported by providing incentives for exports of new products or for new markets. One mechanism is a simplified drawback for products whose export level is below a given amount for a specific period. These incentives should be moderate (helping to place competitive or near-competitive products in foreign markets), limited in time, and subject to performance results in terms of new products or markets.

The public sector can provide institutional support for export activity, especially in the areas of information, financing and export insurance; management training to encourage businesses to focus on exporting; negotiations to improve access to external markets; and promoting exportable supply abroad. Pioneering efforts must also be made in such areas as investing abroad to support export activities, marketing chains, and joint ventures with firms in target markets. Timely, up-to-date information on the requirements of export markets in terms of quality, environmental regulations, standardization, deadlines and volumes would facilitate this task.

Past export-promotion policies often neglected sectors based on non-traditional natural resources. Recent technological advances in microelectronics, data processing, telecommunications and satellite technologies considerably augment the supply of information on the quality and volume of economically available natural resources. This is one more reason for acquiring and strengthening comparative advantages in non-traditional natural resources with significant economic rents.

To be effective, an export-promotion system must be selective. It is impossible to promote everything indiscriminately. The selection of sectors, and export-promotion decisions in general, should be made in close, systematic cooperation between the public and private sectors.

Other aspects of selectivity that have not been accorded due attention in reform efforts in LACs have to do with the sequence with which the State does correct market failures that hamper investment and changing production patterns. Such State action includes policies for supplementing the long-term segments of capital markets, attracting greenfield FDI to new sectors able to build competitive advantage and upgrading physical and social infrastructure, along with the application of effective labor training and technology-enhancing programs.

In order to open up the production sector in a way that will further a country's development, pragmatic corrections ought to be made in the extreme forms of liberalization advocated and implemented in recent years. Trade policy reforms should also be accompanied by a greater role for the exchange rates in bringing about changes in production patterns. It appears to be impossible to steer the private sector's production activities firmly in the direction of tradables unless a more competitive and stable exchange rate (i.e., one that withstands the influence of temporary swings in capital flows and terms of trade) is maintained. The authorities of the region need to devote greater attention to the economic policies required to achieve this objective, one of which will surely be the regulation of short-term and liquid capital flows. Fulfilling the requirements mentioned, implies achieving systemic competitivity.

One essential condition for a successful liberalization effort is a supportive international environment. Unless protectionism is watered down in the central countries, the active linking with the world economy will be weakened as a policy option for the wide range of countries that are currently pursuing export-led development.

Part Three

Financial Reforms for Development

VI
Taming Financial Shocks: How to Manage Boom and Bust*

Introduction

International capital markets have grown dramatically since the mid-1960s. Although international capital movements partly reflect expanding economies, increasing world trade and the globalization of production, they also involve purely financial factors that rose notably faster, particularly since the 1990s. In the 1960s, the growing presence of unregulated international offshore financial centers stimulated capital movements by evading national financial regulations, capital controls and taxes. Then, in the 1970s and 1980s, many countries began to deregulate their domestic financial sectors and to relax or eliminate the regulation of foreign exchange transactions (Díaz-Alejandro, 1985; Devlin, 1989; Eichengreen, 2003). This, together with the revolutionary innovations that have taken place in data-management and telecommunications technology, and the emergence of increasingly sophisticated financial techniques, contributed to a boom in international financial flows. Generally, the financial boom occurred in a framework of lax or incomplete regulations and supervision, and in which existing regulations were in fact pro-cyclical (Griffith-Jones, 2001; Ocampo, 2002; United Nations, 1999; Turner, 2000). Indeed, there is a significant shortage of macroeconomic and financial governance in the present stage of unbalanced globalization.

It is premature to speak of integrated financial markets, since international capital mobility is clearly far from perfect, and still prevails a strong home-bias (Feldstein and Horioka, 1980). Nevertheless, there is no doubt that capital flows and global financial integration are increasing

* Sections 1 and 4 are partly based on Ffrench-Davis (2005, chapter I).

137

rapidly. These developments have aroused controversy. At one extreme, there are those who see rising integration as a sign of greater efficiency; according to this interpretation, markets are overcoming the financial repression characteristic of inefficient government regulation. At the other extreme, there are those who see the boom in all capital flows as high-risk speculation that threatens national sovereignty. Between these two extremes there are diverse intermediate positions that recognize the significant potential advantages of some forms of international capital mobility, but are also concerned about issues such as the sustainability, composition and terms of capital flows, and the need to ensure that they are consistent with real macroeconomic stability, systemic competitiveness, growth and social equity.

This controversy has acquired crucial relevance for Latin America (LACs) in the last decades. In the 1980s, the links with international capital markets were largely severed as a result of the debt crisis.[1] However, the region enjoyed a booming expansion of capital flows during 1991–94 and again from mid-1995 to 1998. At the beginning, these inflows were most welcome because they overcame a binding external constraint (BEC) that was contributing to low investment levels and to a severe economic recession in the region. Nevertheless, these increasing inflows also had, on both occasions, an also increasingly unwelcome and distorting effect on real macroeconomic balances.

We have observed that emerging economies have, frequently led by capital surges, penetrated in *vulnerability zones*. These include (i) high external liabilities, with a large liquid share; (ii) significant current account deficits; (iii) appreciated exchange rates and currency mismatches; (iv) high prices of domestic financial assets and real estate; and (v) sizable increases in money supply as counterpart of the accumulation of international reserves. The longer and deeper the economy's penetration into those vulnerability zones, the more severe the *financieristic trap* in which authorities could get caught, and the lower the probability of leaving it without undergoing a crisis and long-lasting economic and social costs. The absence or weakness of policies moderating the boom – putting breaks during overheating – endangers the feasibility of adopting a strong reactivating policy under the frequent recessive environment following the bust.

---

[1] For comprehensive analyses of the region's insertion into capital markets during the 1970s, the emergence and management of the debt crisis see Devlin and Ffrench-Davis (1995); Ffrench-Davis (1982 and 1984); Devlin (1989); Griffith-Jones (1988).

Capital flows are, potentially, a valuable variable in economic development. However, the intertemporal character of financial transactions and *incompleteness* of available instruments contribute to placing financial markets among the most imperfectly functioning in the market economy. They are prone to considerable ups and downs, to periods of over-optimism and over-pessimism, and they tend to generate outlier domestic prices and ratios during long periods (Kindleberger, 1978; Stiglitz, 1994; Rodrik, 1998). Hence improved information, financial sector regulation, and broad prudential macro management (direct and indirect) of financial flows constitute a public good for which there is a shared role for governments: on the supply side for industrialized country officials and on the demand side for developing country authorities, coordinated – where relevant – by international organizations. A passive stance can render a significant cost, as made evident in the debt crises of the 1980s, in the Mexican crisis of 1994, in the East Asian crises of 1997, and in the long stagnation of LACs in 1998–2003 (see chapter VII).

Section 1 reviews the analytical foundations of the role of external capital flows in development. Section 2 summarizes the evolution of financial liberalization and capital account opening in recent decades. Section 3 focuses on the sources of the recent boom in capital flows, that emerge from the supply side. This is followed by an analysis, in section 4, of why there prevails such pro-cyclical behavior in capital flows. The nature of the most influential agents is the crucial explanatory variable.

1. Capital flows and development: growth convergence or recurrent financial crises?

In recent years increasing attention was devoted to the potential contributions of capital mobility to economic growth, which gave rise to policy recommendations for capital account opening. The arguments in favor of freely mobile capital had been in an overwhelming fashion in orthodox theory. However, the real second best world in which we live do seriously question many of the textbook assertions. Actually, implementing fashionable theories too literally, without attention to the important caveats that arise out of a more empirically-rooted evaluation of the role of capital mobility in the development process, has shown to be extremely costly for EEs. Here we will review the four most commonly cited reasons to promote capital mobility. They are (i) the channeling of external savings from capital-rich toward capital-scarce countries; (ii) the compensatory financing of external shocks, which helps stabilize domestic spending; (iii) flows contributing to diversity risk, and (iv) capital account opening as a leader of macroeconomic discipline.

a) Flows from capital-rich to capital-scarce economies

We have shown in chapter III that GDP per capita is closely associated with the stock of capital per worker. That fact supports the view that the speed of capital formation is a significant determinant of GDP growth.

Mobilization of external savings is the more robust argument in favor of capital flows to LDCs. At the aggregate level, net flows from developed to developing countries are assumed to improve the efficiency of world resource allocation, because real marginal returns on investment in capital-rich countries are expected to be systematically lower than those in (well managed) capital-scarce countries. Consequently, flows to LDCs can benefit both supplier and demander economies.[2] Indeed, net inflows of external savings can supplement domestic savings, raise productive investment and boost growth. In turn, expansion of aggregate income can further increase domestic savings and investment, thereby creating a virtuous circle in which there is sustained economic expansion, eventual elimination of net foreign debt, and transformation of the country into a capital exporter; it is the so-called virtuous debt cycle (ECLAC, 1998, chapter X), that contributes to the convergence of levels of economic development. Actually, EEs concentrate the overwhelming majority of private capital flows to LDCs.

This well-known framework has some powerful policy implications; disregarding them has proven to be extremely costly. First, capital inflows should consistently be directed to augment aggregate investment, and not be diverted to consumption; otherwise, results a crowding-out of national savings. Second, an aggressive domestic savings effort is called for: from the outset of a debt cycle, the marginal savings rate must attain a level much higher than the average rates of domestic savings as well as of investment; thus, it would eventually give way to a savings surplus. Initially, matching interest and profit remittances; subsequently, for the repayment of capital. Third, there must be efficient absorptive capacity in the domestic market; that is, investment must be allocated efficiently (requiring the supply of the other ingredients of the production function – whether domestic or imported, for instance via

---

[2] In 2000, the capital intensity per worker of the US and the Latin American economies, was US$111,000 and US$16,000, respectively, in constant prices of 1995 (see Ffrench-Davis and Tapia, 2004; Ros, 2000, chapter 1).

FDI – and a real macroeconomic environment suitable for productive investment). Fourth, investment must become more intensive in producing tradables, in order to generate an external surplus large enough to transform domestic savings into foreign currency, to service external liabilities. Fifth, creditors must be willing to provide stable and predictable flows of finance on "reasonable" terms.

It is not easy to comply with all these conditions in practice: countries may experience a significant *crowding-out* of domestic savings by foreign savings (see chapter III); investments may not always be efficient or channeled sufficiently into tradables, and creditor behavior may differ from the desired pattern. Indeed, as convincing as the traditional argument for the transfer of international savings to developing countries is, the above problems and ensuing payments crises have often caused this valuable developmental mechanism to miss its target.[3]

b) Compensating shocks

Second, capital mobility can also contribute (i) to balance transitory differences between output and expenditure, or (ii) to spread out over time the adjustment to permanent changes in relative prices; thus, it allows stabilizing consumption and investment, generating a *stabilizing intertemporal adjustment*. Given the smallness of EEs markets, *vis-à-vis* international financial markets, a stabilizing behavior is potentially feasible. However, this counter-cyclical behavior not always does evolve smoothly in practice. Usually, it is not easy to ascertain whether a downturn in the external sector is transitory and, if so, for how long. This uncertainty, coupled with imperfections in international capital markets (especially informational asymmetries, enforcement obstacles, and contagion of changes of suppliers mood; Stiglitz, 2000), represent obstacles to the arrival of matching amounts of foreign financing at those times when they are required.

Compensatory flows have taken place systematically only during periods of generalized abundant supply. For instance, in 1991–97 (except early 1995 for LACs), the specific agent affected by a falling export price could borrow abroad rather easily. On the contrary, in cases of moderate or weak supply, a worsening of the terms of trade has led to sharper dryness or to a consolidation of an already existing BEC, as in 1998–2003; the outcome tends to be a private capital account contributing to a

---

[3] See the research presented in Ffrench-Davis and Reisen (1998), particularly, that of Uthoff and Titelman (1998).

destabilizing intertemporal adjustment.[4] In these circumstances, financial markets, systematically, have pressed EEs authorities to face the negative external shocks with a pro-cyclical recessive policy.

Under pro-cyclical international capital mobility, the costs of adjustment for developing countries can be enormous. That is because in the face of negative external shocks (and easily exhaustible domestic international reserves), any shortfall in capital inflows will require immediate cutbacks in domestic expenditure to restore the external balance. As discussed in chapter II, actual output will almost certainly fall because of the natural rigidities standing in the way of resource reallocation, and a perverse hysteresis comes into action because there also tends to be a cutback in investment, usually an over-proportional one (see chapter III). The crisis-affected economy will be unable to return to the previous growth path; actually, it would be facing multiple market equilibria. These short-term disturbances in financial markets frequently disrupt output and distort returns to capital to a significant degree. It is evident that the phenomenon of hysteresis is extremely relevant in financial matters and their inter-relationship with the real economy.

c) **Diversifying risks**

Third, it is argued that social benefits could be reaped in a multi-way international exchange in financial assets, by allowing individuals to satisfy their risk preferences more fully through greater asset diversification; this is a micro-benefit. This argument has been widely-used for justifying a full opening of the capital account of developed and developing countries alike, particularly including the opening to outflows of domestic funds.[5]

There are several ways to diversify risk or insure against diverse types of risk. For instance at the macro-level, by trade diversification and

[4] It is interesting to recall that it was the public (multilateral and bilateral) supply of funds that behaved counter-cyclically in the 1980s and 1990s (see ECLAC, 2002a, chapter 4). Prasad, Rogoff et al. (2003, section I.c and table 4), conclude that "procyclical access to international capital markets appears to have had a perverse effect on the relative volatility of consumption for financially integrated developing economies." Kindleberger (1978) and Eichengreen (2003, chapter 2) provide interesting historical analysis of financial cycles.
[5] It is relevant that Korea and Malaysia – the two fastest recovering EEs after the Asian crisis – kept restrictions on outflows by residents as a countercyclical macroeconomic device (Mahani, Shin and Wang, 2005). Zahler (2005) discusses the macroeconomic implications of outflows from domestic institutional investors, illustrated with the case of Chilean private pension funds.

stabilization funds (including international reserves policy) to face exports and imports instability as a prudential macroeconomic policy. At the micro-level, by sectoral and geographical diversification by the firm, and producers of goods and services operating with derivative markets (see Dodd, 2003). But, a different matter is capital account opening to diversify financial assets and equity stock portfolio of residents.

It is evident that trade in goods and services, flows of greenfield FDI, and trade in financial assets are not identical (Díaz-Alejandro, 1985; Devlin, 1989; Bhagwati, 1998). The former transaction tends to be complete and rather instantaneous, whereas trade in financial instruments is inherently incomplete and of uncertain value, since it is based on a promise to pay in the future. In a world of uncertainty, incomplete insurance markets, informational costs and contagious changes of mood, *ex ante* and *ex post* valuations of financial assets may be radically different. The gap in time between a financial transaction and payment for it, generates externalities in market transactions that can magnify and multiply errors in subjective valuations, to the point where finally the market corrections may be abrupt, overshooting and destabilizing (Kenen, 1993; Stiglitz, 1998);[6] that would imply micro and macroeconomic costs. Thus, some form of regulation of trade in financial assets may not only make specific markets function more efficiently, and avoid frauds, but improve the overall performance of the economy through the enhancement of real macroeconomic stability and better long-term investment performance.

From the point of view of growth convergence, indeed, this third argument is not too relevant for enhancing development. First, for a given country, financial opening for the implementation of financial risk diversification implies liberalizing outflows by residents. It is doubtful that money would move to LDCs' markets to diversify their risk. Likely, it flows in response to higher returns associated to capital-scarcity (argument 1). In the case of LDCs' opening, most probably, it would

---

[6] Financial markets, which intermediate most capital flows, must fulfill what Tobin (1984) termed fundamental valuation efficiency: that is, market valuations must accurately reflect the present value of the profits that the assets in question can be expected to generate over time. Accuracy for determining prices is extremely important because they are the main signals for the reallocation of capital. Unfortunately, price movements in financial markets are known often not to reflect fundamentals (Kenen, 1993; Stiglitz, 2000). Thus, empirical studies (summarized in Akyüz, 1993), as well as historical analyses (Kindleberger, 1978; Eichengreen, 2003), suggest that severe allocative inefficiencies usually arise in capital markets (Mishkin, 1999; Shiller, 2000).

tend to encourage net outflows from – the more incomplete, smaller, less liquid and less deep – developing or emerging markets, rather than the opposite. Evidently, that may diversify risk for domestic financial investors and agents. However, it is not likely to diversify risk on returns to domestic producers. Additionally, it tends to reduce savings available domestically and the financing for productive investment, and introduces larger pro-cyclicality to the macroeconomic environment faced by producers.

Second, there are some interesting analytical pieces in the literature supporting this third argument. For instance, Obstfeld (1994) develops a model based on the hypothesis that global financial integration implies a portfolio shift from low-risk-low-returns capital to high-risk-high-returns capital. He concludes that that shift could contribute to "enormous welfare gains" (Obstfeld, 1998, p. 10). Three comments in this respect, follow: (i) the assertion that the size of the effects is *enormous* reveals an *a priori* belief or desire; (ii) there is an overlapping of the risk diversification argument with that of flows from capital-rich to capital-scarce markets in response to differential average returns; there is need to identify what is truly different in the pure financial risk diversification argument; (iii) actually, cross-border flows tend to move into better-known and non-high risk assets; a look at stocks (for instance, ADRs) and bonds of EEs transacted internationally, documents it sharply – they usually correspond to large, mature, and better graded domestic firms. In particular, the same happens with financial investment abroad of EEs residents.[7] The exception, covering a broader set of assets, is in the case

---

[7] Another relevant argument is the obvious positive role fulfilled by financial intermediaries in relaxing liquidity constraints and in reducing search costs for small and medium sized agents (SMEs), which is crucial for economic growth with equity. But, it is domestic intermediaries who concentrate that role overwhelmingly. To our knowledge, access abroad of SMEs is notably limited. There is some empirical work that, frequently, misleads the reader by not distinguishing, sharply, between the smaller of the firms traded in stock exchanges (actually, these are among the large firms of the universe of all firms) and SMEs; for instance, see Forbes (2003). Berry and Ruiz (2003) present an interesting research on the impact of financial integration on firms of different sizes. Additionally, there have been sizable acquisitions in the banking activity of EEs, particularly in Central Europe and Latin America. For instance, in Argentina half of banks assets belonged in 2000 to foreign controlled banks. Interestingly, foreign ownership has implied that local lending by those banks represents offshore exposition for their matrixes (see Hawkins, 2003). The conventional argument that the presence in EEs domestic markets of foreign banks would assist in securing external funding when facing financial shocks and in completing capital markets, apparently, has not been supported in practice.

of the bubbles, in which investors actually do not reveal an *appetite-for-risk*, but rather *it implicitly involves the assumption that no risks exist* during the contagion of over-optimism. In brief, there is no well-documented connection of risk diversification with the sources of domestic productivity increases.

Third, international financial diversification has presently achieved evident priority in policy-making; for instance, when eliminating capital gains taxes on cross-border operations and in the encouragement to financial investment in offshore markets. But, the fact is that these activities are quite isolated from the sources of systemic competitivity and productive development. That sort of priority tends to concentrate energy of economic agents in purely financial activities; this implies a *neo-rent-seeking* attitude – to make profits at the expense of other agents, instead of profit derived from increased productivity. Of course, there is not a dilemma of all or nothing, but of a rebalance in favor of "productivism" and longer-term horizons.

d) Enhancing macroeconomic discipline

Fourth, there is the newest argument in favor of capital account liberalization. It states that dependency from inflows can make a significant contribution to deter political authorities from following irresponsible and populist macroeconomic policies. It is argued that, consequently, fully opening the capital account would encourage "sound macroeconomic fundamentals". This is partly true for *domestic* sources of instability, i.e., large fiscal deficits, permissive monetary policy and arbitrary exchange-rate overvaluation. However, systematically before the recent crises in "successful" EEs, we have observed, during booms (in periods of overoptimism of financial agents), that lax demand policies or exchange-rate overvaluation have tended to be encouraged by financial markets. That is, a macroeconomic disequilibria led by capital inflows.

In fact, the so-called discipline of the private financial market has simply not materialized during the expansive side of the cycles. Instead of facing an upward sloping supply curve for loans, with credit rationing, as would be assumed for a market with efficient lenders, many developing countries along the three surges have faced a sort of downward sloping supply curve (with decreasing spreads charged by lenders and appreciating exchange-rates in borrower economies). This feature is highly destabilizing indeed, giving perverse price signals for the savings and investment process.

It is no coincidence that, in all three significant surges of the last quarter century, loan spreads underwent, in a *process*, a continued decline, notwithstanding that the stock of liabilities was rising sharply: spreads fell for 5–6 years in the 1970s, before the debt crisis; over 4 years before the Tequila crisis; over a couple of years between mid 1995 and 1998, before the contagion of the Asian crisis. Figure VI.1 depicts the evolution of EMBI and stock prices for LACs; peaks in 1994 and 1997 illustrate well the market enthusiasm, just before the Tequila and East Asian crises, respectively.

In brief, the opening of the capital account may lead EEs to import external financial instability, with capital inflows engendering a worsening in macroeconomic fundamentals (see section 4). Thus, although this market discipline can serve as a check to *domestic* sources of instability – not necessarily very efficient, given the whims of opinions and expectations characteristic of financial markets – it likely becomes a *source* of externally generated instability. Indeed, it is the market itself which, during the booms, has generated incentives for EEs to enter *vulnerability zones*, whereas excessive punishment during crises has tended to force authorities to adopt overly contractionary policies.

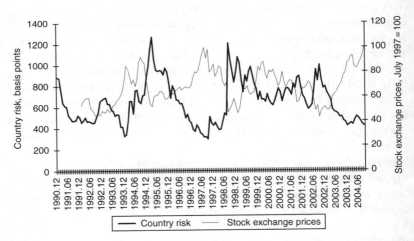

Figure VI.1   Latin America: Country risk and stock exchange prices, 1990–2004 (basis points, indices)

Source: Country risk (measured by the sovereign spread over the US zero coupon curve): JP Morgan, Emerging Market Bond Index (EMBI). Stock exchange prices: IFC, Standard and Poor's. Dollar denominated.

One additional, implication is that legitimate national political authorities may lose the capacity to pursue the policy proposals for which they were elected.[8] To this issue we return in chapter VIII.

2. Liberalization of the capital account: the historical evolution of policy

Most general equilibrium frameworks analyze capital as a whole and take no account of important real-world conditions such as informational bottlenecks, the institutional peculiarities of investors and large heterogeneity among different segments of the supply of funding, the structure or incompleteness of the market within which investors operate, and the allocative implications of the volatility of financing. These factors frequently do not mix, spontaneously, in ways that permit countries to tap the full potential benefits of foreign savings. Indeed, systemic market failure can and does occur. Frequent reminders of this feature are the major financial crises, accompanied by macroeconomic collapse, that have repeatedly appeared in economic history, including the debt crisis in Latin America in the 1980s and the more recent Mexican and Asian crises.

a) From closed to open capital accounts

During the 1950s and 1960s mainstream professional thinking on development predominantly focused on real economic activity rather than questions of money and financial markets. Moreover, the analysis of capital inflows concentrated on a limited number of channels of funding: basically bilateral aid, multilateral lending and FDI. Most developed and developing countries had comprehensive controls on capital flows.

This situation had its roots in the concrete historical circumstances of the Great Depression and the sluggish activity of international private finance in particular, up to the early 1960s. Direct regulations on the structure of interest rates, controls on the allocation of credit, and selective or discriminatory reserve requirements were common. Public property of commercial banks, and particularly of development banks was significant. Administrative or quantitative controls on capital flows were also common, or, plainly, prevailed straight prohibitions for several channels

---

[8] This source of market discipline can also pose obstacles to necessary social reform (for instance, to higher taxes to finance efficient human capital investment) or to the ability to capture economic rents from natural resources exploited by FDI.

of access to foreign exchange markets, and to access from abroad to domestic assets like the stock market. Several of these varied forms of intervention were common, even in the more advanced market economies still by the late 1980s.

This predominant policy orientation, both in developed and developing regions, did not have a monopoly of ideas, however. Indeed, it was confronted by competing paradigms, particularly variants of *laissez-faire* economics or neo-liberalism. It was held that an open capital account was needed as a way of raising savings, deepening domestic financial markets, reducing the costs of financial intermediation through enhanced competition, satisfying individuals' demand for risk diversification and optimizing resource allocation. In short, most of the benefits of capital mobility outlined above were invoked.

Capital-account liberalization in the industrialized countries was fairly slow and gradual, accelerating only in the 1980s as capital markets globalized. It is interesting to note that Ireland, Portugal and Spain reintroduced certain restrictions on capital flows in 1992 to combat exchange rate instability. Once the objectives of stability were achieved, the restrictions were lifted. This highlights the importance of flexible instruments that, according to circumstances, allow some temporary constraints to be imposed on capital movements so to support efforts toward real macroeconomic stability.

b) Sequencing the opening up

Many analysts viewed the world-wide boom in international bank lending of the 1970s as an inherently benign event for development. On the supply side, private financial markets – and especially the unregulated Eurocurrency market – were considered to be highly efficient and capable of imposing market discipline on borrowers, in contrast to the allegedly inefficient and permissive lending of official agencies. Furthermore, it was felt that portfolio and direct investment decisions were based on the long-term key variables (*fundamentals*) of the countries concerned, and therefore inherently encouraged greater market order and discipline. On the demand side, there was also a popular notion that if the borrowers were from the private sector – in contrast to public sector agencies – the resources would be deployed efficiently (Robichek, 1981).

Those attracted to this approach were in broad agreement on the diagnosis and general policy prescription, but there were significant differences of opinion regarding implementation. Some argued that basic reforms were part of a "seamless web" and should ideally be undertaken simultaneously in a type of "big bang." Those who distrust government intervention in foreign exchange and capital markets and/or fear that, otherwise, vested interests would paralyze liberalization programs favored rapid and ambitious opening-up. Others favored the sequencing of reforms, with the capital account being opened up only after consolidation of the other liberalization measures, with domestic financial reform and trade liberalization being given the highest priority (McKinnon, 1991; Edwards, 1989). The capital account was deemed an especially sensitive area because, if it were opened up in conjunction with other reforms, it could induce a capital insurge bringing about premature exchange rate appreciation, with negative consequences for trade liberalization and resource allocation. A competitive exchange rate was crucial to trade reform. Hence, the regulation of capital flows could be justified as a way to temporarily reduce pressures for exchange-rate appreciation.

The different policy approaches began to have real implications for Latin America in the mid-1970s when three Southern Cone countries underwent radical economic liberalization processes, inspired partly by the financial repression hypothesis and the theoretical simplicity of the "monetary approach to the balance of payments" (Díaz-Alejandro, 1985; Ffrench-Davis, 1983). As known (Devlin and Ffrench-Davis, 1995; Ffrench-Davis, 2000, chapter 4), the Southern Cone experiment collapsed in the early 1980s under large price disequilibria and speculative bubbles on asset prices, low domestic savings and investment, a huge external debt, and domestic insolvencies. The history was repeated to a significant extent during the 1990s, when the reforms á la Washington Consensus were implemented in several LACs, *pari passu* with the two capital surges present in that decade. The most popular explanation of the negative experience was, beyond the imperfections of international financial markets, that there had been a flawed sequencing of liberalization.

As far as sequencing is concerned, there is now some consensus that the capital account opening was premature and should have been postponed until other major reforms had been consolidated and equilibrium prices established. The lesson is that during adjustment, open capital accounts (especially in periods of elastic supply of international finance) can induce capital surges, with destabilizing macroeconomic and sectoral effects (ECLAC, 2002b).

First, if productive investment capacity reacts slowly and/or with a lag and domestic financial markets remain incomplete and poorly supervised, additional external resources cannot be absorbed efficiently in the domestic economy, thereby threatening the future stability of flows themselves. Second, fiscal parameters need to be consolidated, tax evasion must be placed under control, and policy must be flexible, for without a sound tax base and flexible fiscal instruments, authorities must rely excessively on monetary policy to regulate aggregate demand. Furthermore, the tax base must be strong enough to sustain adequate levels of public spending consistent with long-term development needs. Third, LDCs are structurally capital-scarce. Since, under capital surges, naturally financial markets adjust faster than economic structures, usually there emerge bubbles in financial assets and real estate markets, together with exchange rate appreciation (and/or inflation). The policy response to avoid all those sources of vulnerability, prone to crises, is to impose a gradual adjustment in financial flows, accommodating its speed to that at which productive structures can adjust. That is, in an economy that gradually is being transformed from intensive in capital-scarce to capital-rich productive activities. In brief, if it is decided to liberalize the capital account, the speed at which it should be done must be tailored to the economy's capacity to absorb and allocate efficiently external resources. Indeed, according to McKinnon (1991, p. 117), "during liberalization, stringent controls on suddenly increased inflows (or outflows) of short-term capital are warranted."

Lastly, in the particular case of Latin America, many countries conducted deep trade reforms in the 1990s *pari passu* with exchange-rate appreciation, directly led by financial surges. More indirectly, since part of the aggregate demand generated by capital flows is inevitably spent on non-tradables, when actual demand comes close to the production frontier, the relative price of non-tradables tends to rise.

Actually, there has been a significant correlation between cycles in net capital flows and the mid-term swings in the average real exchange rate of the region since the 1970s (see figure VI.2, for 1987–2004) This, in turn, usually is reflected in a widened current account deficit. The real appreciation of the exchange rate can obviously distort resource allocation and investment, seriously weakening a country's medium-term structural objective of penetrating external markets with new exports. Real appreciation also tends to bring unnecessary allocative social costs, as domestic resources most probably will later have to be switched back in order to get a larger output of tradables, through real exchange-rate depreciation (Edwards, 1989; Williamson, 2000). This is because the counterpart of the current account deficit is an accumulation of external liabilities, which must eventually be serviced in foreign exchange.

A considerable body of expert opinion has thus emerged which urges that several segments of the capital account should be opened only after

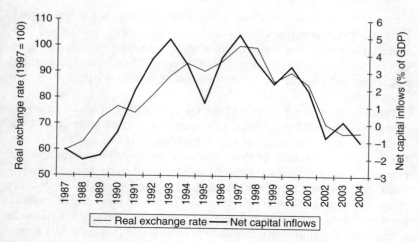

Figure VI.2 Latin America: Net capital inflows and real exchange rate, 1987–2004 (% of GDP; indice 1997 = 100)

Source: Author's calculations based on ECLAC figures. Real exchange rate defined in terms of dollars per unit of local currency.

the consolidation of other major liberalization programs, especially in the areas of trade and domestic finance (IEO/IMF, 2005). Nonetheless, the new consensus comes after the wrong inducement and the wrong action. Already several nations had opened their capital accounts prematurely.

A somewhat different issue refers to the cyclicality of flows. It is not identical to have a given form of opening under a capital surge or under a dry market. Consequently, counter-cyclical devices should complement gradual reforms. In periods when resources are scarce, such as 1995, there would be justification for seeking ways of attracting capital inflows and erecting certain barriers to discourage capital outflows. The reverse would apply when there was an abundance of capital in the markets, as in 1990–94, and 1996–97 for many LACs. It seems desirable in such circumstances that certain kinds of inflows are transitorily restricted and some channels for outflows promoted.

Obviously, sequencing and counter-cyclicality imply the presence of controls – either price-based or quantitative regulations. There are a number of ways to manage capital flows. The more pressing the need for management, and the more underdeveloped fiscal and monetary policies are, the more likely it is that the use of direct regulations, such as quantitative controls, on certain types of capital flows will be warranted, even if only temporarily. Often, controls of any type are considered inefficient and capable of being circumvented by ever more sophisticated capital market operations. But, as Williamson (1993; 2000) has pointed out, "assertions about the ineffectiveness of capital controls are vastly exaggerated."

There have been many cases of ill-designed or ill-managed regulations that have created disequilibria, inefficiency and corruption. But those evils can also be the result of full liberalization. It is a fact that across-the-board liberalization of flows brings-in money laundering and tax evasion, and encourages tax inequities. To avoid those costs, there is a need for capital account regulations, but oriented to make prevail short term values and ratios consistent with the long term market trends, particularly of the exchange rate and aggregate demand; a formula condemned to failure are quantitative controls with a clearly over appreciated exchange rate, as in Venezuela at the outset of this decade.

Anyway, the gradual approach stems from the belief that macroeconomic stability also requires a certain sequence in capital account opening itself. A clear distinction can be drawn between inflows and outflows, and it is suggested that countries should liberalize the former before the latter, partly because the benefits that can be derived from outflows are more evident after accumulating substantial net assets (Williamson, 1993; Rodrik, 1998). There could also be sequencing within the components of inflows and outflows: for instance, long-term inflows could be liberalized before short-term transactions while, in the case of outflows, priority might be given to direct export-oriented investments and trade credit.

Even though developing countries may have made radical reforms, it may take many years before conditions emerge (such as a deep and institutionally diversified domestic financial market; a broad, consolidated tax base; a diversified, internationally competitive export sector; and a wide range of available macroeconomic policy instruments) that will allow their economies to absorb unregulated capital flows in ways that are consistent with sustained growth and social equity.

The proponents of sequencing usually question only the order and timing of liberalization, not the ultimate objective of an open capital account. Yet the overriding importance of real macroeconomic stability, coupled with the overwhelming size of international capital markets compared with the much smaller Latin American economies and the severe imperfections existing in such markets, may make an inflexible commitment in all circumstances to an across-the-board open capital account highly undesirable. Indeed, the increasing volatility of international capital flows, and their huge size, have already given rise to renewed discussion in industrialized countries on the potentially destabilizing behavior of capital markets and the possible need for their additional regulations (Financial Stability Forum, 2000; IEO/IMF, 2005). The Mexican, Korean, Thailand and Argentinean crises reinforce the convenience of prudential macroeconomic regulation of short-term and liquid financial flows in EEs.

3. Origins and composition of the private capital surges in the 1990s

There is well-documented evidence showing that the initial surge of private flows, in the early 1990s, was originated, to a large extent, in the sources of suppliers rather than in the demand side.[9] It was associated to technological innovation, institutional and policy changes in developed economies, and was led by some economic authorities and powerful lobbying forces (Bhagwati, 2004; Pfaff, 2000). The financial surge toward the EEs originated mainly in the USA. Liberalization of financial outflows in the US, its domestic recession in the early 1990s – with a limited local demand for funds, and very low real interest rates – led investors to search for other markets.[10] *Pari passu*, there was a fast opening in the capital accounts of EEs, first in Latin America and some years latter in East Asia; consequently, this opening was implemented under abundant supply. Latin America was a receptive market, with the BEC still prevailing in 1990, and offered the expectation of high rates of return.

a) Massive increase in scale of more diversified flows

There was a massive scale-up of private capital flows to Latin America in the early 1990s. As can be seen in table VI.1, net capital inflows climbed in 1992–94, to 4% of GDP and an average of US$56 billion.

---

[9] The classical paper is Calvo, Leiderman and Reinhart (1993). Diverse interesting approaches and emphasis are found in Calvo (1998); Culpeper (1995); Griffith-Jones (1998).

[10] Between 1989 and 1993, the LIBOR rate in dollars, at 180 days, fell from 9.3% to 3.4% (IMF, *International Financial Statistics*, Washington, DC, various issues). Background on interest rates in Latin America can be found in ECLAC (1998, chapter IX).

Table VI.1 Latin America (19): Composition of capital flows, 1977–2004 (US$ billions and % of trend GDP)

US$ billions	1977–81	1982–90	1991	1992–94	1995	1996–97	1998–2003	2004
1 Current account (2 + 3 + 4)	−24.3	−10.3	−17.0	−43.5	−37.8	−51.5	−41.3	21.8
2 Trade balance	−9.4	20.3	4.5	−21.9	−12.3	−21.4	−12.6	46.9
3 Rents	−16.1	−35.3	−31.4	−33.5	−40.8	−45.2	−52.8	−65.3
4 Unrequited transfers	1.2	4.8	10.0	11.9	15.2	15.1	24.1	40.3
5 Net capital inflows (6 + 10 + 11)	27.8	−12.9	23.3	56.1	19.3	76.5	31.8	−19.4
6 Net FDI (7 + 8 − 9)	5.1	5.5	11.0	15.7	25.8	48.9	57.4	37.8
7 M&A inflows	n.d.	1.5	2.9	5.7	7.4	26.3	33.0	
8 Greenfield FDI inflows	5.4	4.6	9.5	12.7	22.4	28.0	31.0	
9 Outflows	0.3	0.4	1.3	2.7	4.0	5.4	6.6	
10 Portfolio	1.3	0.6	16.4	57.0	2.2	32.7	1.9	
11 Other capital	21.4	−18.9	−4.1	−16.6	−8.6	−5.1	−27.5	
12 Special flows	0.5	23.6	11.8	3.8	31.6	−4.1	12.3	6.8
13 Reserves accumulation (5 + 1 + 12)	4.1	0.4	18.1	16.4	13.1	21.0	2.8	9.3
14 Net transfer of funds (5 + 12 + 3 + 4)	13.5	−19.9	13.7	38.3	25.4	42.4	15.4	−37.6
15 Trend GDP	598	858	1206	1404	1590	1701	1842	1889
Percentage w.r.t. trend GDP								
1 Current account (2 + 3 + 4)	−3.9	−1.3	−1.4	−3.1	−2.4	−3.0	−2.3	1.2
2 Trade balance	−1.5	2.4	0.4	−1.5	−0.8	−1.2	−0.7	2.5
3 Rents	−2.6	−4.2	−2.6	−2.4	−2.6	−2.7	−2.9	−3.5
4 Unrequited transfers	0.2	0.5	0.8	0.9	1.0	0.9	1.3	2.1
5 Net capital inflows (6 + 10 + 11)	4.6	−1.5	1.9	4.0	1.2	4.5	1.7	−1.0
6 Net FDI (7 + 8 − 9)	0.8	0.6	0.9	1.1	1.6	2.9	3.1	2.0
7 M&A inflows	0.0	0.1	0.2	0.4	0.5	1.5	1.8	
8 Greenfield FDI inflows	0.9	0.6	0.8	0.9	1.4	1.6	1.7	
9 Outflows	0.0	0.0	0.1	0.2	0.3	0.3	0.4	
10 Portfolio	0.2	0.0	1.4	4.0	0.1	1.9	0.1	
11 Other capital	3.5	−2.2	−0.3	−1.1	−0.5	−0.3	−1.5	
12 Special flows	0.1	2.8	1.0	0.3	2.0	−0.2	0.7	0.4
13 Reserves accumulation (5 + 1 + 12)	0.7	0.0	1.5	1.2	0.8	1.2	0.1	0.5
14 Net transfer of funds (5 + 12 + 3 + 4)	2.3	−2.4	1.1	2.7	1.6	2.5	0.9	−2.0

Source: Based on official data from ECLAC and UNCTAD.
Trend GDP was calculated by filtering nominal GDP in US dollars (Hodrick-Prescott filter, lambda = 100). Portfolio flows include bonds and stocks purchases. Other capital includes errors and omissions. Special flows include use of IMF credits and exceptional financing.

Furthermore, after the drop in 1995, it jumped to US$76 billion (4.5%) in 1996–97.[11] The two capital surges reached most countries of the region.

Particularly dramatic was the sharp increase in flows to Mexico, where net capital inflows were nearly zero in the 1983–90 period, while in 1992–94 they climbed to 9% of GDP, a ratio well above that in 1977–81.

The sharp increase of international financial flows since the early 1990s was notably more diversified than in the 1970s. The trend was a shift from mid-term bank credit, which was the predominant source of financing in the 1970s, to a set of equity portfolio flows, liquid bonds, medium-and short-term bank financing; short-term time deposits; acquisitions of domestic firms by foreign investors. Overall, these changes in the composition of finance have been seen by many observers as positive, since they involved a greater diversification of capital flows, and flows with variable interest rates (particularly dangerous for funding long-term development, as shown by the 1980s debt crisis) represented a small share of total inflows. However, there have been crucial dangerous features, stressed by other observers. One source of vulnerability has been that current account deficits grew too sharply during each boom. Second, associated to that fact, real exchange rates had appreciated generally. Third, the domestic investment ratio did not grow *pari passu* with capital inflows. Fourth, a very high proportion of net capital inflows in the early 1990s corresponded to short-term flows, in which the risk of volatility is empirically higher (ECLAC, 1998; Rodrik and Velasco, 2000).

Paradoxically, this diversification had potentially brought-in more instability, in as much as, since the 1990s, there has tended to be a *diversification toward highly reversible sources of funding*. If each component tended to respond to different causes of fluctuations, diversification would likely compensate each other, determining more stable total flows. However, the new components not only are more unstable but, additionally, they are prone to be subject to common contagions; frequently, they have shared similar spreads of overoptimism and overpessimism. The reversibility of flows is not observed during the expansive-boom stage of the cycles, but its pervasiveness, for real macroeconomic stability, explodes abruptly with the contagion of negative changes of mood common to diverse financial markets.[12]

---

[11] In order to control for the typical measuring bias introduced by a pro-cyclical behavior of RERs (overestimate of GDP when measuring it in current dollars during booms, and vice versa in recessions), we use a trend RER.

[12] The accelerated growth of derivatives markets contributed to soften "micro-instability" but has tended to increase "macro-instability" and to reduce transparency. See Dodd (2003).

There are two interesting components of private external financing that have risen sharply, and are comparatively stable sources along the cycle. One is traditional; the other is quite novel.

The traditional FDI experienced a sharp rise since the mid-1990s. It expanded fast in the world, to EEs in general, and in particular to LACs, as an important agent of globalization. But, now presents a new feature in that includes a large share of acquisitions (M&A). Greenfield FDI inflows are, by their own nature, reflected in parallel in capital formation, and continue to be more stable (it is a persistent variable, with a unitary root).[13] On the contrary, FDI in the form of M&A is different. (i) M&A is an inflow unlinked with the direct generation of productive capacity.[14] (ii) Private domestic sales of firms to FDI frequently are followed by financial outflows, especially under recessive gaps; it depicts a clearly pro-cyclical behavior. It must be recalled that about one-half of FDI inflows into Latin America in 1996–2003 corresponded to M&A (table VI.1, and UNCTAD, 2004).

On the whole, only greenfield FDI flows seem to be a stable and rather irreversible capital inflow, and flows of FDI that are already in the investment process tend to continue until projects are completed. In parallel, they strengthen domestic capital formation, since they contribute to the creation of new capacity rather than, simply, the purchase of already existing productive assets.

The novel source of inflows to LACs are the remittances from emigrants. They have climbed to US$ 40 billion in 2004, and 2.1% of GDP (ECLAC, 2004c).[15] Over 20 million Latin American and Caribbean people are living abroad, particularly in the USA, with Spain as second destination. Mexico is by far the larger recipient in volume, representing 2.6% of its GDP. However, for several small economies, remittances have become a notably large source of foreign currency. In Dominican Republic, El Salvador, Guatemala, Haiti, Honduras and Nicaragua, remittances inflows represent more than 10% of GDP.

---

[13] Prasad, Rogoff et al. (2003, table 1 and figure 3) report data on volatility of total inward FDI (not controlling for M&A), bank loans and portfolio investment. The authors confirm the conclusion from other abundant research that FDI is less volatile. Recall that the more relevant figure, for policy and econometrics, refers to greenfield FDI (see chapter III).

[14] Another delinking from GKF is related to the reduced relative weight of IFIs development loans, which were tied to their use in capital formation.

[15] These remittances (unrequited transfers) are included as current inflows in balance of payments accounts.

The foundations of a broad liquid market for portfolio investment, that were laid down with the Brady bonds in the late 1980s, developed vigorously in the 1990s, with Latin America as a major destination for both bond and stock financing.

The advantage of bonds is that they are often at fixed interest rates until maturity. However, the average maturity for bonds placed by Latin America is highly sensitive to the cycle. Actually, after a significant extension of maturities up to 1997, experienced a sharp shortening with the contagion from Asia.

Equity investment was a new form of external private funding for LACs. This has the advantage of a cyclical sensitivity of dividends. However, equity flows carry very important volatility risks for recipient countries. Foreign financiers can, suddenly, stop not only investing in equities, but try to sell their stocks quickly, if they fear a worsening prospect. This leads to pressure on the exchange rate and/or to price drops in the domestic stock exchange. This latter could have a negative impact on aggregate demand – via wealth and panic effects – and on the domestic financial system, especially if banks and securities activities are closely integrated either through cross holdings or investor leveraging. As long as markets are led by players who specialize in short-term yields, the risks of great volatility are inherent to this new modality of external financing (Eatwell, 1997; Turner, 2000). LACs actually provided high rates of return during the upswings of the two cycles in the 1990s, as discussed below.

Regulatory changes took place that relaxed the access by EEs to the stock and bond markets in advanced economies, as well as EEs opened their stock markets to foreign investment. Particularly well-advertised were the measures that facilitated placing LACs equities in the US stock exchange (primary ADRs). Equity flows, especially initially, were predominantly from USA-based sources (including the return of Latin American flight capital). Indeed, as Culpeper (1995) reports, US investors provided a significant proportion of flows to major stock markets of LACs, including Mexico, Brazil and Argentina. This has been a determining factor for transmitting cycles among the stock markets of the continent.

It seems worth stressing that an extremely high share of Latin American bonds are raised in dollars, which does give some indication that US-based investors (including Latin American capital flight based in the USA) have been the major source of such funding. The high share of dollar-denominated bonds would seem to reflect both the currency preference of investors and the currency composition of Latin American companies' receipts. In the case of domestic markets' bonds, Latin American borrowers have mainly participated in the US private market placements, where the slackening of regulations (particularly rule 144-A) greatly facilitated funds procurement.

Among the main recent institutional changes affecting capital flows to developing countries, we underline the following two:

(i) The introduction of collective action clauses into bond issues of many EEs, including Mexico and Korea. It is important to highlight that these changes have not increased the cost of borrowing for countries that introduced these clauses. This is a very relevant outcome. Also, there have been some issues of bonds linked to prices of commodities exported by LDCs (Budnevich, 2003; Williamson, 2003a).

(ii) The approval of Basel II, without participation of developing countries, without taking account of their interests. Basel II will tend to restrict the supply of bank flows to developing countries, and to increase their cost. Perhaps most worrying is that it will increase pro-cyclicality of international and domestic bank lending, which is very negative for stable growth and increases the risk of financial fragility and crises (Griffith-Jones et al., 2005).

One outstanding feature behind the supply of funds to EEs, is that in all of them institutional investors, especially pension funds and insurance companies, saw their total assets increase dramatically in the 1990s. At the same time, there has been a clear trend towards an increase of the share of foreign assets in total assets (IMF, 1998; ECLAC, 2002). The rapid growth of financial holdings by institutional investors swelled demand for risk diversification and financial derivatives. Hence the development of specialized markets, such as for the securitization of 'junk bonds', bonds issued by EEs and ADRs. A result of the development of these markets is that the role of credit rating agencies has broadened considerably, as they provide information to investors. However, there has been widespread criticism of the markedly pro-cyclical behavior of agency ratings (see Reisen, 2003). As a result of these trends, there is a large potential supply of funds available for emerging economies but a significant pro-cyclicality.

b) The financial risks of the newer capital flows

The benefits of interaction with private capital flows for the development of recipient economies depend, to a great extent, on stable and predictable access to financial markets. The risk of abrupt stops in supplies and/or inordinately sharp increases in cost and shortening of the maturity terms of external liabilities are partly determined by perceptions of risk and hence host country policies. But from the standpoint of LDCs, access also can be heavily conditioned by exogenously determined supply-side dynamics, related to industrialized country policies in the areas of macroeconomics and prudential regulation.

There is a growing potential for market instability as derivatives become increasingly important in financial activity. On the one hand, these transactions are unregulated with no margin or capital standards; on the other, the up-front fees the seller accrues immediately without risk drive the marketing of these instruments. Finally, information on derivative transactions continues to be extremely incomplete (Dodd, 2003).

Given this more systemic risk, central banks and governments in LACs should seek to participate in global discussions of regulation. There are a number of fora, either global ones, like IOSCO (International Organization of Securities Commissions), or industrial country ones, like the BIS, where issues of systemic risk of international flows are analyzed, and regulations suggested or implemented which are geared to reduce systemic risk and/or to protect investors. Indeed, less systemic risk internationally benefits LACs, which historically have been particularly vulnerable to instability in world financial markets.

c) Some macroeconomic effects

As stressed, in the two surges of the 1990s, the entry of capital had positive Keynesian-like effects, in that it removed the BEC, enabling existing productive capacity to be used more fully and production, incomes and employment to pick up as a result. Inflows, under a BEC tend to be extremely efficient initially.

The BEC disappeared as a result, and aggregate demand was increased. GDP rose faster in countries with large gaps between productive capacity and use of it. Initially, reserves accumulated fast, to build up the Latin American depleted international reserves; the share of reserve accumulation in subsequent inflows steadily decreased with the recovery of aggregate demand and increased absorptive capacity, enhanced by the significant, distorting, exchange-rate appreciations allowed by several LACs.

These trends initially reflected the recovery of "normal" levels of aggregate demand, imports and the real exchange rate, all of which were determined by BECs during the previous period. However, after a while, the continuing abundance of capital generated an overshooting with unsustainable macroeconomic imbalances.

Exchange-rate appreciation was determinant for this outcome. Most LACs revalued their exchange rates between 1990 and 1994 and in 1996–97, appreciation averaging 23% in the first period and 12.5% in the second one. The exchange rate impact was reinforced by significant trade liberalization, executed by various LACs in the early 1990s (ECLAC, 1998, chapter VI). Thus, commercial liberalization took place together with important exchange-rate revaluations, therefore causing the recovery of aggregate demand to be increasingly intensive in imported goods. For example, between 1990 and 1994, regional GDP expanded 15%, while the quantum of imports of goods and services increased 69% (implying a gross elasticity of 4.5); after a sudden stop of imports in 1995, in 1996–98, GDP rose 12% and imports 51% with a similar gross elasticity. These trends reflect to some degree the trade opening of LACs. Actually, exports were rising fast, but they expanded slower than imports. As a matter of fact, the current account deficit in LACs increased from an annual average of US$10 billion in the period 1982–90, to US$52 billion in 1994, and to US$88 billion in 1998.

d) Policy approaches

A wide variety of national policies help to explain why the effects of the new capital inflows have not been identical among LACs. The renewed links with international financial markets caught countries at different stages of their adjustment programs. However, there are strong correlations between generalized capital surges to EEs and their macroeconomic imbalances. The strength of changes in capital flows appears to be stronger than the diversity among LACs, particularly among those with higher GDP per capita.[16]

When the authorities are faced with an unexpected abundance of external financing, which they consider to be partly transitory or as flowing too fast for the economy to absorb efficiently, they can intervene at three levels. First, they can moderate the impact on the exchange rate through the Central Bank purchasing foreign currency (i.e., accumulating reserves). At a second, deeper level, they can adopt sterilization policies (e.g., open domestic market operations) to mitigate the monetary impact of the accumulation of reserves. At the third level, they can implement incentives, surcharges, or quantitative controls to

---

[16] About US$2,000 per capita in 1997, in a classification used in ECLAC (2002a). Includes 10 LACs and 3 Caribbean economies, covering 85% of population and 95% of GDP of all Latin American and Caribbean economies.

regulate capital inflows, thereby influencing its composition and volume. The aim is to encourage flows whose volume and composition is consistent with the domestic absorptive capacity, channeling them into productive investment projects, and, conversely, to discourage short-term or volatile inflows; some countries have directly regulated capital flows in order to bring them in line with their development objectives.

The possible combinations between the three levels yield different mixes of aggregate demand, exchange rate and monetary policies.

The first level includes a variant of non-sterilized intervention, frequently adopted by countries, which especially target price stability as the main objective, anchoring it to a fixed nominal exchange rate. They are willing to accept a passive monetary policy. The bet is that supply will remain abundant but also that national interest rates and inflation rates will converge rapidly with international rates.

An important part of the success of this strategy will ultimately depend on the confidence of economic agents in the capacity of monetary authorities to maintain the nominal peg. Success also depends on the relationship between the nominal exchange rate and inflation. In the face of inertial components of inflation and/or lags in adjustment of imports – which can cause the monetary base to expand beyond desirable levels or the prices of importables to remain high – the use of the exchange-rate as an anchor to stabilize prices can cause marked real exchange-rate appreciation, a growing excess of aggregate expenditure, and a change in the composition of output biased against tradables. An extreme reliance on this approach to attack inflation is clearly a high-risk strategy; should important disequilibria emerge, the policy options often narrow down to a severe recession or abrupt and destabilizing corrective measures. As Peter Kenen (1993) has commented: "no sensible sailor throws out the anchor before the boat stops moving."

Sterilized intervention intends to isolate the money stock from large fluctuations stemming from the mobility of foreign capital. This type of sterilization, if effective, prevents domestic real interest rates from falling and limits the expansion of aggregate demand. Countries that have left behind a recessive conjuncture, maintain an active monetary policy and, at the same time, adopt a more cautious position regarding capital inflows have preferred this second level of intervention. It reflects a concern for the sustained development of the tradables sector, and the channeling of foreign capital towards investment (preferably in that sector).

In economies that have reached full use of their productive capacity, sterilization is needed for helping to control aggregate spending and preventing further appreciation of the real exchange rate. However, if interest rate differentials persist, capital inflows continue to be stimulated, generating further need for sterilization. At the same time, this intervention may be a source of quasi-fiscal deficits, since the Central Bank is placing commercial paper in the domestic market at higher interest rates than those it obtains on its international reserves.[17]

In practice, sterilized intervention has been complemented with other policy measures at the three levels of intervention. At the first level of intervention, designed to influence the foreign exchange market, it is possible to: (i) increase the demand for foreign exchange through transitory incentives for the outflow of capital during surplus periods; this can be done by relaxing the rules governing investment by nationals abroad and the repatriation of FDI, and by authorizing various debtors to make pre-payments; (ii) encourage increased investment intensive in imported capital goods and inputs.

At the second level of intervention, geared to complement monetary policy to control the impact on aggregate demand, it is possible to: (i) introduce mechanisms regulating financial systems in order to avoid distortions and market incompleteness in the sector, and remove weaknesses in consolidated prudential regulation (ECLAC, 1998, chapters VII and XII; Rojas-Suárez and Weisbrod, 1996); and (ii) enhance fiscal discipline avoiding excessive pressures on aggregate demand increasing transitorily takes during booms; that would permit a better policy mix and more stable interest and exchange-rates.

At the third level of intervention, designed to alter the composition of capital flows, it is possible to: (i) apply indirect exchange-rate measures aimed at reducing inflows (and fostering outflows) of short-term capital by introducing uncertainty as to the short-run evolution of the exchange-rate; (ii) adopt direct measures imposing restrictions on capital inflows, which can take the form of reserve requirements, without interest, on bank deposits or other credits from abroad, and various kinds of quantitative controls (requirements as to minimum maturity periods, minimum volumes for bond issues, and regulations on the participation of foreign capital in the stock market, and prohibitions on

---

[17] If net inflows were only transitorily large, this eventual cost would tend to be compensated for by subsequent sales by the Central Bank of foreign currency at prices (during shortages) above those at which it made purchases (during abundance). However, some Central Banks have sold foreign currency in moments of scarcity at appreciated rates in order to avoid inflation or capital looses to private debtors in foreign currency. This is a frequent outcome of allowing appreciation during a previous boom led by capital surges.

some inflows, like in China and India). All these measures contribute to make interventions in the first two levels more efficient and sustainable.

Intervention is based on two assumptions: (i) the monetary authority has a better idea of future macroeconomic trends in the balance of payments and their long-term effects on the economy; and (ii) more fundamentally, its objectives are longer termed than those of agents operating in short-term markets (Zahler, 1998).

4. Why does the market fail to avoid overshooting?

On the whole, in both Latin America and Asia, during the 1990s most authorities took a procyclical approach, allowing capital surges to be transmitted domestically, as illustrated by the data in figures VI.1 and VI.2. As a consequence, they fell into a *financieristic trap*, with appreciated exchange rates, high current account deficit, high stock price/earnings ratios, and large short term or liquid liabilities. From that financieristic trap, it becomes highly unlikely to escape without a traumatic adjustment, involving overshooting to outlier exchange or interest rates, and considerable liquidity constraints that, together, generate a very unfriendly macroeconomic environment for firms and labor.

Most authorities (as well as observers) took the view that there was (i) nothing that should be done during the expansive stages, or (ii) nothing that could be done, or (iii) preferred to "benefit a little longer" from the boom led by capital inflows. *Ex post*, only *ex post*, interestingly, the consensus of observers was that disequilibria had accumulated. Given that voluntary flows cannot take place without the willing consent of both debtors and creditors, why did neither agent act in due time to curb flows well before a crisis?

An outstanding feature of most recent macroeconomic crises in East Asia and Latin America is that currency and financial crises have been suffered by EEs that usually were considered to be highly "successful" by IFIs and financial agents.[18] Actually, they were awarded with growingly improving grades from international risk rating agencies;[19] accordingly, EEs were rewarded with large private capital flows, and falling spreads, in parallel with accumulating rising stocks of external liabilities (see figure VI.1).

---

[18] Complementary analyses are found in Fanelli (2003); Ffrench-Davis (2003); Frenkel (2003; 2004); Williamson (2003b).

[19] Reisen (2003) shows that risk-rating agencies usually follow the market. Nonetheless, they play a significant role because they tend to reinforce overoptimism and overpessimism.

The fact is that both regions moved into *vulnerability zones*. (We repeat the signals discussed in chapter II: some combination of large external liabilities, with a high short-term or liquid share; a credit boom; currency and maturity mismatches; a significant external deficit; an appreciated exchange-rate; high price/earnings ratios in the stock market, high luxury real estate prices; plus low domestic investment ratios in LACs.) In parallel, as discussed below, agents specialized in microeconomic aspects of finance, placed in the short-term or liquid segments of capital markets, acquire a dominant voice in the generation of macroeconomic expectations.

There is an extremely relevant and interesting literature on the causes of financial instability: the asymmetries of information between creditors and debtors, and the lack of adequate internalization of the negative externalities that each agent generates (through growing vulnerability), that underlie the cycles of abundance and shortage of external financing (Krugman, 2000; McKinnon, 1991; Rodrik, 1998; Stiglitz, 2002; Harberger, 1985). Beyond those issues, as stressed by Ocampo (2003), finance deals with the future, and evidently concrete "information" about the future is unavailable. Consequently, the tendency to equate opinions and expectations with "information" contribute to herd behavior and multiple equilibria. Actually, we have observed a notorious contagion, first of overoptimism, and then of overpessimism in many of the financial crises experienced by EEs in the last three decades.

During all three expansive processes there has been an evident contagion of overoptimism among creditors. As said, rather than *appetite for risk*, in those episodes agents underestimate or ignore risk. In this respect, it is interesting to recall the evident parallel, in the 1990s, between spreads of Mexico (today praised as then a well-behaved reformer) and Argentina (today qualified as a non-reformer in that decade) (see figure VI.3). Apparently, creditors did not perceive any significant difference between these two economies until 1998.

With respect to debtors, in periods of overoptimism, the evidence is that most debtors do not borrow thinking of default and expecting to be rescued or to benefit from moratoria. Contrariwise, expectations of high yields tend to prevail: borrowers are also victims of the syndrome of financial euphoria during the boom periods (Kindleberger, 1978).

However, over and above these facts, there are two additional features of the creditor side that are crucially important. One feature is the particular *nature of the leading agents* acting on the supply side (Ffrench-Davis, 2003). There are natural asymmetries in the behavior and

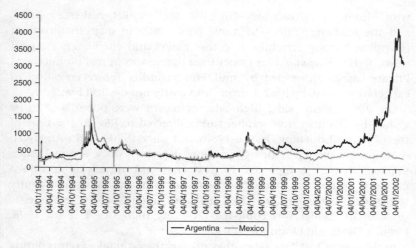

Figure VI.3 Argentina and Mexico: Country risk, 1994–2002 (base points)

Source: JP Morgan. Country risk measured by the sovereign spread over the US zero coupon curve.

objectives of different economic agents. The agents predominant in the financial markets are specialized in short-term liquid investment, operate within short-term horizons, and naturally are highly sensitive to changes in variables that affect returns in the short-run.[20] The second feature is the gradual spread of information, among prospective agents, on investment opportunities in EEs. In fact, agents from different segments of the financial market become gradually drawn into new international markets as they take notice of the profitable opportunities offered by emerging economies previously unknown to them.

This explains, from the supply-side, why the surges of flows to emerging economies – in 1977–81, 1991–94 and mid-1995–97 – have been *processes* that went on for several years rather than one-shot changes in supply. In this sense, it must be stressed the relevance for policy design of making a distinction between two different types of volatility of capital flows, short-term ups-and-downs, and the medium-term instability,

---

[20] Persaud (2003), argues that modern risk-management by investing institutions (such as funds and banks), based on value-at-risk measured daily, works pro-cyclically in the boom and bust. Pro-cyclicality is reinforced by a trend toward homogenization of creditor agents. A complementary argument by Calvo and Mendoza (2000) examines how globalization may promote contagion by discouraging the gathering of information and by strengthening incentives for imitating market portfolio.

which leads several variables – like the stock market, real estate prices and the exchange rate – to move persistently in a given direction, providing "wrong certainties" to the market and encouraging capital flows, *seeking economic rents* rather than differences in real productivity. Private capital flows; led by mid-term volatility (or reversibility) of expectations, usually have a strong and costly pro-cyclical bias.

On the domestic side, high rates of return were potentially to be gained by creditors from capital surges directed to EEs. At the time of their financial opening, in the 1980s and early 1990s, Latin American economies were experiencing recession, depressed stock and real estate markets, as well as high real interest rates and initially undervalued domestic currencies. Indeed, by 1990, prices of real estate and equity stocks were extremely depressed in Latin America, and the domestic price of the dollar was comparatively very high (see ECLAC, 1998; Ffrench-Davis and Ocampo, 2001).

In the case of East Asia, when they opened their capital accounts during the 1990s, the international supply of funding was already booming. As compared to LACs, they were growing notably fast, with high savings and investment ratios. However, equity stock was also cheap as compared to capital-rich countries (exhibited low price/earnings ratios), and liquid external liabilities were extremely low. Naturally, as discussed in section 1, the rate of return tends to be higher in the productive sectors of capital-scarce EEs than in mature markets that are capital-rich. Then, there is potentially space for very profitable capital flows from suppliers in the latter to the former markets. Flows should continue until rates of return (adjusted!) converge, what naturally would take a long term. The expected adjustments in any emerging economy moving from a closed to an open capital account, in those conditions, should tend to be similar to those recorded in LACs. The outcome in both emerging regions, for instance, was a spectacular rise in stock prices, multiplying in average the price index by four in 1990–94 and (after a sharp 40% drop with the Tequila crisis) by two in 1995–97 in LACs, and by two in East Asia in 1992–94 (see table VII.4). All these swings were directly associated to portfolio flows.

In what relates to domestic interest rates, they tended to be high at the outset of surge episodes, reflecting the BEC faced by most countries during periods of sharp reductions in capital inflows, the restrictive monetary policies in place and the short-term bias of the financial reforms implemented in Latin America. Finally, in a non-exhaustive list, the increased supply of external financing in the 1990s generated a process of exchange-rate appreciation in most LACs (see figure VI.2), as well as, more moderately, in East Asia; the expectations of continued, persistent, appreciation encouraged additional inflows from dealers operating with maturity horizons located within the expected appreciation of the domestic currency.[21] The combination of open capital account, large liquid liabilities and expectations of depreciation lead, most naturally, to a large outflow, with a large depreciation if the rate is flexible.

For allocative efficiency and for export-oriented development strategies, a macroprice – as significant as the exchange rate –[22] led by capital flows conducted by short-termist agents reveals a severe policy inconsistency. The increase in aggregate demand, pushed up by inflows and appreciation, and a rising share of the domestic demand for tradables, augments "artificially" the absorptive capacity and the demand for foreign savings. Thus, as said, the exogenous change – opened by the transformations recorded in international capital markets – was converted into an endogenous process, leading to domestic vulnerability given the potential reversibility of flows.

In brief, the interaction between the two sets of factors – *the nature of agents and a process of adjustment* – explains the dynamics of capital flows over time: why suppliers keep pouring-in funds while real macroeconomic fundamentals worsen. When creditors *discover* an emerging market, their initial exposure is low or non-existent. Then they generate a series of consecutive flows, which result in rapidly increasing stocks of financial assets in the EE; actually, too rapid and/or large for an efficient absorption; frequently, the absorption is artificially increased by exchange rate appreciation, and a rising real aggregate demand with an enlarged external deficit as a consequence.

The creditor's sensitivity to negative news, at some point, is likely to, suddenly, increase remarkably when the country has reached *vulnerability zones;* then, the creditors take notice of (i) the rising level of the stock of assets held in a country (or region), (ii) the degree of dependence of the debtor market on additional flows, which is associated with the magnitude of the current account deficit, (iii) the extent of appreciation, (iv) the need of refinancing of maturing liabilities, and (v) the amount of liquid liabilities likely to flow out in face of a crisis. Therefore, it should

---

[21] For short-termist agents the actual and expected profitability were increased with the appreciation process. That same process, if perceived as persistent, would tend to discourage investment in the production of tradables intensive in domestic inputs. Therefore, it is most relevant, because of its policy implications, what happens with the behavior of exchange rates during the expansive or boom stage. It is then when external imbalances and currency and maturity mismatches are, inadvertently, being generated.

[22] The allocative role of the exchange rate was notably enhanced under the deep trade reforms implemented. See ECLAC (1998, chapters III and IV); Velasco (2000); Williamson (2003b). Consequently, its instability became more damaging.

not be surprising that, after a significant increase in asset prices and exchange rates, accompanied by rising stocks of liquid external liabilities, the sensitivity to adverse political or economic news and the probability of reversal of expectations grows steeply (Calvo, 1998; Rodrik, 1998).

The accumulation of stocks of assets abroad by financial suppliers, until well advanced that boom stage of the cycle, and, then, a subsequent sudden reversal of flows, can *both* be considered to be *rational* responses on the part of individual agents with short-term horizons. This is because it is of little concern to this sort of investors whether (long-term) fundamentals are being improved or worsened while they continue to bring inflows. What is relevant to these investors is that the crucial indicators from their point of view – prices of real estate, bonds and stock, and exchange-rates – can continue providing them with profits in the near term and, obviously, that liquid markets allow them, if needed, to reverse decisions timely; thus, they will continue to supply net inflows until expectations of an imminent near reversal build up.

Indeed, for the most influential financial operators, the more relevant variables are not related to the long-term fundamentals but to short-term profitability. This explains why they may suddenly display a radical change of opinion about the economic situation of a country whose fundamentals, other than liquidity in foreign currency, remain rather unchanged during a shift from *overoptimism* to *overpessimism*.

Naturally, the opposite process tends to take place when the debtor markets have adjusted downward "sufficiently." Then, the inverse process makes its appearance and can be sustained for some years, like in 1991–94 or 1995–97, short-lived like in late 1999 and 2000,[23] or since 2004.[24]

In conclusion, economic agents specialized in the allocation of financial funding (I will call it *microfinance*, as opposed to macrofinance), who may be highly efficient in their field but operate with short-horizons "by training and by reward", have come to play the leading role in determining macroeconomic conditions and policy design in EEs. It implies that a "financieristic" approach becomes predominant rather than a "productivistic" approach. Growth with equity requires improving the rewards for productivity enhancement rather than *financial rent-seeking* searching for capital gains. There is a need to rebalance priorities and voices.

---

[23] Vulnerabilities were still significant in EEs when negative signals reappeared in the world economy in 2000, including the subsequent downward adjustment in the USA and the Argentinean crisis.

[24] It is relevant, for equity and average growth, that the upward process usually tends to be more gradual or slower than the downward adjustment, which tends to be abrupt. See chapter II.

VII
The Latin American and Asian Financial Crises: Contagion of Causes and Costs*

Introduction

Latin America's macroeconomy has been strongly affected by changes in capital flows over the last three decades. During the 1970s, a large supply of funds was made available to the region; then, during the 1980s, there was a severe and widespread shortage of financing, and the region became a net exporter of funds. Between 1991 and 1994, it became a net recipient of large capital flows again, only to experience another sharp reduction of some of the main inflows in late 1994 and early 1995, and a renewed access in 1996–97. Since 1998–99, Latin America (LACs) experienced a new shortage of external financing. A crisis centered in Asian countries was now the origin of this new recessive macroeconomic adjustment in the region. When closing this typescript, in early 2005, a new significant recovery of economic activity was at work. In 2004, LACs exhibited the larger GDP growth since the previous peak year 1997. Interestingly, in this occasion, recovery was not led by inflows but by a sharp improvement in export volumes and prices. On all these swings, the changes that were first expansive and then contractionary, began on the international markets and had a strong impact on the national economies. In the times of the Latin American debt crisis of the 1980s and the Tequila crisis of 1994–95, the successful emerging economies of Asia – with the exception of the Philippines – appeared to be immune to the instability associated with capital surges. However, in 1997 they became the place of origin of a widespread financial crisis in emerging economies (EEs). Here we provide data on significant causes of recent financial crises that are common to both regions.

* Sections 2 and 3 are partly based on "Policy Implications of the Tequila Effect," *Challenge*, Vol. 41, March–April 1998, and Ffrench-Davis and Ocampo (2001).

In section 1, the three recent capital surges to emerging economies are summarized. Section 2 examines the gestation and effects of the Tequila crisis. Section 3 analyses, first, the spread of the contagion to the region. It is explained why it was short-lived in the financial surface, but with a long-lasting impact on the real economy; then, the sharply different performance of Mexico and Chile between 1989 and 1995 is discussed. Section 4 takes care of the East Asian experience with their opening to capital flows since the nineties, highlighting similarities and differences with Latin America. In particular, it addresses how Asian countries became vulnerable to external crises. Section 5 focuses on the recovery-cum-vulnerabilities in Latin America in 1996–97 and its financial and real consequences in 1998–2004. Section 6 introduces the next chapter.

1. Capital surges to emerging economies

After the decade long shortage of external financing during the 1980s, there was a vigorous resurgence of capital inflows between 1991 and 1994. But, vulnerability to volatility was being built. In fact, a sharp scarcity ensued, especially in Mexico and Argentina, with a rather generalized portfolio outflow from LACs in late 1994 and early 1995. The so-called Tequila crisis was followed by a renewed access in 1996–97, but in 1998–2003 a new shortage of external financing set in, as a result of the contagion effect of the crisis detonated in Asia in 1997, which was aggravated by worsening terms of trade, and the Russian default in 1998. On all those occasions, changes in external financing were supply-led. They had a strong impact on the national economies on both sides of the cycle, with contagion first of overoptimism and then of overpessimism.

As discussed in chapter VI, the domestic conjuncture has crucial implications for the link between capital flows and economic activity. When there is a binding external constraint (BEC), any inflow will contribute to relax it, thus facilitating a recovery of economic activity. BEC has been predominant during several episodes in many LACs, and was particularly widespread from the early 1980s up to 1990, in 1995, in 1998–99, and in 2001–03.

Thus, renewed capital inflows contributed to a recovery of economic activity in all those situations. Moreover, they facilitated the adoption of successful anti-inflationary adjustment, anchored to appreciating real exchange rates. The monetary effects of reserve accumulation and the wealth effects of exchange-rate appreciation tended to push-up aggregate demand, facilitating the recovery of economic activity. The existence of the BEC provided an automatic capital inflows/GDP growth link.

A recessive environment brought by the debt crisis still prevailed, by the end of the 1980s, in most LACs. Capital inflows contributed to a significant recovery of economic activity in 1991–94 and in 1996–97. Annual GDP growth rose from 1.3% in the 1980s to 4.1% in 1991–94 and 4.4% in 1996–97 (table VII.1). This growth was meager, however. First, the comparison with the previous golden age is shocking. As already underlined, along the three decades spanning between 1950 and 1980, Latin America had averaged a GDP growth of 5.5% per annum; this dynamic growth lasted beyond that of industrial countries, since it covered all the 1970s.

Second, domestic investment had been rising fast, as a source of that vigorous growth. In the 1980s there was a sharp drop of the investment ratio, of 7 points of GDP, with a negligible recovery in the 1990s. In fact, investment grew much less during this decade, than did capital inflows; thus, most of the external flows financed increased consumption, and

Table VII.1 Latin America and East Asia: Business cycles, 1981–2004 (annual average GDP growth, percentages)

A. Latin America

	1981–89	1990	1991–94	1995	1996–97	1998–99	2000	2001–03	2004
Latin America (19)	1.3	−0.5	4.1	1.0	4.4	1.3	3.7	0.4	5.8
Argentina	−1.0	−2.0	8.0	−2.9	6.7	0.2	−0.8	−2.5	9.0
Brazil	2.3	−4.6	2.8	4.2	2.8	0.5	3.9	0.8	5.2
Chile	2.8	3.3	7.5	9.0	6.8	1.4	4.5	3.0	6.0
Colombia	3.7	4.1	4.2	4.9	2.6	−1.5	2.4	2.2	3.5
Mexico	1.4	5.1	3.5	−6.1	6.1	4.4	6.7	0.5	4.4
Peru	−0.7	−5.4	4.9	8.6	4.7	0.2	2.5	3.1	5.1
Uruguay	0.4	0.5	5.7	−2.4	5.3	0.4	−1.9	−4.6	11.8
Venezuela	−0.3	6.0	3.2	4.8	3.4	−2.5	3.8	−5.1	17.3

B. East Asia

	1981–90	1991–96	1997	1998	1999–2004
East Asia (6)	7.0	7.2	4.5	−5.6	4.9
Korea	8.6	7.4	4.7	−6.9	6.0
Philippines	1.7	2.8	5.2	−0.6	4.0
Indonesia	5.1	7.4	4.5	−13.1	3.6
Malaysia	6.0	9.6	7.3	−7.4	5.2
Thailand	7.9	8.1	−1.4	−10.5	4.9
Taiwan	7.9	6.9	6.7	4.6	3.6

Source: Latin America: based on ECLAC data at 1980 prices for 1980–89 and at 1995 prices for 1989–2004. East Asia: based on data from the Asian Development Bank and the IMF.

crowded-out domestic savings. Third, as shown in chapter III, a significant share of GDP growth, in those two occasions, was a recovery of economic activity rather than an increase in productive capacity. In the early nineties, Argentina (see Fanelli and Machinea, 1995) and Peru are two outstanding cases of countries, featuring huge underutilization of capacity and hyperinflation; the disappearance of the BEC, which allowed an exchange rate appreciation, and the reintroduction of fiscal discipline were strongly complementary in combating hyperinflation.

However, there were outstanding exceptions. Mexico, for instance, actually received notably large financial inflows but did not experience any significant growth in 1991–94. One explanation underlying that fact is that by the late 1980s, the Mexican economy was placed close to its potential output. Consequently, there was no room for a recovery of economic activity. Thus, a positive capital inflow/GDP growth link was contingent upon the capacity to transform foreign savings into productive investment. Actually, foreign funding did not flow into productive investment, and a significant exchange rate appreciation had led, by 1994, to huge imports.

Net capital inflows to all Latin America amounted to between 4 and 5% of GDP in 1977–81, 1991–94 and 1996–97. As documented in the couple of tables that follow, in the three periods, the deficit on current account rose sharply, and exchange rates appreciated; naturally, imports grew more rapidly than exports, and external liabilities rose steadily. Indeed, all the variables taken together reflect growing macroeconomic imbalances, which, before the explosion of the crisis, were not recognized as disequilibria. As discussed in chapter II, there is a frequent misunderstanding of what are, really, macroeconomic balances. The strong fact is that those recipient countries having large deficits on current account, high shares of short-term and liquid external liabilities, and appreciating exchange rates,[1] had penetrated *vulnerability zones*. Thus, they became increasingly vulnerable to changes of mood of external creditors who, given the high and rising exposure of financial assets placed in the region, subsequently became more sensitive to any "bad news."

External financing is obviously a vital ingredient of development in capital-scarce economies; however, it also tends to be very volatile, and to fluctuate between excessive surpluses and shortages. Consequently, it is important to design economic policies that will ensure that funds flow in

---

[1] It should be recalled that several LACs were implementing sharp liberalization of import regimes *pari passu* with exchange rate appreciation, led by capital inflows. See chapter IV.

quantities that are sustainable and are allocated mainly to long-term investment rather than to consumption.

2. Causes and costs of the Tequila crisis

Most LACs moved suddenly from shortage to abundance in the early 1990s. Nevertheless, recovery of access to international private finance came earlier and with greater intensity in some countries, particularly Chile (analyzed in chapter IX) and Mexico.

Far-reaching economic reforms had been implemented during the second half of the 1980s in Mexico, while gradually recovered from the debt crisis of the 1980s. This recovery continued up to 1990. Subsequently, GDP growth and investment only picked up moderately, despite huge capital inflows. The large supply of funds coming into Mexico in the early 1990s entered the domestic market, with only a few limitations, which principally restricted bank indebtedness (Gurría, 1995).

The real exchange rate appreciated quickly, encouraging the utilization of the large supply of foreign currency. The nominal exchange rate remained practically fixed since November 1991 until March 1994, even though officially it was a flexible crawling rate within a band with a rising ceiling and a constant floor. The inflation rate in Mexico, which was larger than that of its trade partners at the beginning of the period, involved a rapid real exchange-rate appreciation. A bending inflation, anchored by the sticky nominal exchange rate, took place with a lag, leaving as heritage an overvalued price of the peso (see table VII.2), a large external deficit, and a huge stock of rather liquid liabilities.

How were these resources from abroad used? The answer was to finance expenditure, growingly intensive in imported consumer goods. Total expenditure greatly exceeded production. This trend was mediated by a domestic credit boom, supported by a lack of prudential regulation and supervision (ECLAC, 1998, chapter XII; Sachs, Tornell and Velasco, 1996). The consequent deficit on current account rose from US$7 billion in 1990 to US$15 billion in 1991; it continued to rise in subsequent years, and reached US$30 billion in 1994 (see table VII.3).[2] The credit boom reached also the stock markets, leading to a sizable rise in asset prices (see table VII.4). These trends were becoming a significant source of vulnerability. However, they continued to be deepened by the agents of financial markets.

[2] In 1994, the authorities projected that it would rise by another US$4 billion in 1995.

Table VII.2 Latin America: Real exchange rates, 1987–2004 (average 1987–90 = 100)

	1987–1990	1994.IV	1995.I	1998.I	2001.III	2002.IV	2004.III
Weighted average (16)	100.0	76.8	84.6	73.5	90.0	119.8	112.2
Argentina	100.0	62.8	63.3	63.4	54.4	135.8	127.6
Brazil	100.0	70.4	68.3	61.8	112.1	143.2	113.1
Chile	100.0	95.9	96.1	83.4	105.4	104.1	102.1
Colombia	100.0	77.4	76.3	73.9	92.4	105.1	96.6
Mexico	100.0	76.0	116.4	80.4	65.6	69.0	77.7
Peru	100.0	59.0	59.3	56.5	61.2	62.1	63.7
Uruguay	100.0	87.2	86.2	82.7	78.0	110.6	119.7
Venezuela	100.0	96.4	88.7	64.8	50.1	71.2	74.9

Source: Based on official figures processed by ECLAC.

Real exchange rate indices (main official) for each country with respect to the currencies of their main trading partners, weighted by the share of exports to those countries; inflated by external CPI and deflated by domestic CPI; for Brazil we weighted the Rio CPI index (2/3) and the new official series of inflation (1/3) for 1992–97. Selected quarters correspond to significant peaks and minimum levels for the average of Latin America. For 1987–90 annual average; for 1992–2004, quarterly average.

Table VII.3 Latin America: Balance on current accounts, 1983–2004 (US$ million per year)

	1983–90	1994	1995	1997	1998	1999	2004
Total (19)	−6,560	−51,604	−37,912	−64,552	−88,510	−55,370	21,845
Sub total (18, without Venezuela)	−8,235	−54,145	−39,926	−68,284	−84,078	−57,482	6,251
Argentina	−1,413	−11,148	−5,175	−12,240	−14,530	−11,966	3,653
Brazil	−1,564	−1,153	−18,136	−30,491	−33,829	−25,400	11,094
Chile	−997	−1,586	−1,350	−3,660	−3,918	99	2,904
Colombia	−671	−3,673	−4,527	−5,751	−4,858	671	−1,267
Mexico	−241	−29,662	−1,576	−7,666	−16,073	−13,999	−7,200
Peru	−1,034	−2,785	−4,640	−3,428	−3,390	−1,518	−1,061
Uruguay	−6	−438	−213	−287	−476	−508	28
Venezuela	1,675	2,541	2,014	3,732	−4,432	2,112	15,594

Source: ECLAC.

The balance on the current account includes unrequited private and public transfers as current income. Preliminary figures for 2004.

Table VII.4 Latin America and East Asia: Stock exchange prices, 1990–2004 (indices, July 1997 = 100)

	Dec-90	Sep-92	Sep-94	Mar-95	Jul-97	Aug-98	Mar-00	Sep-01	Mar-02	Sep-02	Oct-04
A. Latin America (7)	**21.7**	**44.6**	**92.5**	**52.3**	**100.0**	**47.2**	**88.3**	**54.8**	**71.8**	**43.5**	**102.2**
Argentina	13.4	46.9	78.2	53.5	100.0	53.4	90.3	37.8	23.5	16.1	59.8
Brazil	8.0	22.1	71.8	42.8	100.0	44.4	76.9	39.0	54.6	25.2	78.8
Chile	24.5	51.4	93.1	89.4	100.0	48.0	78.4	54.2	61.8	45.8	102.4
Colombia	16.6	65.0	113.1	96.3	100.0	49.9	41.2	29.0	31.2	28.0	74.5
Mexico	38.6	72.7	132.1	45.9	100.0	49.7	118.5	83.3	116.2	78.1	137.9
Peru	n.a.	n.a.	72.9	56.4	100.0	57.3	67.7	54.1	60.2	59.1	141.0
Venezuela	84.9	82.2	50.8	37.9	100.0	26.2	36.2	46.3	31.7	22.4	43.8
B. East Asia (6)	**n.a.**	**49.9**	**110.0**	**97.9**	**100.0**	**37.0**	**107.9**	**45.1**	**77.0**	**55.5**	**82.6**
Indonesia	n.a.	53.7	84.2	71.6	100.0	11.1	27.6	13.7	17.3	16.0	32.9
Korea	n.a.	87.6	187.2	161.9	100.0	30.2	120.1	54.9	109.6	88.0	129.7
Malaysia	n.a.	63.7	119.0	103.5	100.0	16.8	61.3	35.6	46.1	39.5	52.2
Philippines	n.a.	67.1	134.6	108.6	100.0	30.4	47.9	25.5	30.9	24.5	35.6
Taiwan	n.a.	37.1	80.9	73.5	100.0	47.6	99.1	31.6	55.5	34.1	48.6
Thailand	n.a.	133.9	279.8	236.3	100.0	19.0	48.0	25.2	36.1	31.3	66.9

Source: Based on IFC/Standard & Poor's, *Emerging Stock Market Review*, several issues. The averages of East Asia and Latin America are weighted by amount of transactions. Values at the end of each period, expressed in current US dollars; distributed earnings are not included. Selected dates correspond to peaks and minimum levels for the average of Latin America.

Over a four-year period, the stock of net external liabilities rose by US$92 billion, of which only around US$24 billion were accounted for by FDI. This large stock of liabilities, most of which tended to be eventually volatile, along with the significant exchange rate appreciation and the correspondingly high deficit on current account, were the main variables that made Mexico so vulnerable and caused the far-reaching recessive adjustment which exploded in December 1994. The deterioration of the financial portfolio, associated with the credit boom,[3] and the large issue of short-term government bonds in dollars (*Tesobonos*), which were mostly bought by foreign investors, also had a great deal to do with the intensity of the Mexican currency and financial crises (Ros, 2001).

These sources of vulnerability, together with several dramatic non-economic shocks, which took place in Mexico in 1994,[4] and the increase in US interest rates, made the ground fertile for a crisis. However, there are other popular explanations in the literature, to which we refer now.

It is said, surprisingly often, that the Mexican crisis of 1994 could not have been foreseen because of the concealment of information. While the provision of official information on international reserves was admittedly only sporadic, the key data – on real exchange rate appreciation, the high current account deficit and its financing with volatile resources, and low GDP growth despite booming inflows – were available on a regular basis. For instance, in 1992, it was already known that the deficit on current account was rising fast encouraged by exchange rate appreciation (see Box VII.1);[5] also there were data recording a significant crowding-out of domestic savings.

Notwithstanding these facts, by 1993 Mexican policies were praised loudly by financial institutions, the media and risk rating agencies

---

[3] The worsening of the financial portfolio is not an exogenous phenomenon. Amongst others, it responds to the slackening of standards of prudential supervision and to a large bank credit boom (Sachs, Tornell and Velasco, 1996). A credit boom was closely associated to a capital inflows surge in Chile 1982, Mexico 1994, and Thailand 1997.

[4] A number of significant non-economic events included the Chiapas uprising, the assassination of the leading presidential candidate and the election of a new president. But, in 1994, also Mexico became a member of the OECD, and NAFTA was born.

[5] By mid-1992, we had already advised that a significant tendency to exchange rate revaluation was in process, which would become dangerous if not stopped (reproduced in Ffrench-Davis, 2000, chapter 9). In parallel, since early 1991, the Central Bank of Chile was moving forward in the regulation of capital inflows and the strengthening of active exchange-rate and monetary policies (see chapter IX).

Box VII.1 The return of private capital to Latin America: A word of caution, in 1992, for "successful" economies*

Optimism has replaced pessimism in Latin America since 1991. A large number of LACs faced a sharp rise in their access to international capital markets, particularly to new financing sources. The relaxation of the foreign exchange constraint allowed actual GDP to recover. Some countries show annual increases in GDP as high as 8%, notwithstanding low investment ratios. Actually, it is not that LDCs suddenly became highly productive, but simply that the previously available output capacity had been constrained by a binding foreign exchange shortage. Money inflows in 1991 were much greater than the foreign financing actually absorbed in the domestic economies of LACs. Thus, roughly one-half of net capital inflows went to build up reserves.

What does this imply? That the absorptive capacity of domestic economies was limited. Nonetheless, capital kept flowing. Why? Not because Latin America needed more capital for macroeconomic balance or growth, but because interest rates or profit differentials were wide and expected to remain so by operators of "hot money". So these signals of the market kept drawing capital into LACs, with large reserve accumulation leading to exchange rate appreciation.

In fact, domestic currencies appreciated in real terms in 15 of the 18 main LACs in 1991 – between 1 and 20% – as compared with the 1990 average. Most of these currencies continued to appreciate during the first half of 1992. Additionally, in 1991 many LACs reduced restrictions on imports, in most cases correctly. However, if a country is appreciating the exchange rate, *pari passu* with reducing import barriers, it will be giving two negative signals for import-competing activities, which may result in a strong negative adjustment. Depreciation is required to avoid the resulting imbalance.

Macroeconomic management, and exchange-rate policy in particular, are crucial for stability to be sustainable: how to get a volume of capital flows that does not disturb the performance of the real sector, especially via a destabilizing influence on the exchange rate and aggregate demand. This poses, I think, an unavoidable dilemma, with macroeconomic and microeconomic implications. One alternative is a policy that aims to achieve sustainable macroeconomic equilibrium by regulating the exchange rate and controlling short-run capital flows. On the other hand, lies an across-the-board full liberalization of the capital account; this move tends to lead to outlier exchange rates as a likely consequence, after a while followed by sharp capital outflows and macroeconomic cycles. The history of crises, and present events, very clearly signal that one has to make a choice. Chile made a choice in 1991, against the neo-liberal approach in fashion. In view of the abundant supply of external funds recorded during that year, introduced regulations discouraging short-term capital inflows. We can add now, that the implementation of an adjustable reserve requirement on capital inflows in 1991, proved later, during the 1994 Mexican crisis, to have been quite an efficient decision (see chapter IX, and Ffrench-Davis, 2002, chapter 10).

* Excerpts from a note I published in J. Williamson et al., *Fragile Finance*, edited by J.J. Teunissen, FONDAD, Den Hague, June 1992, and reproduced in Ffrench-Davis (2000, chapter 9). Only the last phrase is new.

(see Gurría, 1995), while the incorporation of Mexico to two clubs of wealthy nations in 1994 – NAFTA and the OECD – intensified the trend toward macroeconomic disequilibria. What was lacking was a more comprehensive analysis of information available, with a concern for macroeconomic sustainability rather than for short-term returns to financial investors. The crucial problem was that neither those on the supply side nor those on the demand side paid enough attention to the available information, not until after the crisis erupted.

Other variables that are usually blamed for the crisis are the deterioration of the fiscal balance, the monetary policies implemented in 1994, the absence of a pension system based on capitalization (see discussion below), and the inexcusable way in which the devaluation of December 1994 was implemented. Although all these variables had some effect, they were of only secondary importance in the light of the (i) significant exchange rate appreciation; (ii) the magnitude and duration of the current-account deficit that prevailed between 1991 and 1994; (iii) the fact that a high share of external liabilities were short term or liquid, and (iv) the poor response of productive investment to large capital inflows.

As indicated previously, the real exchange rate appreciated heavily along the way. This occurred after 1988, and the trend was even more marked during the first half of the 1990s (table VII.2). Exports grew, but imports rose even more rapidly. The investment rate recovered, but much less than the increase in capital inflows; actually, by 1993, when Mexico received inflows of US$31 billion, the investment ratio had merely risen 1.8 points of GDP with respect to 1990, while the external deficit did jump 4.1 points. Consequently, these external funds further reinforced consumption and crowded-out national savings. The disequilibria cannot be attributed to government expenditure, inasmuch as Mexico had achieved a fiscal balance after having made a tough and successful effort to eliminate the large deficit of the mid-1980s. Hence, the excess expenditure occurred mostly in the private sector, and was financed with private funds from abroad; one part was intermediated by the banking credit boom, and the other by traders of imported goods. The savings ratio fell significantly, between the late 1980s and 1994: national savings (measured at current prices) diminished five points.

After some reserve losses, in March 1994, a devaluation, which represented an 8% jump, from the floor to the ceiling of the existing exchange rate band, was implemented. The financial markets were not severely disturbed by this devaluation. Flows into Mexico and the other LACs continued at high levels. The Mexican economy remained relatively strong during that year; GDP rose somewhat more than during the preceding biennium, the investment coefficient rose slightly (0.8% of GDP) and the consolidated public sector balance showed a small surplus (0.2% of GDP).

Nevertheless, during that year there were several attacks on the peso, while the exchange rate was at the top of the band and the Bank of Mexico was selling reserves. However, in November 1994, once the presidential elections were over, analysts of international risks gave Mexico good grades financially, and recommended investing in its assets (Ros, 2001).

In the meantime, the deficit on current account had continued to rise. On December 20, the new elected authorities reached the conclusion that they could not postpone making a major correction in the exchange rate and drastically reducing the external deficit: 15% devaluation took place; the market then expected additional devaluations and conducted a massive attack on the peso. Authorities liberalized the exchange rate, which depreciated in total by 125% between the end of 1994 and of 1995.

Essentially, the seeds of the crisis date back to the period between 1992 and 1994, when there was a massive capital inflow, mostly liquid and short-term (Rodrik and Velasco, 2000). Aggregate demand grew rapidly exceeding by an unsustainable amount the potential GDP; domestic expenditure leaned increasingly toward imports (tradables), especially encouraged by exchange rate appreciation.[6] Thus, in those years, there was a maladjustment that would most likely have to be reversed in the future. What is extremely policy relevant is that disequilibrium was led and encouraged by capital inflows.

Downward adjustment is always painful, and it was extremely painful for Mexico in 1995. GDP fell 6.1%, open unemployment doubled, investment dropped by nearly 30%, and the financial sector experienced liquidity problems and large non-performing portfolios; this had a fiscal cost, arising from support to banks and debtors of over 10% of annual GDP (Reisen, 1997, table 11).

The Mexican crisis, with its explosion in 1994, illustrates the harm that can be caused by the absorption, in the preceding years, of an excessive volume of capital inflows, giving way to the accumulation of a large

---

[6] Despite the fact that expenditures exceeded GDP, potential output was probably larger than actual GDP, with an underutilization of the production capacity of importables and of potentially exportable goods under a less appreciated exchange rate. This might explain the subsequent sizable response of the output of tradables to the real devaluation in 1995.

stock of external liabilities – especially dangerous when the composition of such financing is short-term or liquid – and to a domestic credit boom. Between 1990 and 1994, producers and consumers accommodated to a level of overall expenditure that rapidly outstripped potential GDP: expenditure exceeded actual GDP by 7% in 1992–94.

The natural shortsightedness of suppliers led to only see the undoubtedly great merits of many achievements recorded by Mexico – such as the dramatic improvement of its fiscal position – but was unable to recognize the problems that were still there (poverty and low levels of investment) and those that were being created (such as the external deficit and a growing stock of volatile liabilities).

When expectations of profitability to creditors were reverted, *pari passu* the well-known events of 1994, the amounts involved became unsustainable. Then, creditors cut financing sharply, forcing Mexico into a highly contractionary adjustment and a huge devaluation after the authorities adopted the flexible exchange rate. Despite a large package of international support that Mexico received in 1995 (Lustig, 1997), it experienced the mentioned drop of 6.1% in GDP.

GDP recovered strongly shortly afterward, peaking at a growth rate of nearly 7% in 2000. But, in spite of that jump, the overall GDP rise averaged only 3.5% per year in 1995–2000: a recovery is not net growth, but just returning to zero; in the process, there is an unavoidable loss of welfare. Significantly, GDP growth continued to be slow despite the fact that Mexico was benefiting from a significant positive shock as a result of a United States boom. This boom was reflected in the vigorous expansion of export volume by 16% per year in 1995–2000, nine-tenths of which were directed to the US markets. After a sharp drop in 1995, the investment ratio did not fully recover until 1998. Poverty increased from 45% to 53% of the population between 1994 and 1996. As well, average real wages decreased substantially during the crisis, and by 2003 had not recovered the 1994 level yet (ECLAC, 2004d).

In this new decade, the growth performance of Mexico was also poor. Actually, GDP per capita has stepped back, reaching in 2004 a level below that of 2000. Mexico, rightly so, has been praised as a distinguished pupil of the Washington Consensus. Has kept inflation under control and fiscal discipline, both positive features, but has been unable to generate a macroeconomic environment perceived as *friendly* by productive investors and has been unable to pull-up systemic competitivity and potential GDP growth.

3. The brief and limited contagion of the Tequila crisis to Latin America

The shock waves of the deep Mexican crisis did not trigger a widespread recessive contagion throughout the region in 1995, in contrast to 1982. The most notable exception was Argentina, which was seriously affected by contagion, with significant drops in GDP, employment and investment in 1995. The negative impact on expectations of financial markets was short-lived.

Nonetheless, during 1995 many countries experienced negative flows in several segments of the supply of financing, particularly bonds, deposits and flows to stock markets. Stock market prices, which usually fluctuate a great deal, dropped throughout the region (table VII.4). Issues of primary ADRs were also discontinued, falling from US$6 billion in 1993 to less than 1 billion in 1995.

Subsequently, the flow of funds became extremely abundant, again across all Latin America. GDP recovery in Argentina and Mexico was particularly vigorous; given the sharp drop in both countries in 1995, which had generated a large gap between actual GDP and productive capacity. This enabled a significant reactivation to take place, which led to a complacent view – in those countries, in International Financing Institutions (IFIs) and nearly everywhere – of the effects of crises and the capacity to recover from them. Even more, as known, the IMF was pressuring member countries in 1997 so that the board was to decide to endorse a proposal requesting the formal adoption of a policy enforcing capital account opening in member countries.[7] That complacent view was based on a shortsighted perspective of what was really happening. Recovery was in the financial surface, but not in the forces behind economic development.

a) The Tequila impact on Latin America

The negative impact on Latin America as a whole is quite obvious (see, again, table VII.1). GDP growth fell to 1% in 1995, and per capita GDP suffered a drop of 0.7%, for the first time since 1990. The investment ratio declined close to one point, capital inflows (discounting the non-market packages of support to Argentina and Mexico) fell to less than half the level of the preceding three-year period, which shows how unstable capital flows can be), and the unemployment rate rose in

---

[7] See critical appraisals of this proposal in Bhagwati (2004) and Stiglitz (2002).

countries such as Argentina, Costa Rica, Mexico, Paraguay, Uruguay and Venezuela. As said, all stock markets experienced a sharp drop and outflows of capital. By early 1996, several countries showed GDP drops in various quarters. In fact, average growth in Latin America was negative in the four quarters ending in the first quarter of 1996.

Aside from Mexico and Argentina, GDP also fell 2.4% in Uruguay; in early 1996, it also diminished in Peru. Thus, the sharp reduction of external funds did have an impact in LACs where most financing was short-term and volatile, or in countries that engaged in heavy trading with the economies that were affected by the financial shock (as in the case of contagion to Uruguay).

b) Why was the dryness of supply so brief in 1995?

The fast return of financial inflows is commonly associated to the good behavior that, according to those markets and IFIs, Latin America had exhibited in previous years. It was a reward, it was stressed, for implementing the reforms of the Washington Consensus (see Camdessus, 1997; World Bank, 1997). There is no doubt that financial markets were well impressed by the intensity of reforms, the improved budgetary discipline in Mexico, as well as across several other LACs. However, there were other significant variables that also contributed to the recovery of inflows. Actually, the return of capital inflows was notably faster than in the nearly one-decade dryness with the debt crisis of 1982.

Here we outline four other relevant variables, favoring a fast capital surge in 1995 as compared to the highly delayed return in the 1980s. First, the 1982 crisis in Mexico came after cutbacks in flows that had first been evident in Argentina (1981) and Brazil (1980), which had no contagious effects on other LACs. Most of them continued borrowing heavily until the explosion of August 1982, that was, consequently, the third critical episode in a row.

Second, the 1994 explosion in Mexico is equivalent, in terms of the duration of the financial boom, to the expanding cycle of the 1970s being restrained in 1980, or by early 1981 at the latest, when the stock of external liabilities and the deficit on current account were much smaller than when the debt crisis actually erupted in August 1982. Evidently, the cumulative effect of the imbalances influences the scope and the cost of the subsequent adjustment. In this regard, the Tequila effect came at an earlier time and enabled many LACs to halt the imbalances, even if only temporarily, that were under way in their own economies. The adjustments made by Brazil and Peru in 1995–96 are good examples of timely holdback, which allowed them, subsequently, to resist at a lesser cost the Asian crisis in 1998–99.

Third, during the first half of the 1980s, the shock of the sudden stop of external financing was further aggravated by the fact that international prices (expressed in dollars) were falling, the terms of trade of LACs had deteriorated, the volume of world trade became more unstable and less dynamic, and real interest rates had risen dramatically. In 1994–95, on the other hand, the negative shock in the supply of funding was accompanied by just a moderate rise in interest rates, a significant increase in the volume of world trade (9%), a 4.5% improvement in the terms of trade over the biennium, and a 9% increase in the overall level of external prices (expressed in dollars), which was associated with the devaluation of the US dollar during that period. The set of multiple negative shocks, to emerging in external markets around 1982, implied a sharp contrast with several positive shocks that were present around 1994.

Fourth, in 1995, the US and the international institutions took a more active and pragmatic approach to the situation (Lustig, 1997). The financial support package offered to Mexico was four times bigger in real terms than in 1982, and it was also organized more expeditiously. It was a positive shock, arranged in short time, that brought in massive lines of credit in excess of the amount needed, which helped to moderate expectations. In 1995, actually provided a net total of US$25 billion in exceptional financing, that is about one half of the official funds made available. The large package was effective in bringing tranquility to financial markets, in signaling that the recession had bottomed, and recovery of economic activity was at hand. The rapid support engineered by the US government not only put a break to the financial panic in Mexico, but also was quite effective in undermining the contagion of the Tequila crisis to the rest of Latin America.[8]

There is no question that the impact of the Mexican crisis on the other LACs, as well as on Mexico itself, would have been much greater had it not been for all these positive shocks and a more opportune timing for global cooperation, than when facing the debt crisis of the 1980s.

c) The macroeconomic contrast between Chile and Mexico

It is relevant to make a brief reference to the contrast, during 1994–95, between Mexico and Chile, the other pole of economic performance in Latin America. Towards the late 1980s, both countries had already opened up their trade considerably, their budgets had improved substantially, privatization was well under way, annual inflation was around 20%, and

---

[8] The positive shock articulated by the US government revealed a significant learning in contrast with the ineffective piecemeal approach to the debt crisis of the 1980s (see Devlin and Ffrench-Davis, 1995; Ffrench-Davis, 2000, chapter 4).

the two countries had similar domestic savings rates. Regardless of these numerous similarities during the late 1980s, both countries exhibited sharp divergences in 1994–95. Some observers state that the superior performance of Chile rested in the privatization of the pension systems in 1981. Notice that, by 1988, the new pension regime had already being operating for seven years in Chile, but in this year its saving rates were similar to those of Mexico. However, by 1994, Chile's savings rate had risen by 3 points, while Mexico's had fallen 4 points with respect to 1988 (Uthoff and Titelman, 1998). These data suggest that the main determinant of the difference between Chile and Mexico was not a mechanism that had existed in Chile since 1981, but rather the different policy approaches implemented principally in the early 1990s. The most pronounced divergences refer to, rather than to fiscal policy, to the other macroeconomic policies more related to the external sector (mainly regulation of capital inflows, exchange rate and monetary policies, and prudential supervision of the financial system, see chapter IX).

Indeed, a determinant policy variable of why Chile performed better in 1995 is that, faced with an abundance of external funds in 1990–95, it deliberately followed a prudential macroeconomic policy so to discourage short-term financial inflows and their distorting effects (see Agosin and Ffrench-Davis, 2001; Ffrench-Davis, 2002, chapter 10; Le Fort and Lehmann, 2003).[9] Instead of taking and spending all the large supply of external resources available, which would have led to a significant appreciation of the peso and to a rising deficit on the current account, it chose to discourage short-term capital inflows. In 1991 a tax was imposed, and substantial non-interest-bearing reserves for external liabilities were required. The set of measures adopted effectively discouraged inflows of speculative capital, mitigated exchange rate appreciation, avoided the crowding-out of domestic savings (that both Argentina and Mexico suffered to a large degree), and allowed to manage aggregate demand in a way consistent with the evolution of potential GDP.[10]

In brief, the major differences between the Chilean and Mexican economic policies and outcomes of the first half of the 1990s do not have to do with structural reforms, such as those carried out in trade, state ownership or fiscal balance, but rather with the nature of the macroeconomic policies adopted in the 1990s: Mexico illustrates the neoliberal

---

[9] A similar approach was followed by Colombia. See Ffrench-Davis and Villar (2005), and Ocampo and Tovar (1998).

[10] Econometric support can be found in Ffrench-Davis and Tapia (2005).

macroeconomic approach, and Chile provides a proof of how rewarding can result the approach that we have termed here a macroeconomics-for-development.

4. The new casualty of globalizing financial volatility: emerging East Asia

Up to 1996, the successful emerging economies of Asia appeared to be immune to the instability associated with capital surges, as illustrated by their performance during the Tequila crisis. Actually, part of the out-flows from LACs was reallocated to Asia, and other EEs such as South Africa (see Gelb, 2005), during that episode. The subsequent events have shown that immunity was no longer a feature of the East Asian economies, which implied that the two regions now faced common destabilizing external forces.

During 1995 there were negligible effects of the Tequila crisis over the Asian region. This was so even in economies with large deficits on current account, such as Malaysia and Thailand. As a consequence, the year 1996 saw many outstanding researchers and observers asserting that those deficits were not relevant if investment ratios and growth were high. Thailand was one of those cases. By late 1996, just a few months before the start of the East Asian crisis precisely in that nation, a report published by the IMF praised Thailand as a road to sustained growth (Kochhar et al., 1996).

A few Asian countries had rather free capital flows, but several of them had regulated capital inflows and foreign exchange markets suc-cessfully for long periods. Several had quite high saving ratios that made exotic the argument that they needed to open their capital accounts in order to capture foreign savings.[11] Growth was actually sus-tained and extremely high. In 1970–95 GDP yearly growth averaged between 6% and 8% in the Republic of Korea, Indonesia, Malaysia and Thailand; the investment ratio exceeded 33%, with domestic savings ratios close to that notable level; inflation was low (in the 5% annual range) and fiscal budgets were generally balanced or in surplus. Nonetheless, in 1997, financial capital rushed away from the region, and brought in the East Asian crisis.

---

[11] This critical argument is neatly presented in Helleiner (1997); Jomo (1998); Amsden (2001); Stiglitz (2002). See the country cases of Indonesia, Malaysia and Thailand, in Sachs, Tornell and Velasco (1996); Korea and Taiwan in Agosin (2001); Korea and Malaysia in Mahani, Shin and Wang (2005).

What explains the sudden inverted comparative perceptions of Asia and Latin America in 1997? First, what works for some time might see its efficacy reduced after a while. A relevant feature relates to exports. In fact, the exports of several Asian economies were experiencing oversupply. What had been until then products with a notably dynamic demand, appeared to be facing tightening markets (Radelet and Sachs, 1998).

Second, even if exports behave well, a disequilibria can emerge if imports experience a boom. In both Korea and Thailand imports rose sharply in 1995–96. This boom was related to expanded aggregate demand and to cheaper imports (due to some import liberalization together with exchange-rate appreciation, a recent *Latinamericanization* of some Asian economies). Rising capital inflows were behind both factors.

Third, sound policies can be reversed under exogenous pressures. The strong drive towards financial liberalization prevailing in the world had also permeated Asia in the 1990s. Actually the deficits on current account increased substantially since 1993. Data show that they were not led by public deficits and did not imply losses of international reserves. Neither were they due to a sudden rise in corruption or to an exogenous increase of private expenditure. On the contrary, the cause was an endogenous private expenditure rise, led by short-term capital inflows. In Indonesia, Korea, Malaysia and Thailand international reserves were accumulating persistently between 1992 and early 1997, fed by capital inflows, pressing local authorities to purchase foreign currency. Consequently, international reserves more than doubled in those countries in that period. It must be stressed that it was a phenomenon led by capital inflows, which sustained appreciating exchange rates (though a moderate trend) and a strongly increased aggregate demand (with a significant enlargement of the deficit in current account of 4.4 points of GDP in Korea, 2 points in Indonesia, and 3 points in Thailand).

Fourth, the additional financing was mostly short-term (IMF, 1998). Inflows contributed to a domestic lending boom, with bubbles in real estate and stock market prices. Weaknesses in prudential regulation and supervision of the financial system, not so relevant in the previously repressed domestic markets, became evident. Domestic balance sheets thus became quite vulnerable as a result of maturity and currency mismatches, and the rapid rise of firms' leverage (see Krugman, 1999). But it is also evident that poor supervision was not the main cause, but just a reinforcing factor in the macroeconomic disequilibria that was made possible by increased capital inflows. The disequilibria was recognized by financial markets only in 1997, and charged a high bill in 1998.

The policy failure was an error shared with the financial reforms of Chile in the 1970s and of Argentina, Mexico and others in the 1990s.

In the particular case of Korea, until the early 1990s it had extensive capital account regulations, based on a combination of market forces and State guidance (see Agosin, 2001; Furman and Stiglitz, 1998; Wang, 2000). In 1991, the country began implementing a broad range of measures aimed at liberalizing the capital account. Contrary to common assumptions by observers, greenfield FDI – not acquisitions – was deregulated. Also, local firms and banks were allowed to issue securities abroad, and foreigners were authorized to purchase stocks in Korean companies subject to limits that were raised progressively as of 1992. Foreign-currency loans to local firms, trade credit and short-term financing were also liberalized. Only long-term borrowing and acquisitions remained restricted. Under the new regulations, Korean banks and firms were permitted to engage in arbitrage between international lenders and local markets, by borrowing short abroad and in several cases lending long-term at home and in neighboring economies. Korea's image of sound creditworthiness afforded local firms lower spreads and more expeditious access to funding, which they used partly to borrow for financing investment and lending in other Asian markets.[12]

Capital inflows expanded hugely after liberalization, including purchases of stock shares, bond issues and private loans to banks and non-financial firms; liabilities became highly liquid, with short-term debt duplicating international reserves in 1996. Actually, in the outset of the crisis, liabilities becoming due within a year included the majority of external debt (see Dean, 1998). In the process, the exchange rate appreciated with respect to the currencies in which borrowing took place, which encouraged further borrowing. Korea accommodated to the capital surplus through a relaxation of domestic liquidity constraints, some import liberalization and currency appreciation.[13] The combined effect of increased imports and worsening export prices explain the rise in its current-account deficit to nearly 5% of GDP in 1996.

The East Asian countries suffered deep recessions in 1998, after decades of sustained annual GDP growth of around 8%. Indonesia

---

[12] In May 1995, one of the large international risk-rating agencies had upgraded the sovereign credit rating of Korea (see Wang, 2000). Then, in June 1997, the World Economic Forum had classified Korea as the fifth most secure place to invest in the world (cited in Agosin, 2001).

[13] Mahani et al. (2005) estimates that real appreciation was around 5% between January 1993 and July 1997.

exhibited a 13% recession, similar to the spectacular drop of Chilean GDP in the recession of 1982. For Korea, Malaysia and Thailand reductions of 7 to 10% were recorded. The specific nature of the crises varied within Asia. However, most appeared to be directly associated with the capital surge of the 1990s and the resulting excess liquidity.

During 1999–2000, Korea and Malaysia recovered faster than the other countries of the region. Notwithstanding their impressive GDP growth in 1999 and 2000, the costs have been significant: for instance, in the period 1998–2000 the Korean GDP was about 12% below where it would have been had the historical trend continued, and a drop of over one-fifth was recorded in investment in the biennium 1998–99 as compared with the quatrienium 1993–96 (28.9% and 36.4%, respectively).

These recessions in East Asia are comparable to those of Latin America in 1982–83, with drops in productive investment, banking crises and social regression.[14] Apart from the intrinsic strengths of the Korean economic structure and of other Asian economies, four general features of the international economic environment and one specific feature of the domestic approach, explain to a large extent why the shift from recession to recovery came sooner than during the Latin American debt crisis. In the external environment there were (i) the plentiful supply of official external financing; (ii) a rapid action spearheaded by the United States authorities to refinance private credits, particularly inter-bank lending; (iii) a significantly lower interest rate in the advanced economies, and (iv) higher growth rates, particularly in the United States.

On the domestic front, a salient feature was the strong counter-cyclical policies implemented by the Korean and Malaysian governments that played a significant role in the recovery. Heterodox macroeconomic policies were in line with the approach exposed in chapter II, in response to the external shock that had generated a significant output gap in the two economies. In fact, notwithstanding significant differences with respect to outflows of foreign capital and to FDI acquisitions, both countries implemented a sharp positive shock based on a strong fiscal stimulus (see Mahani et al., 2005). For instance, the Korean fiscal balance swung from a surplus of 0.3% of GDP over the period 1993–96 to a deficit of 4.2% in 1998; in 1999, GDP recovered 11% and 7% in Korea and Malaysia, respectively. Particularly, the vigorous counter-cyclical policies of Korea and Malaysia diverge from the more passive

---

[14] See various interpretations of the Asian crisis in Akyüz (1998); Dean (1998); Furman and Stiglitz (1998); Krugman (1999); Perry and Lederman (1998); Radelet and Sachs (1998).

stance of LACs. It contributes to explain why GDP growth in 1998–2004 averaged 3.4% in East Asia and 1.9% in LACs.

However, in all, the crisis was costly too for East Asia. This region moved to growth paths of actual GDP that were 2–3 points below their record in previous decades. Potential GDP paths shifted downward as well. In brief, the opening of the capital account represented a powerful source of vulnerability, exacerbated by poor bank regulation and supervision; it left East Asian economies prone to contagion, even though economic fundamentals were generally sound.

5. Back to recovery and then a long-lasting contagion in Latin America

The fast recovery from the Tequila effect in LACs caused a generalized optimism in the international financial environment, which was based on the notion that the international community had learned to handle international crises episodes and that virulent episodes were gone forever. A rapid return of inflows during 1995 opened a new strengthened cycle, with economic recovery and a new wave of overoptimism. One reflection of this overoptimism was the attempt by the IMF, at its meeting in October 1997, to achieve a mandate to promote capital account liberalization among member countries. The meeting took place in the mid of East Asia, at Honk-Kong; paradoxically, in the core of the origin of a new international financial crisis. In the preceding years, it happened that lobbying pressure from international capital markets and the US authorities, and a strong fashion toward financial liberalization were enormous factors influencing policy makers in many EEs, and explaining the audacious extreme position of the IMF (see Bhagwati, 2004, pp. 204–5, for what he calls "the energetic lobbying of Wall Street firms and the Wall Street-Treasury complex," as leaders of that process).

a) A recovery-cum-vulnerabilities: clonating the previous cycle?

The flow of funds was reactivated by mid-1995. Economic recovery, led by the new capital surge, was particularly significant across LACs, for nearly three years, until the arrival of the Asian contagion.

In 1996–97, net capital inflows climbed to the pre-crisis levels. They were larger than in 1992–94, both in real terms and as share of GDP. A rise in aggregate demand, led by inflows, implied that the previous GDP decline in various LACs was reversed, notably in Argentina and Mexico; but as well, economic activity accelerated in several other LACs (table VII.1). In fact, a dynamic growth for the region as a whole was

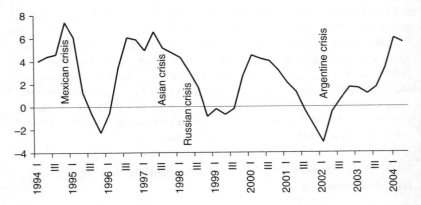

Figure VII.1 Latin America: Gross domestic product instability, 1994–2004[a] (annual growth rates)

Source: ECLAC, based on official figures.

[a] Includes Argentina, Brazil, Chile, Colombia, Mexico, Peru and Venezuela.

observed from 1996 until mid 1998 (see figure VII.1); interestingly, for different reasons, Colombia lost speed and Brazil continued rather depressed.

As a consequence of capital inflows, (i) real exchange rates tended to appreciate, with the average level rising by almost one-seventh (table VII.2); (ii) the overall deficit on current account more than doubled (table VII.3); (iii) as in other booms led by capital surges, prices of financial assets climbed; stock prices doubled with respect to the trough of early 1995 (table VII.4). In fact, again all the signals of increasing vulnerability we have stressed along this book were present; as well, risk rating agencies improved the grades of the region, and together they and IFIs applauded the trends they were observing: low inflation, rising exports, improved fiscal balances, and actual GDP growth. Nevertheless, they ignored or underestimated the severe vulnerabilities being built in the real macroeconomic sphere.

It should be noted that, again, the average actual GDP increase comprised a large recovery share (see chapter II). However, the production frontier moved upward slowly, because productive investment was still low, as well as overall productive innovation. As has been documented in a most robust way (chapter III), as long as productive investment does not increase substantially, that rate of growth is not sustainable. Meanwhile real exchange rates, deficits on current account, and asset prices had retaken a path inside of *vulnerability zones*.

Once again, the increased availability of external financing in 1995–98 had had clearly beneficial short-term effects by removing the binding external constraint (BEC), which had reemerged in 1995. However, renewed access to external capital once more posed challenges in regard to the stability and sustainability of macroeconomic equilibria, and jeopardized chances for attaining sounder development. Indeed, the capital surge led to a dangerous vulnerability in face of future negative external shocks, as the long six-year period of stagnation, since 1998, attests. Thus, when the Asian contagion arrived, several LACs were in need to correct external and domestic real disequilibria, now in an unfavorable international environment.

b) The Asian contagion to Latin America and a "lost half a dozen years": 1998–2003

As said, policy pitfalls displayed in 1991–94 reappeared in 1996–97, and actually collected a heavy bill for several years that followed. With the contagious effects of the Asian crisis, reinforced by the Russian crisis in late 1998 (Baig and Goldfajn, 2000; Palma, 2005), actual GDP growth in LACs contracted to 1.3% in 1998–99. Actually, GDP growth was negative during four quarters in that biennium (see figure VII.1).

In 1998–99 there were sizable trade shocks (terms of trade worsened 5% and growth of volume fell some 3%) and financial shocks (a sudden stop of portfolio inflows), both associated to the crisis contagion.

Nonetheless, there were factors attenuating the intensity of the vulnerabilities built, which softened their incidence on Latin America. First, the new financial boom had lasted only 2–3 years. Second, there was a rise in the share of (greenfield) FDI inflows, which exhibit more permanence than flows to the stock market or short-term credits. Third, owing to a sharp reduction of the current account deficits (and a significant exchange rate depreciation, particularly in Mexico), a high deficit had been recorded only in one year (1997). Fourth, considering the banking crisis of Mexico and Argentina, following the "tequilazo," these and other countries introduced reforms to their financial reforms which strengthened the prudential regulation of their banking systems. Consequently, the required adjustment in 1998–99 took place in economies with a more moderate stock of external liabilities than in 1982 and 1995, and with healthier bank portfolios. Fifth, significant support from IFIs, particularly to Brazil.

The balance of strengths and vulnerabilities implied that, in 1998–99, there were no sharp recessions and banking crisis, as there had been in 1982 and 1995. In parallel, it was well-known that Korea and Malaysia had experienced a sharp recovery in 1999 (see section 4), and USA was heading for a boom. A short-lived recovery took place in 2000, associated with the boom in the USA, but subsequently, a recession, by which we imply a significant output gap, prevailed until 2003. Actual average annual GDP growth in the recessive sexennium was a shocking 1.2%, similar to that in the lost decade. The crude fact is that the bill did include heavy costs until even 2003.

The notable length of the recessive environment, for half dozen years, left a quite negative economic and social heritage. Even a healthy economy, such as that of Chile, suffered a drop of its growth from 7.1% in 1990–98 to 2.5% in 1999–2003.

In contrast with the two East Asian cases discussed above, LACs were unable to make room for a strong counter-cyclical macroeconomic policy. Consequently, their economic environment remained subject to the transmission of external shocks. Output gaps were significant from 1998 to 2003, depressing capital formation and employment. Temporary improvements in the terms of trade and world trade pulled up LACs economies in 2000, while worsening in both variables pushed most LACs into depression in 2001–03.

With regard to capital inflows, large FDI inflows (climbing to 3.1% of GDP in 1998–03; see table VI.1) included over one-half of acquisitions of domestic firms. Most frequently the corresponding "inflows" never crossed the national border and stayed abroad. Additionally, the persistent liberalization of the capital account by LACs included freeing outflows by residents.[15] A consequence was what we predicted in chapter II, that risk diversification tended to imply net outflows, particularly under a pessimistic environment.

After the Tequila crisis, significant policy differences emerged between Argentina and Mexico. Mexico moved in 1995 from an actually quasi-fixed nominal exchange rate to a flexible rate, which facilitated the adjustment to the financial shocks generated by the Asian crisis. Also, the country experienced the sizable positive shock associated with the rapid growth of the US economy during the late 1990s, up to 2000, during the contagion of the Asian crisis. As said, Mexico was exempt from a new recession, but average growth has been mediocre in the full decade since the Tequila crisis (2.7% in 1995–2004).

---

[15] For an analysis of the liberalization of outflows from private social funds, and the strong pro-cyclical implications in the case of Chile, see Zahler (2005) and Ffrench-Davis and Tapia (2001).

Many other LACs adopted flexible exchange rate regimes after 1998 (among them, Brazil, Chile, Colombia). For fear of an inflationary impact, some countries waited until recessions were at work before changing the regime. Only then, flexibilization allowed an equilibrating depreciation in exchange rates. Since exchange rate began to float in a context of recessive output gap, there were no significant inflationary pressures. The problem that emerged under the new regime was that exchange rates became extremely responsive to transitory changes in the supply of external funding.

Meanwhile, Argentina, tied to the currency board, was experiencing negative shocks from Asia, from the devaluation of currencies in neighbor countries (especially in Brazil) and the revaluation of the US dollar until 2002. As a consequence, the incapability of Argentina to correct relative prices with the active use of the nominal exchange rate (self-imposed when adopting the full peg to the dollar in 1991), gave way to a critical pro-cyclical situation. A delayed sharp recession emerged in Argentina and Uruguay.[16] The adverse additional effect of the persistent dryness in the supply of external funding, explain a sharp 15% drop of GDP in 2001–02. Again, there was a contagion of disequilibria from Argentina toward Uruguay (now, both via trade and financial variables); the GDP of Uruguay dived 16% in the biennium.

c) A trade-led recovery in 2004–05

In 2004 Latin America experienced a sharp GDP recovery, climbing to 5.8%, a figure even above the peaks achieved in 1994 and 1997. What was a novelty within the last third of a century is that recovery was led by trade improvements. All medium and large LACs exhibited rising terms of trade, under a boom in the prices of traditional commodities.[17] The volume of exports, after the stagnation suffered in 2001–03, expanded 11% in 2004. Economic activity, employment (urban employment rose nearly 4%; ECLAC, 2004d) and profits improved in 2004.

Indeed, the improved real value of exports financed the 6.3% increase in aggregate demand, particularly the 4.6% expansion in the demand

---

[16] Another sharp recession took place in Venezuela in 2002 and 2003, with GDP drops of 8.9% and 9.7%, respectively. This crisis, however, was not associated to financial contagion but to domestic political and economic events.

[17] On several occasions smaller economies – Central American and Caribbean – have been more intensively effected by variables other than those prevailing in the rest of LACs. The broad trends reported in this book reflect more accurately the case of medium and large LACs; these cover some 90% of regional GDP and population.

and output of the rest of GDP (that is non-exports GDP; see table V.2); as shown in chapter V, in 1998–2003 non-export GDP had fell persistently in per capita terms.

It is noticeable that trade expansion and economic recovery took place with net capital outflows (equivalent to 1% of GDP) and a current account surplus (US$22 billions). Trade dynamism was so vigorous that allowed an average exchange rate appreciation, notwithstanding the capital outflows. LACs such as Argentina, Brazil, Chile, Colombia, Paraguay and Peru experienced real revaluation. Generally authorities have not expressed concern for revaluation. An exception has been Argentina that has intervened in the floating regime in order to sustain a more depreciated rate.

Actual GDP growth more than doubled the increase of potential GDP in that year. Actually, the investment rates exhibited a negligible change. Again, as in 1994 and 1997, the new peak GDP growth did not reflect a sudden improvement in productivity but a higher rate of use of the stock of productive factors.

For a sustainable economic growth in the range of 5–6%, LACs need to increase investment ratios by some 4 to 6 percentage points (ECLAC, 2002b, chapter 4), implement comprehensive programs of labor training and incentives to technical and management innovation. In broad terms, LACs must *reform the reforms* in capital markets and macroeconomic policies, and strengthen productive development policies.

6. Introducing a major conclusion

It is unwise to make an inflexible commitment to indiscriminately keeping the capital account open, particularly (i) in light of the crucial importance of achieving sustainable real macroeconomic stability, along with (ii) the disproportionate volume of the international capital markets compared with the small size of LACs markets, and (iii) the severe shortcomings of financial markets. As long as market movements depend to a significant extent on short-term transactions and domestic securities markets remain shallow, there will be a risk of great real macroeconomic instability in this modality of linkages with the global economy.

There are systematic signals indicating that EEs have been unable to manage capital surges, in order to avoid costly currency and financial crises. Evidence shows that they are costly both for growth and for equity. It is true that several crises are caused by irresponsible or populist policies. But, in the normal or boom stages of the business cycle, it has been quite common in successful emerging economies, that a capital surge flowing into stock markets and private financing, has been the leading variable behind an excessive increase in aggregate demand associated with an exchange rate appreciation and bubbles in the stock market. The consequence has been a growing trade deficit, led by the capital surge, with a deficit placed in the private sector.[18] This "wrong" policies have been supported by suppliers of international financing and encouraged by financial analysts, risk rating agencies and IFIs: recall the enthusiastic praises to Argentina in the 1990s, or to Mexico in the first half of the 1990s.

Understanding better the working of domestic and international financial markets is at the core of the future of the world economy. More systematic efforts should be at work in order to include pragmatism in the highly ideologized approach to capital account liberalization that prevails today. In chapter VIII, that follows, we provide what we take to be robust conclusions and policy lessons, based on recent experiences and on consistent analytical interpretations.

---

[18] One test of the origin of disequilibria is that in most EEs experiencing crises in the 1990s, *pari passu* with ER appreciation and rising external deficits, during the preceding boom stage were accumulating large international reserves.

VIII
Policy Lessons for this Decade*

Introduction

One of the outstanding features of modern financial crises is that they have taken place in emerging economies that were generally viewed as highly successful, until crises exploded. Recent crises have been radically different to those typical from the 1940s to the 1970s in Latin America. They displayed three major features that have been absent or relatively less important in recent experiences. They used to involve, first, large fiscal deficits that were financed with external loans or, in the absence of such financing, with money issuing by central banks. Second, domestic financial systems were "repressed", a fact that was generally accompanied by private sector access to rediscount or bank loans at negative real interest rates. Finally, balance of payments crises were frequently associated with a sharp worsening in terms of trade and/or by explicit domestic policy decisions to overvalue exchange rates.

Over the past quarter century, a "new" variety of crises did gradually develop in East Asia and Latin America, with four features that differentiate them from the "old" type. First, the international capital market has been the major source of shocks to emerging economies (EEs), whether positive or negative. Second, flows have largely originated from and been received by the private sector, i.e., they have been of the "private-private" type. Fiscal deficits have, on the contrary, played a secondary role and, indeed, in most experiences public finances have been sound. Third, these financial crises have been suffered by EEs that

* Based on overview chapters in three of the projects I have coordinated recently. They are cited as Ffrench-Davis and Ocampo (2001), Ffrench-Davis (2003) and Ffrench-Davis (2005).

usually were considered to be highly "credible and successful." In fact, the bulk of private flows has been concentrated in a small number of better-off and more organized developing nations. Fourth, these flows have been characterized by a lack of regulation, on both the supply and demand sides. Domestic financial systems have often been liberalized without the parallel development of a significant degree of domestic prudential regulation and supervision.

In practice, the differentiation between "old" and "new" crises is naturally somewhat less clear-cut than the above description would suggest. An early example of the "new" variety was the Chilean crisis in the early 1980s, but the "old" type of crises was still predominant in most of Latin America during that period. In the 1990s, the "new" kind generally predominated in both Latin America (LACs) and East Asia, but there were some mixed episodes in which new and old crises features were intermingled, with budget deficits and terms of trade fluctuations.

Section 1 takes five common assertions in the literature of the last decade, which we consider to imply, frequently, costly damages to the EEs that follow the advice based on those assertions. Section 2 summarizes our concluding policy lessons.

A strong fact, we want to stress, is that there is significant room for policy diversity. Actually, Chile, China, India and Taiwan provide diverse striking examples of policy diversity and successful prudential macroeconomic management of the capital account. They have contributed to successfully avoid crises led by volatile capital inflows. As well, Korea and Malaysia provide two successful cases of economies that were able to recover faster from a crisis that had been led by capital inflows.

1. Five misleading recipes and misconceptions in fashion

A series of widely accepted hypothesis or beliefs form part of the "conventional wisdom" of the financial world, including IFIs, though these have undergone some positive change in their perceptions in the wake of the Asian crisis. We have selected five common assertions, that we believe have significant policy and welfare implications for both labor and capital. We contend that they have shown to be wrong by the actual performance of international financial markets and domestic markets in EEs. They are: (i) recovery from crises is rapid; (ii) open capital accounts discourage macroeconomic disequilibria; (iii) corner exchange rate regimes are the only viable today; (iv) financial inflows complement domestic savings, and (v) prudential regulation of banks suffices for deterring financial crises.

a) Recovery from recent crises is (not) rapid

A first, common assertion, is that the recovery from crises has proven to be fast. This is a fundamental assumption for claims that authorities should allow the free, self-correcting operation of markets, since it is assumed that attempts to adopt policies to counter booms or accelerate recoveries tend to generate additional instability. Given the fact that financial markets have become the major source of economic instability for EEs, this line of reasoning implies that instability is inevitable but not excessively costly.

This assumption is inconsistent with evidence in financial and real economy markets. For one thing, crises generate medium- or long-term effects on financial markets. The most significant case in recent decades was the effect of the Latin American debt crisis on the long-term syndicated bank loans that were then the principal mechanism of financing. This form of lending disappeared for a decade long and, indeed, bank lending never returned to being a major source of financing for LACs in the 1990s. Equally important, the Asian crisis had negative effects on bond and stock market financing, which had not been surmounted seven years after its outburst. The usual assertion that markets have had a rapid recovery has been based, in fact, on a very partial view of what are the relevant variables, generally focused on the ability to leave behind panic situations, but without due regard to the conditions of access to finance in terms of volume, stability, costs and maturity of financing.

Something quite new is the liberalization of outflows by residents. Across-the-board liberalization opened a broad way for outflows in moments of uncertainty, expectations of depreciation and domestic recessive gap. The fact is that dealings that in the past were restricted or forbidden and performed illegally, denominated "capital flight," today are an active component of capital account opening. They tend to be highly pro-cyclical, and actually they have tended to delay recovery of real macroeconomic balances in LACs (discussed in chapter VI, section 1).

With respect to the real economy, a return to positive rates of actual GDP growth is by no means a basis to assert that the effects of crisis are short-lived. All countries which have undergone severe crises – including Korea and Malaysia, where recovery was very strong – display evidence that they are pushed into a lower GDP path. Three channels through which these medium-term or even permanent effects on GDP are transmitted are particularly important: (i) the sharper reduction of investment that occurs during the crisis, which affects the path of productive capacity; (ii) the loss of capacity associated with firms going bankrupt, which generates a permanent loss of the goodwill, productive and commercial networks and the "social capital" of those firms; even those that do not go bankrupt may pass through a long period of debt restructuring, in which "property rights" are indeterminate; and (iii) the domestic financial crises that may ensue if the portfolio of domestic financial institutions deteriorate severely; the experience of EEs (and Japan) indicate that restoring a viable financial system takes several years, generating adverse effects throughout the period in which it is rebuilt.

Moreover, there is a growing body of evidence that boom-bust cycles have ratchet effects on social variables (Lustig, 2000; Morley, 2001; Rodrik, 2001a). The deterioration of the labor market (through open unemployment, a worsening in the quality of jobs or in real wages) is generally very rapid, whereas the recovery is painfully slow and incomplete. This is reflected in the long-lasting worsening of Argentinean unemployment, and real wages in Mexico after the Tequila crisis, and has been reflected even in Brazilian and Chilean joblessness after the 1999 recession. The evidence on the number of Latin Americans under the poverty line (24 million more in 2004 as compared to 1990), also indicates that such a ratchet effect is present.

b) Opening capital accounts discourage (does encourage) macroeconomic disequilibria

It is also commonly argued that fully opening the capital account deters domestic macroeconomic mismanagement and encourages good macroeconomic "fundamentals." This is partly true for *domestic* sources of instability, i.e., large fiscal deficits, permissive monetary policy and arbitrary exchange-rate overvaluation. However, the volatility in market perceptions makes this type of control highly unreliable: in fact, lax demand policies or exchange-rate overvaluation tend to be encouraged by financial markets during booms (during periods of "irrational exuberance", to borrow Alan Greenspan's term), whereas excessive punishment during crises may actually force authorities to adopt overly contractionary policies ("irrational overkill").

Actually, the opening of the capital account may lead EEs to import external financial instability, with capital inflows engendering a worsening in macroeconomic fundamentals. It is the market itself, which, during the booms, has been generating incentives for EEs to enter the *vulnerability zones*, inducing deviations of macro variables from sustainable levels.

Financial operators evidently fulfill a crucial microeconomic function as intermediaries between savers and users of funds, as hedgers of risk, and as providers of liquidity. In practice, however, perhaps unwittingly, they have come to play a role that has significant macroeconomic implications. With their herd-prone expectations, they have contributed to intensify the financial flows towards "successful" countries during capital surges, thus fostering in recipient markets unsustainable increases in financial assets and real estate prices, and sharp exchange-rate appreciation. Apart from the poor quality of prudential regulation and supervision in these markets, these macroeconomic signals contribute to prolonging an expansive process that appears, misleadingly, to be efficient and sustainable (with good profits and loan guarantees, supported by high stock prices and low value in domestic currency of dollar-denominated debt). But, in fact, bubbles are being generated with outlier macroprices, which sooner or later will tend to burst.

Indeed, in times of booming flows, the general practice – by the international financial institutions, investment funds and financial specialists – has been to encourage the recipient countries to accept the increasing supply of resources, and to praise them for doing so. Moreover, the cost of external financing has typically taken a downward trend during boom periods, which implies that the market actually operates with a sort of downward sloping mid-run supply of funds (see figure VI.2). Excessive indebtedness and periods of massive outflows ensue, prompting admonishment, in many cases, by the very agents who praised the economic performance of the EEs during the boom. There is an obvious contradiction between these two attitudes: it is the opposite to the accountability we are claiming to achieve.

There is a consensus that "fundamentals" are essential. However, there is wide misunderstanding about what constitutes "sound fundamentals." The inappropriate conventional definition, together with "irrational exuberance", led to high positive grades being given to Chile just before the crisis of 1982, to Korea and Thailand in 1996, and Mexico and Argentina in 1994. Something "fundamental" was thus missing in markets' evaluation of "market fundamentals"! Obviously, the severe crises of these five countries could not all be due to bad luck or contagion alone. Rather there was a deterioration of crucial components of a comprehensive set of fundamentals, led by massive capital inflows. A reformed definition of fundamentals should thus include – alongside low inflation, sound fiscal accounts and dynamic exports – sustainable external deficits and net debts, low net liquid liabilities, non-outlier real exchange rate, and strong prudential regulation, supervision and transparency of the financial system. During capital surges, the regulation of capital inflows becomes a requirement for maintaining real macroeconomic balances; if entering a recession, having at hand regulations on outflows by residents and foreigners contribute to softening depressing effects and accelerating recovery.

c) Corner exchange-rate regimes are (not) the only right policy alternative today

In today's open developing countries, the exchange-rate regime is subject to two conflicting demands, which reflect the more limited degrees of freedom that authorities face in a world of weaker policy instruments. The first demand comes from trade: with the dismantling of traditional trade policies, the real exchange rate has become a key determinant of international competitiveness. The second is from the capital account. Boom-bust in international financial markets generate a demand for flexible macroeconomic variables to absorb, in the short run, the positive and negative shocks generated during the cycle. Given the reduced effectiveness of traditional policy instruments, particularly of monetary policy, the exchange rate can play an essential role in helping to absorb shocks. This objective, associated with short-term macroeconomic management, is not easily reconcilable with the trade-related goals of exchange-rate policy.

The relevance of this dual demand is not captured in the call by many analysts to limit alternatives to the two corner exchange rate regimes, either a totally flexible exchange rate or a currency board (or outright dollarization). Intermediate regimes, of managed exchange-rate flexibility – such as crawling pegs and bands, and dirty floating – attempt to reconcile these conflicting demands (Williamson, 2000; Ocampo, 2003).

Currency boards certainly introduce built-in institutional arrangements that provide for fiscal and monetary discipline, but they reduce or even eliminate any room for stabilizing monetary, credit and foreign exchange policies, which are all necessary to prevent crisis and facilitate recovery in a post-crisis environment. They thus allow the domestic transmission of shocks originating in international capital markets, generating strong swings in economic activity and asset prices, with the corresponding accumulation of domestic financial vulnerability, and average rate of use of resources significantly below the production frontier.

On the other hand, the volatility characteristic of freely floating exchange-rate regimes is not a problem, for resource allocation and export quality, only when market fluctuations are short-lived, returning periodically to a sustainable equilibria; but, it becomes a major concern when there are longer waves, as has been typical of the access of EEs to capital markets in recent decades. In this case, volatility tends to generate perverse effects on resource allocation, provoking a "Dutch disease." Moreover, under freely floating regimes with open capital accounts, anti-cyclical monetary or credit policies exacerbate cyclical exchange-rate fluctuations, with their associated allocative, wealth and income effects. This severely weakens the mid-term objective of penetrating external markets with non-traditional exports and strengthens the negative *vis-à-vis* the positive effects of trade reform.

Consequently, the ability of a flexible exchange-rate regime to contribute to efficiently smoothing-out the effects of externally-induced boom-bust cycles, depends on the capacity to effectively manage a counter-cyclical monetary policy, without enhancing pro-cyclical exchange rate patterns. This is only possible under intermediate exchange rate regimes-*cum*-capital account regulations. It is only in this case in which we can speak of effective, albeit certainly limited, "monetary autonomy." These intermediate regimes, of managed flexibility, thus provide the best opportunity to respond to the dual demand on exchange-rate policy.

Obviously, such regimes may generate costs that should be borne in mind by the authorities (as discussed in chapter II). But, all things considered, intermediate regimes offer a sound alternative to costly untamed volatility.

d) Financial inflows tend to complement (substitute) domestic savings

There is a strong correlation between investment ratios and GDP growth rates, with a significant interaction between capital accumulation and technical progress. The Latin American experience in recent decades, provides compelling evidence that the way investment is financed is not irrelevant, as external savings tend to be unstable and may crowd-out domestic savings. Moreover, the induced real exchange rate effects of non-sustainable capital surges frequently lead to misallocation of resources.

In the 1950s and 1960s capital flows to developing countries were mostly tied to official project lending to public users, or to financing imports of capital goods, or through greenfield FDI. The nature of financing tended to generate strong complementarities between external and domestic savings. Commercial bank lending in the 1970s, and private portfolio investments and acquisitions by FDI in the 1990s, however, have made the link between foreign savings and domestic investment weaker and less direct.

This delinking between capital flows and actual investment has three implications: (i) financial inflows tend to increase consumption rather than investment; (ii) inflows do not necessarily enhance the recipient country's ability to earn foreign exchange through expanding productive capacity in tradables; and (iii) the reversibility of foreign investment is facilitated, insofar as foreign liabilities are liquid or short-term commitments.

The first of these effects is associated with the empirical fact that consumers and financial asset markets tend to respond more quickly to released liquidity constraints than productive investors, who have a longer response lag because of the irreversibility and long maturity of their decisions. Nonetheless, one form of investment, construction, generally responds faster than other forms of capital formation and is more prone to investment overshooting, given the effects of liquidity surges on asset prices.

The diverse behavior of agents explains why the degree of stability of flows has a significant effect on the relation between foreign and domestic savings. Uthoff and Titelman (1998) distinguished between trend and deviations from the trend for foreign and domestic savings. On this basis, they found a strong crowding-out of domestic savings by foreign savings when capital inflows are unstable: above the average trend they tend to be consumed; below the trend they tend to generate a recessive gap.

e) Prudential regulation and supervision of banks is sufficient (insufficient) for facing external volatility

Lax or poor prudential regulation and supervision of domestic financial institutions obviously reinforces disequilibria. Strong regulation and supervision *per se* does not solve the problem, however. First, a significant share of capital inflows usually is not intermediated by domestic financial institutions; cases in point are Chile before the 1982 crisis, and Korea and Mexico in the 1990s (see chapter VII). This is because the significance of non-bank to non-bank flows has increased as a result of the type of diversification that has taken place in the supply. Second, expectations are in themselves volatile. This applies not only to expectations of financial intermediaries, but also to those of national authorities and IFIs. Regulation and supervision may influence the transmission mechanism but it can hardly affect the source of instability (volatility in expectations). Third, normal regulatory practices (including Basel I and II criteria) have pro-cyclical features. In particular, during booms, standard regulations are generally ineffective in dampening the strong incentive to lend, as overdue loans and provisions are low, prices of assets used as guarantees are biased upward, and the high level of profits captured by financial intermediaries facilitate meeting the capital requirements necessary to increase lending. On the other hand, during crises the level of overdue loans increases and therefore provisions must be increased also; this reduces the capacity to expand lending by biting into capital requirements, at the same time that lower profits also reduce the funds available to increase the capital base of financial intermediaries.

2. Robust policy lessons

We have grouped into five areas of action the policy lessons that we developed in earlier works (see Ffrench-Davis, 2000, 2003, 2005; Ffrench-Davis and Ocampo, 2001).

a) Absorptive capacity depends on the sustainability of volume and composition of capital inflows

It is crucial to ensure that the volume of inflows is consistent with the absorptive capacity of the host country. The failure to address this point is at the core of recent macroinstability in EEs. Absorption capacity must refer to both the use of existing productive capacity and to the creation of new one. The composition of flows is relevant on three dimensions. First, greenfield FDI (excluding acquisitions of existing assets) feeds directly into capital formation, as do long-term loans to importers of capital goods. Second, volatile flows tend to impact more directly on foreign exchange and financial assets and real estate markets; they carry a weaker association to capital formation, which requires long-term financing. Third, temporary capital surges tend to leak into consumption, due to the faster release of liquidity constraints and capacity of consumers to respond as compared to the more lagged response of irreversible productive investment.

Allowing an excessively large share of capital inflows, to drain off into the stock exchange and consumption of imported goods, will usually create bubbles in asset markets and imbalances in the external sector, which tend to generate growing vulnerability. Particularly, fast rising stocks of net liquid foreign liabilities generate deep vulnerabilities. Consequently, higher ratios of stable long-term flows and of productive investment imply a higher capacity for efficient absorption. Under these conditions of composition and stability, the domestic economy can absorb more efficiently a higher volume of capital flows.

Recent experience offers a dramatic demonstration that recipient emerging economies can pay a high cost for allowing the financial markets, dominated by agents with short horizons, to determine the volume and composition of capital flows. This is why the microeconomic costs associated with the use of regulations on capital inflows should therefore be balanced against the social benefits in terms of macroeconomic stability, investment and growth. Diverse forms of effective and efficient regulation can result in higher and sustained GDP growth, demonstrated by countries such as Chile, China, India and Taiwan in the 1990s.

b) Avoid outlier prices and ratios

Economic authorities must ensure that capital flows do not generate outlier prices or significant distortions of basic macroeconomic indicators, such as interest and exchange rates, aggregate demand, the composition of expenditure in terms of consumption and investment, and the production of tradables. An artificial increase in the absorptive capacity of capital inflows, with outlier appreciation and reduced interest rates, usually leads to subsequent costly recessive adjustment. First, real appreciation during booms tends to distort the allocation of investment, seriously weakening the structural goal of increasing competitive export capacity. Second, if productive investment capacity reacts with a lag and domestic financial markets remain incomplete and poorly supervised, capital surges cannot be absorbed efficiently in the domestic economy and leak to inefficient investment or consumers imports that crowd-out domestic savings.

An interesting feature of the gestation of modern financial crises is that "overheating" has taken place, frequently with falling inflation rates, led by exchange rate appreciation and rising external deficits. In this sense, countries have reached stability in prices, improved expectations of consumers and full employment (real domestic balance) at the expense of real external balances. A notorious case is that of Argentina in 1996–97, with zero inflation in that period and a strong economic recovery (its GDP grew 6.7% per year on average in that biennium). Then Argentina faced a 4-year recession, with an accumulated 18% drop in GDP in the 1999–2002 period.

The two corner solutions for foreign exchange policy tend to throw other major variables off balance. It is risky to remain bound to a fixed nominal rate or to dollarize permanently, unless the economy shares an optimum currency area with the United States. As we have seen, a fully flexible rate implies an unstable currency price led by decisions of short-termist financial investors. Intermediate exchange-rate regimes – which cover a broad diversity – are generally preferable, as they are better adapted to managing the dual demands from external and domestic balances faced in EEs today.

c) Adopt flexible and comprehensive macroeconomic regulation

Across-the–board opening-up of the capital account has been premature and should have been postponed, proceeding selectively until the conclusion of a long-term process in which other major reforms had been consolidated and new equilibrium prices established. The lesson to be learned from these experiences is that during structural adjustment, open capital accounts tend to allow capital flows to increase too fast (especially when international financing is abundant), which has destabilizing macroeconomic and sectoral effects and negative effects on social equity.

The recent experiences of EEs attest to the wisdom of discouraging, with domestic prudential macroeconomic regulations, the accumulation of large short-term and liquid financial liabilities.

It has been argued that the regulation of capital inflows increases domestic interest rates and reduces access to financing of SMEs. Evidently, the first assertion is quite true during non-crisis situations. In effect, that regulation is directed to avoid an excessive supply of foreign currency that would worsen macroeconomic balances and seeds the next crisis. However, two points support the opposite interpretation of the welfare implications of that fact. First, it is well documented that crises punish more than proportionally SMEs and lower income workers, as a consequence of which crises are usually are regressive (see Caballero, 2000; Rodrik, 2001a), as compared to large local firms and MNCs. Second, if regulations are effective, as they were in Chile, the economy operates closer to potential output, thus with a high rate of use of capacity and high capital formation. Actually, Chile in 1990–97 achieved the higher recorded rate of growth of potential GDP, a negligible output gap and an investment ratio notably high (10 points above the average ratio recorded in the 16 years of the dictatorship of Pinochet, see Ffrench-Davis, 2002). It is hard to sustain that SMEs are better off in a cyclical economy than in an economy able to avoid overheating and recession thanks to a set of active macroeconomic policies.

Sustaining economic growth in the face of volatile capital flows requires the deployment of a battery of policy instruments, including: (i) prudential price-based capital account regulations to deter speculative inflows and improve their maturity structure; (ii) a crawling-band with intramarginal intervention or a managed flexibility; (iii) the sterilization of the monetary effects of capital inflows, in order to have an effective demand consistent with potential GDP; (iv) strong prudential regulation and supervision of the financial system, with counter-cyclical devices; (v) regulations on outflows by domestic agents, particularly institutional investors, and (vi) strong fiscal accounts also with counter-cyclical mechanisms. A flexible management of all these policy tools, accommodated to the changes in the intensity of the external supply of funding, is required for stabilizing the flows into the domestic market and for making them complementary with domestic savings. As said, there is growing evidence that the greater the instability of flows (or deviation from the trend), the lesser the share directed to productive investment.

It should be stressed that capital controls alone, such as reserve requirements (or any other policy that increases the cost of financial flows), while clearly crucial, are not sufficient to deter speculative attacks when large exchange-rate fluctuations are anticipated. Obviously, this implies that an effort must be made to avoid cumulative exchange-rate disequilibria and sharp changes in the macroeconomic environment. Usually, when a significant exchange rate appreciation has been accumulated, authorities have to wait for the achievement of a recessive situation (with a large output gap), to become able to get a real depreciation. Argentina, Brazil, Chile and Mexico, in the 1990s, illustrate well the case: you have to incur a real cost in order to correct that outlier price. The lesson is that costs can be avoided with prior counter-cyclical policies that avoid the accumulation of an appreciation and large liquid external liabilities (see lesson f, below).

d) Avoid a dual constituency syndrome

The integration of capital markets has remarkable implications on governance, on room for domestic policies, and on the constituencies to which national governments respond. The increasing complexity and globalization of the economic system is raising the distance between decision-makers and financial agents *vis-à-vis* the domestic agents (workers, firms and tax proceeds) bearing the consequences. Governments in developing countries are facing a growing duality, worrisome for democracy, in the constituencies they take into account in making their policy decisions.

Indeed, some leaders in EEs are living a *"dual constituency syndrome"* (Pietrobelli and Zamagni, 2000): on the one hand, political authorities are elected by their countries' voters, and promise to implement a platform designed before their election, but on the other hand some feel forced to seek, after being democratically elected, the support of those who "vote" for their financial investments (not necessarily productive investments or, even, at their expense). Recent cycles in financial markets have revealed a significant contradiction between the two constituencies, in a negative-sum game, with large output gaps and discouraged capital formation.

With the upsurge of "autonomous" or independent national institutions, such as Central Banks, care must be taken to avoid "independency" from elected governments and from the democratic process, with poor accountability to the society they belong. Sometimes that "independence" is matched with a high "dependency" from the opinions and vested interests of international financial markets. As a consequence, a more general trend has been the prevalence of a financieristic macroeconomics at the expense of real macroeconomic balances.

e) Reform the international environment for a more efficient and balanced globalization

The "governance" of domestic and international financial markets is key to the future of the world economy. A common factor in recent crises has been the great volatility of the most rapidly growing segment of international financial markets: short-term and speculative funds. Successive waves of over-expansion, followed by financial panic, indicate that the market tends first to grow and then to contract more than is justified by economic fundamentals. These features are inconsistent with a balanced and efficient globalization. More energy is being spent on resolving crises than on avoiding them (Martin, 1997). It is to be stressed that while an appropriate prudential regulation of domestic financial markets has obviously been lacking in most of the emerging economies affected by the crises, the lack of appropriate international and regional institutions to monitor such a sophisticated, but unstable, financial market is even more notorious (United Nations, 1999; ECLAC, 2002b; Griffith-Jones, 2001; Ocampo, 1999 and 2002).

f) Focus on crisis-prevention policy, based on prudential macroeconomic management of booms

We close this Part Three emphasizing that the focus of attention for international and domestic institutions should be the management of booms, rather than crises. It is a fact that usually crises are the consequence of badly managed booms. Existing international institutions and instruments have been ineffective in warning of impending turbulence and even have encouraged unsustainable booms. Consequently, it is particularly relevant to design domestic prudential macroeconomic policies and appropriate domestic regulatory frameworks, aimed at controlling booms before they become unsustainable.

Externalities, the nature of the main financial agents (short-termist agents by training and rewards), and major imperfections of international capital markets give rise to frequent cycles of abundance and scarcity of resources and systemic crises. Accordingly, it is always advisable for governments to exercise a degree of caution where capital inflows are concerned, in order to promote a situation where their aggregate amount and main components are consistent with macroeconomic stability, investment, and growth based on systemic competitivity. Particularly if the size and composition of capital flows are inconsistent with these parameters, sooner or later their sustainability will be threatened, making it necessary to resort to socially costly national adjustments. This problem of the level and quality of domestic absorptive capacity – a typical feature in developing economies – is compounded by the inherent risks of short-term external shocks in international financial markets.

Capital flows clearly are not always consistent with the objectives of macroeconomic stability in its broad sense, sustained economic growth and social equity; a degree of direct or indirect public "management" in order to influence the volume and composition of these flows is therefore justified. There have been numerous past experiences, successful and unsuccessful, in applying this approach.

Anyway, any costs of the management of capital flows must be measured against the global social benefits in terms of macroeconomic stability, investment and growth as well as against the feasibility and reliability of possible alternative ways to achieve the same goal.

The reorganization of financial systems, including the opening of the capital account, should give priority to channeling resources into savings and investment. Thus the relationship between the financial system and national savings and investment processes, and between the domestic financial system and external markets, must also be considered carefully. Latin America's performance with respect to this has been, in general, notably deficient.

Concern about risks associated with financial markets, such as the generation of speculative "bubbles", implies the need to introduce regulatory and supervisory mechanisms to ensure the stability of financial institutions operating in capital markets. Such mechanisms are particularly essential in open, free-market economies. Strengthening prudential regulation can soften the above risks and contribute to a more orderly, stable process of attracting portfolio investments from abroad (ECLAC,

1998, chapter XII). Of course, effective regulation will require countries to improve their monitoring systems for external capital flows. This must be done not only at the micro level for individual financial institutions, but especially at the macro level to ensure that the volume and composition of flows are consistent with economic stability.

Volatility is partly due to the bubbles generated within developed economies, the lack of macroeconomic coordination between the nations that have the greatest influence on world markets, and the limitations of international institutions that should be responsible for enforcing regulation and policy coordination, and real macroeconomic stability. Present policies are not in tune with a needed trend toward a balanced well-working globalization.

Part Four
A Case of Real Macroeconomics

IX
A Macroeconomics-for-Growth in the Democratic Transition in Chile*

Introduction

Chile became one of the most dynamic emerging economies (EEs) in the 1990s. Key macroeconomic indicators show a remarkable accelerated growth of GDP, an increase in savings and investment ratios, a sustained reduction in inflation, unemployment and poverty, and a strengthening of the external position, thus diminishing the vulnerability of the economy to external shocks. In the past, these shocks have been a principal source of macroeconomic instability, particularly in 1975 and 1982.

Chile has awakened considerable international interest and is often referred to as a *model* of structural reform, liberalization and stabilization for other countries in the region, as well as for Eastern European economies in transition. International interest in the Chilean economy heightened in 1990 when, after 16 years under a dictatorship, Chile emerged as a renewed democracy. It was led by a center-left coalition of parties, the *Concertación de Partidos por la Democracia* (Democratic Concertation).

The extended conviction that the "Chilean model" is one unique and uniform paradigm of economic reform is misleading. Since 1973, Chile has experienced a series, not a unique "model", of diverse approaches to build a market economy. Obviously, there are several extremely different ways of implementing and targeting reforms; not taking this diversity

* Partly based on Ffrench-Davis (2002, chapters 1 and 10) and Ffrench-Davis and Tapia (2001). We have avoided, in general, bibliographical references on Chilean reforms, policies and outcome. Some two hundred references can be found in Ffrench-Davis (2002). This book covers the last three decades of Chilean economic history.

213

into account can be very costly. Actually, the Pinochet regime includes two rather divergent subperiods: 1973–82 and 1982–89. Subsequently, since 1990, a different stage is started, where significant *reforms to the reforms* were introduced to macroeconomic and social policies.

In fact, with respect to the Pinochet dictatorship, several of the tougher reforms such as drastic liberalization of imports and of domestic financial markets, were implemented in the 1970s; that first half of the regime ended with a huge economic crisis in 1982. This experience implied enormous economic costs whose pro-cyclical and regressive effects were long-lasting; even by the mid-1980s, evaluations of this experience seemed to conclude that it had failed to accomplish its main objectives (Foxley, 1983; Edwards and Cox-Edwards, 1987).

The evidence suggests that gross mistakes, based on market fundamentalism, were made in social and economic policy, which artificially increased the duration and magnitude of recessive adjustment and the associated welfare costs, after the crises of 1975 and 1982.

A more favorable judgment of the Chilean experience of transforming and stabilizing its economy is to be found in the economic performance of the economy in the second half of the Pinochet government, when there was a more pragmatic macroeconomic management that concluded with a fast recovery based on the idle capacity existing after the 1982 crisis. Nonetheless, in the whole 16 years of dictatorship GDP growth averaged merely 2.9%. Likewise, there is abundant evidence that the neoliberal reforms disproportionately affected the poorest sections of the population, increasing poverty and worsening income distribution.

The new democratic administration, in power since 1990, emphasized a medium-term development strategy of growth-with-equity. The program of the new regime gave priority to reducing the high levels of poverty and improving income distribution, both essential requirements for achieving genuine development; it stressed (i) rising "investment in people"; (ii) a redressing of exports toward diversification and value-added and (iii) achieving a sustainable macroeconomic equilibria (built on active fiscal, foreign-exchange and monetary policies).

In the 1990s, Chile made significant progress in its process of productive transformation and stabilization, while at the same time successfully re-establishing a democratic system; in the fifteen years elapsed since 1990, GDP growth averaged 5.5%. Nonetheless, it faces several economic and social challenges, which must be met, if comprehensive and sustainable development is to be achieved. This chapter presents, in section 1, a brief overview of the three "models" and discusses the main results achieved. Section 2 focuses on the reform of macroeconomic policies in the return to democracy, particularly in 1990–95, that is the period of a more coherent implementation of a macroeconomics-for-development. Section 3 summarizes challenges faced today.

1. A brief overview of three decades of economic reforms and policies[1]

a) Neo-liberal reforms of the military regime, 1973–89

(i) Pure neo-liberalism in 1973–81

In the immediate aftermath of the September 1973 coup, Chile began its transition to a free market economy by means of a series of deep economic and institutional reforms. It was a period of pure neo-liberalism, with a consistent set of neutral policies, a market fundamentalism. One immediate objective was controlling the hyper-inflation inherited in 1973. The stabilization effort concentrated on correcting fiscal imbalances and biases in the goods markets – assumed to be caused solely by excessive state intervention – and on reducing the balance of payments deficit caused by a severe shock in the terms of trade (1974–75).

Between 1974 and 1978 a large part of the assets which had been transferred to the state during the Unidad Popular (1970–73) were privatized. By late 1973 controls were lifted on most prices, domestic capital markets were abruptly de-regulated in 1975, without prudential regulation, and an across-the-board trade liberalization was completed by mid-1979, with a uniform import tariff of 10%; liberalization was expanded to international financial flows, under the capital surge then present in international financial markets. In parallel, the authority adopted the "monetary approach to the balance of payments" (thus resigning foreign exchange and monetary policies), pegging the nominal exchange rate to the US dollar in 1979. Due to a broad indexation of nominal prices and a fast increasing excess of aggregate demand over actual output, the alignment of domestic inflation with the international level was gradual. The result was a sharp appreciation in the real exchange rate, and, consequently, a significant loss of competitiveness in tradables.

During these years, economic performance fluctuated hugely. As a result of the implementation of a structural adjustment and macroeconomic stabilization program, coupled with a severe external shock in

---

[1] For a more detailed discussion of economic development during the military regime, see, among others, Bosworth, Dornbusch and Labán (1994); Edwards and Cox-Edwards (1987); Ffrench-Davis (2002); Fontaine (1989); Foxley (1983); Meller (1991); Zahler (1998).

the terms of trade, the economy experienced a sharp recession during 1974–75, with a drop of 17% in GDP (1975), an increase in the unemployment rate to 20% (1975–76), and an abrupt decrease of 24% in real wages (1974–75).

Since this recession was followed by several years of accelerated recovery in economic activity, a fiscal surplus and a negative inflation (sounds like Argentina in 1997?), the economic program of the military government was pronounced successful (also like Argentina in 1997). It was an ill-informed and premature evaluation. In the social front, there was a continued high level of unemployment (an average of 18% of the labor force in 1976–81, compared to 6% in the 1960s), real wages in 1980–81 were on average 7% lower than in 1970, and income distribution had worsened sharply. Actual GDP growth, disregarding the 1975 recession, averaged 6.7% in 1977–81. But the complete outcome since the start of reforms in 1973, that is in 1974–81, averaged a mediocre 3.0% (see table IX.1). In the macroeconomic front, there was a huge deficit on current account (21% of GDP) and the real exchange rate was an outlier price; notwithstanding huge capital inflows, a low average investment ratio prevailed (see Ffrench-Davis, 2002, chapter 2).

As a consequence, potential GDP was increasing merely 4.2% by 1980–81, while actual GDP expanded 5.5%, and aggregate demand was rising 11.4% yearly. These speeds were inconsistent among themselves, *pari passu* with an outlier exchange rate, a huge external deficit and high domestic and foreign private debts. They were all signals of vulnerability (see chapter VI). It was a situation ripe for a deep crisis if negative

Table IX.1   Chile: Macroeconomic indicators, 1974–2004

	1974–89	1990–2004	1974–81	1982–89	1990–95	1996–2004
GDP growth[a]	2.9	5.5	3.0	2.9	7.8	4.0
Potential GDP growth[b]	2.9	5.9	2.5	3.3	7.5	4.8
Average output gap	10.3	3.3	8.8	11.9	−0.1	5.6
Export growth[a]	10.6	8.7	13.6	7.8	10.1	7.8
Non-exported GDP growth	1.6	4.6	1.5	1.7	7.3	2.8
Inflation rate	79.9	8.1	138.9	20.8	14.7	3.3
Fiscal balance	0.3	0.8	1.6	−1.1	1.6	0.1
Fiscal structural balance	n.a	0.7	n.a	n.a	0.8	0.6

Source: Central Bank of Chile and Ffrench-Davis (2002).

[a] Here we use data from the Central Bank of Chile and historical corrections detailed in Ffrench-Davis (2002). These figures can differ from those of tables I.1 and VIII.1 for Chile, calculated by ECLAC at constant US dollar. [b] Growth of Potential GDP "generated" in each period.

external shocks happened to emerge, as they actually did in 1982 across all Latin America.

Euphoria abruptly vanished when the economy collapsed in 1982, as a result of several external shocks: the disappearance of voluntary external funding, a sharp drop in the terms of trade, and a significant increase in international interest rates.

(ii) Crises and economic recovery in the 1980s

Between 1977 and 1981, the Chilean economy had adjusted to rising levels of external financing, but these inflows began to slow down in late 1981. However, the external gap continued to widen, and thus the reserves that had been accumulated began to be depleted rapidly. The Government continued to hold the view that in a "sound and free" economy, the proper course of action was to pursue passive, neutral policies in the face of a loss of reserves and the decline of monetary liquidity. As a result, during the first half of 1982 (before devaluation) GDP fell sharply, industrial production dropped by 19%, open unemployment rose to 20%, and bank portfolio deteriorated. It was not until June 1982 that the Government partially corrected its economic policy and implemented a major devaluation of the exchange rate, among other measures. Since this response was already overdue, it obviously had a traumatic impact, particularly in view of the fact that a serious recession had already been underway for several months.

The sharp macroeconomic disequilibria, together with permissive banking practices and a liberal regulatory framework, laid the foundation for an enormous financial crisis, which forced the government to intervene in several financial companies that were experiencing problems, including all the country's largest private banks in 1983. The government reacted to the financial crisis by implementing an aid program for local debtors and banks (with a cumulative cost of 35% of the 1986 GDP), which included, among other measures, a preferential rate for dollar debts, loans at subsidized rates for the financial sector, and the Central Bank's purchase of the banks' non-performing portfolios, with a commitment from the latter to repurchase them. Subsequently, prudential regulation and supervision and the power of the Superintendence of Banks were strengthened.

The depth of the Chilean crisis of the early 1980s helps to explain why democratic economic authorities managed in the 1990s, so cautiously but actively, the macroeconomic variables and the regulation of the financial system so as to avoid the risk of another crisis (see chapter VII; and Zahler, 1998).

During 1982–83, the authorities dealt with the shortage of foreign currency by means of a contractionary policy, in order to reduce the huge spending-output gap, and sharp exchange rate devaluation. Chile then experienced the highest recession in all Latin America, with a GDP drop of 14% in 1982, an increase of unemployment to 30% in 1983 (including emergency work programs), and a drop of 11% in real wages in that same year. It is useful to recall that Chile had already implemented far-reaching financial and trade liberalization reforms reforms, it had carried out a broad privatization effort, and had achieved a large fiscal surplus since the late 1970s. The deep crisis should not be blamed to lack of neoliberal reforms.

In order to switch expenditure towards domestic output, the peso was devalued again and the uniform import tariff was increased, in two steps, from 10% to 35% in 1984. In reaction to the recessive adjustment, the external imbalance was reduced by bringing imports down to half their 1981 level, with exports not yet reacting significantly to the adjustment program.

Beginning in 1985, a more pragmatic economic policy, aimed at expanding non-traditional exports, increasing domestic savings, and strengthening the corporate and financial sector, was put into practice. In order to induce an increase in export volume and diversification, several measures were adopted: improvement of the competitiveness of the tradables sector through a series of devaluations, followed by a stabilization of the real exchange rate at a "competitive level" more than double that of 1981; reduction of the uniform import tariffs from 35% to 15%, though short of the 10% in force from 1979 to early 1983; adoption of a 10% simplified refund for non-traditional exports.

Starting in 1986, the Chilean economy experienced a new period of economic recovery, accompanied by an improvement in external accounts. An increase in exports of over 10% per year, a drop in international interest rates, a remarkable rise in the terms of trade since late 1987, and an expansionary policy towards the end of the decade for electoral reasons,[2] contributed to a sharp recovery of GDP. Actual growth was achieved with low average investment rates, and was based on absorbing the underutilized productive capacity, generated as a result of the 1982 crisis, which became completely used up by 1989. Again, as in the late 1970s, if the 1982–83 recession is disregarded, actual GDP

---

[2] Domestic and international pressures forced Pinochet to call a plebiscite in October 1988. Pinochet lost the plebiscite, which implied the return to democracy one year later.

growth is high. A period commonly mentioned successful is 1986–89, with GDP growth averaging 7.5%. But if bad years are counted, actual growth in 1982–89 is mediocre as 1974–81 had been. Overall, growth of GDP was comparatively low in 1974–89, averaging 2.9% per year.[3]

It is interesting to note that export dynamism – a major achievement during this period – was unable to significantly increase the rate of permanent GDP growth. The reason is that non-exported GDP grew only 1.6% per year, even less than the population (see table IX.1).

Average annual inflation was reduced to around 20% (though it had risen sharply to over 30% by late 1989); the unemployment rate dropped steadily, real wages partially recovered, though by 1989 were still lower than in 1981 and even lower than in 1970; and in 1989 there was a surplus of the non-financial public sector of 1% of GDP.

The *military government* managed to target some social programs better, such as care of pregnant mothers and unweaned infants. Likewise, it achieved improvement in some relevant indicators (overall and infant mortality, literacy, and life expectancy) even faster than improvement in some of these indicators around the world. However, performance in terms of income and consumption distribution was negative, both during the process of restructuring and stabilization in the 1970s and 1980s. This is not surprising, if one bears in mind the two sizable depressions experienced by Chile during this period, and the subsequent painful adjustments. In both periods, unemployment increased and real wages dropped significantly.

Figures for Santiago (40% of the Chilean population), show that the highest quintile's share in household consumption increased from 44.5% in 1969 to 51% in 1978, and to 54.9% in 1988. The share of the two lowest quintiles decreased from 19.4% in 1969 to 12.6% in 1988, despite the sharp recovery of economic activity in 1988. Poverty worsened considerably as a result of macroeconomic instability, costly adjustment programs, and the subsequent ill-defined economic reforms in the 1970s and 1980s. In 1987, 45% of the population lived below the poverty line.

Unequal income distribution and high levels of poverty, the still low savings and investment rates, and considerable vulnerability to external shocks – with the corresponding macroeconomic instability – were evidence that, towards the end of the military regime, Chile was still far from achieving sustained, stable, and equitable growth.

These brief accounts show that it is misleading to present both halves of economic policies of the Pinochet regime as identical. They actually

---

[3] In the 1960s, the Chilean potential GDP grew at an average of 4.5% per year.

Table IX.2   Chile: Social indicators, 1970–2004

	GDP per capita (1995 US$)	Poverty as a share of		Real wage index (1970=100)	Income distribution (Q5/Q1)	Unemployment (% of labour force)
		households	population			
1970	2,905	17.0	n.a.	100.0	13.5	5.9
1981	3,212	n.a.	n.a.	96.8	14.9[d]	16.9[d]
1989	3,536	33.3[a]	38.6[a]	91.6	19.9[e]	19.2[e]
1995	5,004	19.7[b]	23.3[b]	118.3	15.2[f]	7.4[f]
2004	6,345	15.4[c]	18.8[c]	143.1	16.4[g]	8.7[g]

Sources: CEPAL, Central Bank of Chile and Ffrench-Davis (2002).

Notes: Income distribution is measured here as the ratio between the richest quintile and the poorest quintile. These figures are for the Greater Santiago. The rest of the variables have national coverage. [a] 1990, [b] 1996, [c] 2003, [d] 1974–81, [e] 1982–89, [f] 1990–95, [g] 1996–2004.

imply two different versions of how some markets work. The first half of naïve neo-liberalism was followed by a more pragmatic approach; however, with interventions heavily biased in favor of high-income sectors. We can term it "regressive pragmatism". In fact, the eighties is the period with the worst recorded income distribution and highest poverty recorded in Chile (see table IX.2). Some of the more significant policy changes under democracy, which implied a third model or variant, are discussed in what follows.

b) Reforms to the reforms in the return to democracy, 1990–95

In 1990, Chile began its transition to democracy, inheriting an economy that had completed most of the structural reforms recommended by international financial institutions for other countries in the region and in Eastern Europe.

President Aylwin's government took office in March 1990. Besides the marked deterioration in income distribution brought by the economic system in force at the time, during the years of the plebiscite and presidential and parliamentary elections, the Chilean economy had grown at rates that were unsustainable in the medium term, using up the installed capacity which had been idle in 1982–87; a spectacular rise in the world price of copper had contributed to a boom in economic activity.[4]

Thus the new administration concentrated its early efforts on accomplishing three main objectives: (i) stabilizing the economy after the

---

[4] The main Chilean copper producer (CODELCO) had remained in public hands.

1988–89 electoral boom; (ii) with the economic recovery already exhausting underutilized capacity, imprinting a stronger increase of potential GDP, which would require, among other things, increasing the investment ratio, implementing a new macroeconomic management that achieved sustainable equilibria, and diminishing the vulnerability to external shocks; and (iii) in a context of sustainable real macroeconomic stability, making progress in solving the most urgent social demands, thus enabling a larger share of the population to benefit from modernizing the economy. The aim was to reconcile macroeconomic and *macrosocial* balances.

This was meant to benefit groups which had suffered more intensively the effects of the long period of adjustment in the 1980s, including minimum wage earners (the real minimum wage was one-third lower than the peak of 1981), those receiving family allowances (the allowance had decreased 65% since 1981), the average worker (with a real wage 5% below 1981), pensioners from the public sector (whose pensions in real terms had decreased by 10% since 1984), extremely poor families (whose subsidy had decreased in real terms by 50% since 1981), and, in general, recipients of social spending (whose per capita level had decreased by one-fifth in the subset of education, health and housing).

There existed a wide-ranging political consensus that permanently reducing social problems and extreme poverty required sustained growth; denying a large part of the population access to the benefits of economic growth can be politically unsustainable in democracy (not to mention the ethical considerations involved) and creates pressures for instability in public policies. If expectations of investors are modeled under this environment, then their response to investment incentives will be weak until the uncertainty regarding the permanence of current conditions has been dissipated. This, in turn, delays investment and social progress, eroding political support for continuing the policies implemented.

The authorities took into account that the stability and credibility of economic institutions and policies can be more important for boosting capital formation than tax incentives and artificially low interest rates. Consequently, one of the costs of political instability is its negative impact on capital formation and, thus, on economic growth (Dornbusch, 1989; Pindyck, 1991). Macroeconomic instability has that effect, generating a gap between potential and actual productivity, and, consequently, reducing expected profits. All of the above discourage investment (see chapters II and III).

The government platform assumed that achieving sustained growth required gradually increasing the productivity of people and their capacity to generate income. This was the basis for the proposal to "invest in people" and, as a result, a significant part of public policy was devoted not so much to improving short-term cash income, but rather to raising the quality of education and job training. In coping with a potential conflict between macroeconomic stability and the demand for more resources to be allocated to lower income groups, the new administration increased the share of social spending in the budget, and had a tax reform approved, which would contribute more resources for social spending.[5]

Fiscal revenue increased significantly from 1990 to 1995, as a result of the 1990 tax reform, a strong growth in economic activity and imports, a higher than expected price of copper, and a decline in tax evasion. Coupled with a lowering of international interest rates, this enabled the government to increase public spending (especially social expenditure) and simultaneously, increase non-financial public sector savings to nearly 5% of GDP. This savings ratio compares favorably with an average of 2% during the 1980s. This increase in savings over-financed public investment, generating an average surplus in those six years of 1.6% of GDP (see table IX.1).

In 1990, a tripartite agreement was also reached between the government and the representatives of unionized workers and employers, which provided for an increase of 28% in the real minimum wage between 1989 and 1993. In April 1991, it was agreed that, after this recovery stage, any future real increase in the minimum wage would be linked to labor productivity gains, and that the criteria for the increase would be future, and not past, inflation. An agreement was also reached in these negotiations to increase the family allowance and welfare benefits for poor families, and to implement an increase in the real minimum pension, which had been frozen since its reduction in 1985.

An increase in capital formation was essential if unemployment was to be kept down, reconciling wage adjustments with improvements in productivity. Criticism of the new reforms, mostly from economists associated with the Pinochet regime, predicted that the combined impact of the constraints imposed by a labor code reform and the supposedly negative impact of the tax reform on investment incentives would reduce capital formation, the economy's capacity to generate productive employment and, as a result, the "natural" unemployment rate would increase. None of these predictions came true. Targets were

---

[5] Likewise, in 1990 the government proposed a reform of the labor code to Congress, aimed at recovering bargaining powers for workers, seeking to endow current legislation with greater social legitimacy.

reciprocally consistent: growth was achieved with some (modest) improvement in equity.

During 1990–95, the real mean and minimum wages averaged annual increases of 4.4% and 5.6%, respectively; employment increased 2.6% per year, while population rose 1.8. Furthermore, the budget raised 40% more in real terms the per capita social spending inherited in 1990 from Pinochet's regime. As a result, there was a significant reduction in poverty levels: data for 1996 show that poverty covered 23% of people as compared to 39% in 1990 and 45% in 1987. These results were strongly influenced by the vigorous 7.8% average GDP growth in 1990–95. Additionally, social expenditure is highly progressive (with the exception of pensions and university education). About 70% of the public expenses in health and education benefit the poorer 40%. Therefore, increased social expenditure contributed both to a reduction in poverty and to investment in people.

The results shown by data on income distribution are less clear. By the mid-1990s income distribution had improved somewhat, with the support of (i) exogenous forces of increased minimum wages, monetary subsidies and social programs and (ii) the better macroeconomic environment and higher employment of labor and SMEs capital. There was an overall, but modest improvement with respect to the late 1980s: a smaller GINI and lower ratio of higher income/lower income quintiles. But, distribution remained notably worse than in the 1960s (see Ffrench-Davis, 2002, chapter 9).

In 1990–95, exports grew as vigorously as during the Pinochet regime (10% per year), while – as mentioned – GDP growth jumped from 2.9% to 7.8%. Indeed, this time, macroeconomic conditions – a friendly environment for producers with full utilization of the productive capacity and *right macroprices* – allowed an impressive dynamism of non-exported GDP (by that time, still 80% of the economy), that grew 7.3% per year (see table IX.1).

c) Back to vulnerability: 1996–2004

In 1995 Chile consolidated a position of economic leadership in Latin America. While Mexico – a praised reformer country by 1994 – suffered a huge crisis (the Tequila) that affected several LACs (see chapter VII), the Chilean economy had been almost immune to contagion from the Tequila effect, recording full utilization of capacity and solid domestic fundamentals. This outcome was helped by a positive shock in terms of trade but was primarily the result of the macroeconomic prudence of the first half of the nineties (see section 2).

In 1996–97, GDP growth averaged 7% in Chile, with a similar rate of expansion of potential GDP. The unemployment rate lowered to 6% and the investment ratio reached a historical record. This time, however, there were imbalances in the external front.

Active counter-cyclical macroeconomic policies lost strength. After the Tequila crisis there was a new vigorous capital surge to most countries in the region, but particularly to Chile that had escaped from the Tequila contagion. This surge should have been met with increased restrictions on rising inflows. Instead policy-makers underestimated risks of external vulnerability, favored an inflation target, and consequently adopted a passive approach in the macroeconomic management of cycles (see section 2). As a consequence, sharp real exchange-rate appreciation and rise of the deficit on current account were observed over the biennium, which pushed Chile into a *vulnerability zone*.

The effects of contagion from the Asian crisis began in late 1997 and were felt strongly in 1998–99. This time, Chile experienced a sharp drop in the terms of trade, equivalent to 3% of GDP per year. At the same time, the large 1996–97 capital inflows gave way to outflows of domestic and foreign funds.[6] The Central Bank resisted market pressures for devaluation by raising real interest rates in 1998,[7] causing a costly adjustment in the real sector. Finally, it allowed the exchange rate depreciating adjustment in September 1999 by adopting a floating regime.

Social and economic costs were significant. Production in 1999 fell 1%, which opened a gap of approximately 8% between actual GDP and productive capacity that year. Together with the increase in interest rates, this gap caused gross fixed investment to fall 17%, and unemployment exceeded 10% of the labor force, which reversed some of the progress that had been made in reducing inequality since 1990.

However, the strengths built by the Chilean government in the previous years allowed an increase in social expenditure after the crisis. Partly, this was the result of a new fiscal scheme of *structural balance* based on a

---

[6] A hurried financial deregulation runs the risk of leaving too many exit doors open, which can be a massive oversight when the market becomes nervous and expectations are shifting to the devaluatory side. This tends to make it more difficult to sustain exchange rate and macroeconomic stability, and it makes international financial crises more painful. Such was the case in Chile in 1998–99, when the pension funds were the main responsible for the capital flight that worsened the external imbalance (see Zahler, 2005).

[7] The Central Bank was concerned that exchange-rate depreciation would result in higher inflation, and in worsened balance sheets of large domestic firms highly indebted in foreign currency liabilities in the biennium.

rule that linked the current budget to structural fiscal revenues (consistent with a normalized copper price and with a cyclically adjusted GDP) instead of current revenues. Thus, the government implemented new and targeted social programs that contributed to make additional progress in the reduction of poverty (that fell to 19% of population in 2003) in spite of the recessive environment.

In 1998–2004, average growth fell to 3.1%; although much better than the rest of Latin America, was about 40% of its growth in 1990–95, and lower than those of Korea and Malaysia (notwithstanding that these had experienced drops significantly more severe in 1998) since the Asian Crisis. The macroeconomic approach is at the core of the differences: acknowledging that a pro-cyclical approach was successfully avoided, compared to Korea and Malaysia (see Mahani et al., 2005), Chile was too cautious in the implementation of counter-cyclical policies during the downturn.

2. A macroeconomics-for-development: the Chilean experience in 1990–95

Chile's recent history includes three interesting episodes of capital surges since the 1970s. The first episode ended with the 1982 debt crisis; the second started in the early 1990s and continued until the Tequila crisis; and the third took place for a couple of years preceding the Asian crisis. All three originated in (i) a capital surge that flew into the private sector of EEs; (ii) each of these financial booms was followed by an international financial crisis; (iii) host EEs held an outstanding image as "successful" economies; and (iv) in the 1990s several EEs exhibited balanced or surplus fiscal budgets, particularly Chile and the East Asian economies. However, Chile experienced different outcomes in each of the three surges. A severe financial and currency crisis in 1982; a continued vigorous and sustainable economic growth in 1995, while Argentina, Mexico and Uruguay suffered deep crises; a soft but long-lasting recession (with recession defined as a significant actual/potential GDP gap) in 1998–2003, while most LACs experienced a deeper recession with drops in per capita GDP during this sexennium. Here we focus in the second episode.

The return to democracy in 1990 coincided with the beginning of a new episode of abundant foreign capital flowing into emerging economies. Conscious of the risks involved, policy-makers adopted a set of active macroeconomic policies to regulate the capital surge in order to achieve real macroeconomic balances (see chapter II). As a result, during this period, potential GDP expanded vigorously and the economy was running close to full capacity. This was a determining factor in creating a virtuous circle of rapid capital formation.

a) Capital Surges in 1990–95

Chile was one of the LACs earlier to attract renewed inflows of private capital in the 1990s, and was among the countries facing the largest supply in relation to its economic size.

Chilean policy in the first half of the 1990s represented a significant step toward a pragmatic approach to macroeconomic management. In brief, policy-makers responded to the massive availability of foreign capital by moderating short-term inflows while keeping the door open to long-term flows. Specifically, an unremunerated reserve requirement (URR) was established to raise the cost of bringing in short-term capital; this is a market-based instrument affecting relative costs. Authorities also used exchange rate intervention to hold down the appreciation of the real exchange rate in face of those flows that surpassed the reserve barrier, and sterilization of the monetary effects of foreign exchange operations. These tools were used in support of a development strategy that encouraged export growth and its diversification.

The policy was highly successful, in the sense that in 1990–95 the current account deficit was moderate, the currency appreciated less than in most of the LACs, and the total short-term external debt was held to a fairly low magnitude. When the Mexican currency crisis exploded in late 1994, the Chilean economy proved to have significantly reduced its vulnerability.

For a country to be the target of interest rate arbitrage, domestic interest rates must exceed international rates by a margin that more than offsets the currency's expected depreciation and the country risk. Such conditions obtained in Chile starting in the early 1990s. On the one hand, in 1992 and 1993, international rates on dollar loans were at their lowest level in 30 years, and though they later rose, they remained far below their levels in the 1980s. On the other hand, Chile is a capital-scarce country with a stock consistent with a GDP, at present, of about one-fourth of that of developed economies. Because scarcity entails a higher price, the interest rate in EEs tends to be higher than in developed countries.[8]

---

[8] Our policy implications are consistent with the idea that the fastest growing economies have higher interest rates associated with their GDP growth rates.

Other conditions for interest rate arbitrage also encouraged inflows. After a cumulative real depreciation of 130% in the 1980s, the exchange rate began to appreciate gradually in the 1990s. As in the case of other countries in the region, Chile's country risk premium fell. An atmosphere of emerging markets mania (à la Kindleberger) on the part of international investors generated a spectacular drop in perceived country risk. Private short-term capital inflows were heavy well into 1992, after which they began to fall as a result of the policy measures taken to regulate them.

Portfolio inflows took two forms: investment through large international mutual funds and the issuing of American depositary receipts (ADRs) by major Chilean firms. Primary issues of ADRs represent an opportunity for a firm to expand its capital at a relatively low cost, given that costs of capital in international markets naturally tends to be below that in the Chilean financial market. Secondary issues of ADRs occur when foreigners purchase securities available on the Chilean stock market and subsequently convert them into ADRs. This operation constitutes a change of ownership from nationals to foreigners, without a direct financial effect on the firm. These changes of ownership exposed the economy to an additional degree of uncertainty and volatility, since foreign investors can easily withdraw their investments.[9] Such flows actually played a destabilizing role in the economy. They contributed to the bubbles in the securities market in 1994 and 1997 and depressed the market in 1995 and 1998, operating procyclically.

b) The response of macroeconomic policies and their effects

Monetary authorities in Chile deployed a wide range of measures to regulate the surge in financial capital in 1990–95. The Central Bank took steps to discourage inflows of short-term, liquid capital by means of the URR. It moderated the impact of those waves of capital by (i) intervening in the foreign exchange market to prevent an overabundance of foreign currency from appreciating the real exchange rate too much (seeking a deficit on current account not larger than 3% of GDP), (ii) sterilizing the monetary effects of the accumulation of international

---

[9] When firms issue ADRs, the prices of securities on the domestic and US markets tend faster toward one common price through arbitrage. In fact, equity price movements of Chilean firms that have issued ADRs on US markets are closely linked with movements on the Santiago stock exchange. This trend, evidently, implies converged prices of capital in economies whose factor intensity has not converged.

reserves that crossed the barriers of the reserve requirements, and (iii) active regulation of the domestic interest rate.

Four other policies contributed to the success in managing capital inflows. First, fiscal policy was extremely responsible. Increases in social spending were financed with new taxes. Consequently, Chile had a significant non-financial public sector surplus of 1 or 2% of GDP. This prudential approach, which included observing the regulations of a stabilization fund for public copper revenues, facilitated the monetary authorities' task of regulating capital inflows. Of course, running a fiscal surplus does not guarantee, by itself, financial stability. The great 1982 crisis occurred despite Chile's having had several years of budget surpluses; the soft recession of 1999 was preceded by three years of a 2% GDP surplus. A similar fiscal behavior happened in Mexico before the tequila crisis, and in Korea before the Asian crisis. In all these cases, the external deficit was led by the private sector, misinformed by a two-pillar rather than three-pillar macroeconomic balances (see chapter II).

Second, there was an active exchange rate policy, with a crawling band, directed to keep the real exchange rate at a level consistent with the external balance in the mid-term. Allowing a significant appreciation evidently makes notably difficult the regulation of capital flows.

Third, prudential banking regulations had been introduced in response to the banking crisis of 1982–83, and the regulatory system had then been improved over the years. Authorities effectively resisted pressures to weaken supervision when lobbying, financial and academic sectors argued that the system was mature enough to self-regulate; in fact, prudential supervision was strongly intensified by democratic economic authorities. This made it difficult for capital inflows to trigger another unsustainable credit boom in the commercial banks, which in turn helped keep the current account deficit and exchange rate within sustainable limits until 1995. It is important to note that, usually, a significant share of financial flows is not channeled through local banks. This phenomenon became decidedly more pronounced in the 1990s, with the development of portfolio investment funds and derivatives markets.

Fourth, authorities continually monitored aggregate demand and its consistency with productive capacity; actually conducted several *mini-adjustments* in monetary policy. Consequently, macroeconomic disequilibria were not allowed to accumulate. When the Tequila crisis exploded, Chile had a moderate external deficit, large international reserves, and space for increasing economic activity. Those conditions would not have been feasible without regulating capital inflows, managing the exchange rate, and pursuing an active monetary policy.[10]

i) Managing capital inflows

Strategic features of the policies used went against the fashion of capital account liberalization. The two main targets of exchange rate and inflows management policies were, first, achieving sustained macroeconomic stability in an economy prone to huge cycles (recall that Chile experienced the sharpest recessions in all Latin America in 1975 and 1982) and, second, supporting the growth model adopted by the authorities, which gave the expansion and diversification of exports a crucial role.

In face of a plentiful supply of foreign funds, Chilean authorities opted to regulate the foreign currency market in order to prevent large misalignments in the real exchange rate relative to its medium-term trend. The natural short-term horizon of financial markets can lead to exchange rate values that are inconsistent with medium- and long-run trends, which negatively affects decisions in the productive sector. The authorities sought to preserve the predominance of medium-term fundamentals over short-term factors influencing the exchange rate.

In June 1991, the financial environment featured accelerating growth in available external funds and a high copper price – factors considered to have a significant transitory component. The authorities reacted by establishing an URR of 20% on foreign credit (covering the entire spectrum of foreign credit, including a spectrum from loans associated with FDI to trade credit). The reserve was to be on deposit at the Central Bank for a minimum of 90 days and a maximum of one year, according to the time frame of the operation. It was heavily onerous for very short-term inflows. At the same time, an up to 1.2% tax on domestic loans was extended to foreign loans.

Since capital inflows persisted, the reserve requirement was tightened and its coverage expanded. In January 1992 it was extended to cover time deposits in foreign currency; in May the rate was raised to 30%, and in July 1995 the coverage enclosed the purchase of Chilean stocks (secondary ADRs) by foreigners.[11] The term of the deposit was raised to

---

[10] Good luck also played a role, with a sharp improvement in the terms of trade in 1995. Even so, the other factors provided strong macroeconomic insurance.

[11] It is not difficult to impose URR on foreign portfolio investments. If funds to be invested are deposited in a Chilean bank, they remain subject to the reserve requirement there. For funds not using a Chilean bank as an intermediary, the reserve requirement can be enforced at the time the asset is registered to a party with a foreign address. Registration with the Central Bank is also necessary when converting securities into ADRs.

one year, independent of the maturity of the loan.[12] With some lag, authorities took measures to eliminate a loophole that made it possible to circumvent the reserve requirement by means of FDI (since risk capital was exempt, though had to be held in Chile at least for a full year). This was accomplished by scrutinizing FDI applications. Permission for exemptions from reserve requirements granted to productive FDI was denied when it was determined that the inflow was disguised financial capital.

Beginning in 1991, measures were put in place to facilitate capital outflows as a way of lightening pressure on the exchange rate. The most relevant one, with strong pro-cyclical effects several years later, was a change allowing Chilean pension funds to invest a given percentage of their total assets abroad.[13] The greater profitability of financial assets in Chile compared to financial investments abroad, along with expectations of an appreciating exchange rate, discouraged, until 1998, investments abroad by pension funds and by the mutual funds created at that time.

The immediate effect of deregulating outflows was probably to encourage new inflows thanks to the greater certainty that it gave potential investors coming into Chile. This scenario may actually produce the opposite of the desired effect, because the market takes advantage of the opportunity to move foreign currency abroad principally when expectations of appreciation are replaced by expectations of depreciation, which is precisely when the economy is most vulnerable and likely to suffer from speculative attacks (see Williamson, 1993; Labán and Larraín, 1997). The progressive deregulation of outflows can thus imply a risk of capital flight not only from the sudden exit of capital that previously came in, but also from domestic funds seeking to speculate against the peso. This procyclical feature weakens the effect of measures such as the reserve requirement on inflows, as was sharply proved in 1998–99.

ii) Exchange rate policy

In the late 1980s Chile was coming out of the depths of a debt crisis, that had been faced with exchange rate depreciation. The real exchange rate had reached historic highs, such that there was room for some

---

[12] The 30% rate was reduced to 10% by the end of June 1998, and to zero in September, in order to accommodate to the new shortage of external financing associated to the Asian crisis.

[13] It was argued that this would contribute to diversifying risk and increasing the profitability of the private pension system. See a critical view in chapter VI.

appreciation. However, the economy was moving from a shortage to a very abundant supply of foreign savings, and authorities wanted to avoid an excessive and overly rapid adjustment in the exchange rate (see Zahler, 1998). One particularly problematic aspect of the situation involved foreign expectations: as pessimism turns to optimism, foreign investors tend to rapidly define a new stock of desired investments in the emerging market; this generates excessive inflows of capital, whose high levels flows are naturally transitory, not permanent.

In response to the capital surge, the crawling band was broadened in January 1992. This produced a wave of revaluatory expectations fed by capital inflows, stimulated by the understanding that the Central Bank would not intervene within the set band. For many months, the Central Bank had been analyzing a proposal to initiate a dirty floating within the crawling band. The sudden revaluation of almost 10% in the observed rate between January and February 1992 contributed to the Bank's initiating the dirty float in March. The observed rate then fluctuated generally off the bottom of the band, with frequent active purchases by the Bank, though also with sales from time to time.

By establishing the intra-band intervention, the Central Bank regained a greater macroeconomic role over short-term and speculative participants, which allowed the Bank to strengthen the long-term variables that determine the exchange rate facing producers of exportables and importables.

In subsequent months, US interest rates continued to be reduced by the FED, putting pressure on the Central Bank of Chile. Nevertheless, since the domestic economy was experiencing a notable boom, the Bank wanted to rise rather than lower domestic interest rates for the sake of domestic macroeconomic balances. To deter arbitrage, it increased the rate of the URR. The effectiveness of the reserve requirement and its flexible application at that juncture facilitated monetary policy and avoided accumulation of macroeconomic imbalances.

The actual market performance strongly indicates that the exchange rate appreciation during this period represented equilibrating movements. This is consistent both with reverting the adjustments brought by the 1980s crisis, thus allowing the elimination of the overdevaluation, and with the net improvements of productivity for Chilean tradables in the 1990s. A revealed proof is the fact that the current account deficit was quite moderate in 1990–95: 2.3% of GDP.

iii) Stronger banking supervision

Some of the elements of prudential regulation and supervision adopted after the Chilean banking crises of 1981–86 include the continuous monitoring of the quality of bank assets; strict limits on banks' lending to related agents; automatic mechanisms to adjust banks' capital when its market value falls beneath thresholds set by regulators; and the authority to freeze bank operations, prevent troubled banks from transferring funds to third parties, and restrict dividend payments by institutions not complying with capital requirements.

Despite the quality of prudential supervision, however, macroeconomic imbalances that suddenly lead to massive devaluations and very high interest rates can unexpectedly affect the quality of banks portfolios, as can exploding bubbles in asset markets. Sustainable macroeconomic balances are an essential partner of sustainable prudential regulation and supervision of financial markets.

c) Effectiveness of policies for stabilizing macroeconomic variables

The Chilean mechanism for prudential macroeconomic regulation attracted considerable international attention, and many studies attempt to measure its effectiveness.[14] Various tests seek to determine how the URR affects the composition and volume of flows, as well as their impact on the exchange rate and the authorities' ability to make monetary policy and regulate aggregate demand. There is robust evidence that Chile's regulations on foreign capital changed the maturity structure of inflows, reducing the short-term component.[15] This evidence points to a very positive feature of the instrument, since the liquidity of foreign liabilities is a major factor in the probability and severity of crises (see chapter VI, and Rodrik and Velasco, 2000).

Disagreement arises, however, on the effect of the overall volume of flows, since some econometric studies fail to find an impact on the total volume or exchange rates, notwithstanding the effect on the composition of flows. The implication of critics is that there is a high substitution between short- and long-term flows. Three counter-points are relevant here. First, part of this compensatory phenomenon between flows of different maturities should be expected, if long-term investors

---

[14] References to Chilean-style policy for dealing with capital flow instability are frequent in the main circles where these issues are discussed, for example by Andrew Crockett, Stanley Fischer, Paul Krugman, Dani Rodrik, Joseph Stiglitz (then Vice-President of the World Bank), and John Williamson; see also *El Diario*, Santiago, March 30, 2000, which quotes Horst Köhler, then the Managing Director of the IMF.

[15] References and a discussion on diverse empirical research is presented in Ffrench-Davis and Tapia (2005).

(greenfield FDI) are attracted by a more stable economy (as it resulted in Chile from the implementation of the URR); that actually is a point in support of the URR. Second, as discussed in chapter VI, FDI flows normally encompass a different investor with a different behavior, closely connected to productive investment. Third, it has been tested robustly that FDI in Chile has behaved as a permanent variable, while other flows have acted as transitory disturbances (Agosin and Ffrench-Davis, 2001). One outstanding implication is that FDI creates new capacity, which contributes to capital formation (higher GDP) and increased imports of capital goods (higher demand for foreign currency). Given a size of FDI inflows, therefore, the foreign currency market experiences a smaller excess supply than in the case of identical volume of financial inflows.

Some observers have stated that the effectiveness of measures to discourage capital inflows is only temporary, since private sector agents generally find ways around such measures. In principle, a number of loopholes facilitate such evasion. But, they usually imply costs, and some may have undesirable repercussions on the tax liabilities of those circumventing reserve requirements. Though a certain level of evasion is inevitable, there is no evidence suggesting large-scale evasion of measures to discourage short-term capital, as shown by the reserve deposits actually made and the collection of the equivalent fee by the Central Bank (Le Fort and Lehmann, 2003).

The most recent studies tend to confirm that the reserve requirement also reduced total inflows and moderated exchange rate appreciation. Qualitative analysis reinforces the conclusion: Chile confronted a supply of foreign funds that was proportionally greater (in relation to its GDP) than other LACs, owing to its more attractive economic performance and its greater political stability in the early 1990s. Nevertheless, exchange rate appreciation and the current account deficit (as a fraction of GDP or exports) were smaller, on average, than in the other LACs that received large amounts of foreign capital (see table VII.2).

All of these studies coincide in their assessment that the reserve requirement, by maintaining an adequate spread between domestic and international interest rates, provided room for effective counter-cyclical monetary policy during a capital surge. This factor was important in the process of sustained growth seen throughout the decade, since frequent *mini-adjustments* by the Central Bank prevented the need for *maxi-adjustments* and allowed the economy to remain persistently close to its production frontier. Actual output thus coincided with potential output. The resulting perception of real sustainable stability stimulated capital formation and the growth of productive capacity and employment.

Based on the Chilean case, some authors have highlighted the microeconomic costs of capital controls (see Forbes, 2003; Gallego and Hernández, 2003). The crucial point is what is the net effect of capital controls on overall welfare, after contrasting both their eventual microeconomic costs and their macroeconomic benefits. From the point of view of investment and growth, the impressive growth performance of the 1990s indicates that the positive effect of the whole macroeconomic Chilean approach, including the capital controls and their management, was much stronger than any associated microeconomic costs. Actually, the investment ratio of Chile in the 1990s was the highest recorded in its history. In this sense, "financial constraints" as defined and reported by Forbes (2003) were far from being an impediment for expanding the productive capacity. Moreover, the microeconomic switch from debt to retained earnings in the financial structure, as well as the shift toward longer-term liabilities of "small" firms, found by Gallego and Hernández (2003), can be considered as a positive by-product of Chilean capital controls. Indeed, the main source of private savings in EEs, as has been well documented for Chile, tends to be non-distributed profits and depreciation reserves of firms.

The combination of policies used involved financial costs for the monetary authority, since accumulation of large volumes of foreign currency implies a significant cost. This also generates a social cost for the economy, since the profitability of these assets abroad is naturally less than interest payments on the Central Bank liabilities issued to sterilize the domestic monetary effects of accumulating reserves. However, evidence shows that disincentives to short-term, liquid capital inflows tended to reduce the magnitude of the financial costs of sterilization and generated substantial macroeconomic benefits. Even more timely management of the intensity and coverage of the reserve requirement and additional mechanisms by the monetary authority would undoubtedly have kept the financial costs lower.[16] Furthermore, the existence of high levels of reserves has frequently been a very significant stabilizing

---

[16] Another potential source of real compensation for the Central Bank losses is the exchange rate band, which allows to buy cheap (near the floor) and to sell expensive (near the top). This would generate profits only if there is not an excessively strong revaluation of the band.

factor in EEs facing crisis situations, as was proved in Chile in the episode of the contagion of the Asian Crisis.[17]

d) The price of success?

In 1996–97 Chile recorded vigorous growth that could be judged sustainable thanks to high domestic investment rates, but the economy was becoming vulnerable to changes in the international environment. As emphasized in chapter VIII, crises are usually the consequence of badly managed booms.

Paradoxically, satisfactory performance was one of the causes of the disequilibria built in 1996–97. In the first place, foreign investors' confidence in the strength of the Chilean economy encouraged them to invest massively, which created additional pressure on the exchange rate and tested the economy's capacity for efficient absorption. Second, a generalized optimism characterized the world financial environment, based on the notion that the international community had been learned how to handle international crises and that virulent crises were gone forever. Lobbying pressure and a strong fashion toward financial liberalization were well received by many actors in Chile, which immune from the effects of financial crises. Third, some officials, particularly from the Central Bank, understandably let themselves be swayed by this euphoric atmosphere, accepting as sustainable a rising external deficit and a sharp appreciation of the real exchange rate.

Chile thus gave in to the pressures of the dominant international and domestic environment at the time (the *financieristic* forces). It indeed managed to reduce inflation quickly, but it paid a price in the form of the imbalances this generated. The general policy was kept in place, against the fashion, but the authorities failed to strengthen measures in the face of the very abundant supply of capital during 1996–97. The combination of policies and the intensity with which they were applied remained constant. The capital surge clearly weakened the fundamentals of the Chilean economy: the current account deficit rose, the exchange rate appreciated, and the stock of liquid foreign liabilities grew somewhat. The deterioration certainly could have been checked during the boom by means of higher reserve requirements and other measures. Nevertheless, a notorious complacency reigned while the new boom made the country increasingly vulnerable to external shocks.

---

[17] This only argues that the country is better prepared to cope with external shocks; it does not evaluate, however, whether the policy tools and amounts involved are optimal or not.

Imbalances were externally generated and overwhelmingly private. The government's responsibility in this case lay in its failure to enforce coordination between the Central Bank and the Ministry of Finance.[18] This shortcoming was related to the Central Bank's specific form of autonomy (there is not a single form of autonomy in the world, but rather several alternative ones).

As a result of the lack of timely and sufficiently strong measures, the Asian crisis found Chile with a significantly appreciated exchange rate, an overstimulated aggregate demand, and a high current account deficit that in 1996–97 doubled the 1990–95 average (4.5% and 2.3%, respectively). Financial capital began to flow out in late 1997 and accelerated in 1998–99. The outlier nominal exchange rate depreciated to correct for misalignment. This time the impact of the capital outflow was aggravated by the outflows associated with pension funds, which intensified the devaluating pressures on the exchange rate. The channels that had been progressively opened up over the course of the decade, under the argument they would moderate the abundance of foreign currency in boom periods and diversify risk, were effectively used only during the bust. Actually, the mechanism caused a significant loss of international reserves during the crisis, a monetary contraction, and a sharpening of the recessionary adjustment in 1998–99.

The cumulative current account deficit was moderate during the whole decade thanks to the active management of inflows in the first half of the 1990s and the persistence of regulations in the following years with only gradual liberalization. The stock of foreign liabilities was relatively low, and volatile funds played only a minor role, creating external imbalances only in 1996 and 1997. These conditions, together with the country's considerable international reserves, put Chile on a better footing than in the previous crises for confronting the hardships of trade and financial shocks caused by the Asian recession. The domestic financial system did not suffer radically, as a result of the strictness of the Chilean banking commission. Non-performing loans as a percentage of total loans rose from 0.97% in December 1997 to 1.8% at its worst moment in April 1999 – a level comparable to 1992, a crisis-free year. This is remarkable given that aggregate demand fell 6% in 1999.

---

[18] The lack of coordination between the Central Bank and the government was evident. The Central Bank authorities expressed about imbalances in the external sector, while the Minister of Economics, for instance, held that "it is necessary to intensify and strengthen policies such as the reserve requirement to reduce exchange rate appreciation", *Estrategia*, September 26, 1997.

In September 1999, the Central Bank allowed the exchange rate adjustment by adopting a free-floating exchange rate regime. From 2000 on, the government and the Central Bank moved together to a new macroeconomic framework featured by the removal of most of the remaining regulations on the capital account. Thus, in May 2000 the minimum holding period for financial foreign investment was eliminated and, in April 2001, the URR was suspended as instrument as well as many other administrative controls: at that moment economic authorities claimed that Chile had reached the full openness of its capital account. However, capital outflows by residents are subject to some regulations.

3. Concluding remarks

The rich experience of Chilean policy in managing foreign capital surges throws light on key principles and specific instruments for exploiting the benefits and minimizing the costs of financial globalization. Despite the extent to which globalization increases the likelihood of contagion and reduces the space for action, there is still room for each country to foster its objectives.

In this chapter lessons arise from a history of failure and success. Indeed, Chile deployed three types of capital account policy in the last quarter of a century in the face of capital surges (Ffrench-Davis and Tapia, 2001). The first was the plain neo-liberal experiment of the 1970s, which culminated in a major crisis in 1982, with a 14% drop in GDP, and then a rise in open unemployment to 30% in 1983. The second was the approach taken from 1990 to 1995, which – in contrast with the recipe in fashion – consisted of a set of active counter-cyclical macroeconomic policies that included the prudential regulation of financial inflows. Consequently, Chile remained practically unaffected by the Tequila contagion. The third case took place after 1995, with a relative relaxation of macroeconomic prudential policies. This allowed significant appreciation, and accommodated a rising external deficit, which made Chile vulnerable once again. Therefore, the country was forced to undergo a new downward macroeconomic adjustment, which led to a recession (though with a moderate GDP drop of 1% in 1999).

The Chilean experience teaches that the challenge of making good use of foreign capital in EEs, ensuring the healthy domestic absorption of funds, and keeping vulnerability to external factors low requires a comprehensive set of measures. It requires taking an active, pragmatic approach to checking the development of imbalances. Policy-makers (for instance Central Bank and Ministry of Finance) must be able to respond to shifts in domestic and external variables, and to work in close coordination with a solidly structured financial sector, (i) to implement a foreign exchange policy that prevents excessive misalignment of the real rate, (ii) to design counter-cyclical fiscal and monetary policies that put a brake on spending surges, and (iii) to take a flexible prudential approach in managing the capital account. Measures taken must be consistent with the realities of a developing country where capital is not only scarce in absolute terms, but also minuscule in comparison with the volume of capital that can flood a country through an imperfect and volatile international financial market. Chile's experience in 1990–95 proves that all of this is possible and that the challenge is ongoing. It also shows that dangerous temptations can exact a heavy price tomorrow for today's success.

Taking into account both good and bad years since the nineties, the Chilean economy has grown vigorously, in a time in which the world economy exhibited declining product and trade growth rates, and the rest of LACs had a disappointing performance. Chile is the only country in the region that converged with developed economies in 1990–2004 (see chapter III). Correspondingly, poverty has been sharply reduced and living standards have improved noticeably in the last decade and a half. Investment rates during this period rose considerably and, as a result, a potential GDP growth of around 5.5% per year was sustained without inflationary pressure, and with an external savings contribution that was consistent with a competitive tradables sector.

Chile has made significant progress but, if it intends to become a developed and egalitarian society, there are still demanding challenges to be overcome. Here we emphasize two issues, relating to ingredients of sustainable growth that bring in the link with equity.

First, in Chile, as well as in several other places around the world, one can observe a long-run increase in the spread between high and low wages (notice that the real minimum wage only in 1996 exceeded that in the early 1980s, and the average wage just in 1992 exceeded that of 1970). A spectacular effort must be made to improve the quality of education for future members of the labor force, and to develop a comprehensive national training system for workers already out of the educational system.

A second key factor is to ensure a sustainable and vigorous growth path, based on real macroeconomic balances (see chapter II). In order to do so, the country's vulnerability to external shocks must be reduced; a serious risk is to be a victim of own success during booms, and taking larger inflows than those Chile can absorb efficiently and in a sustainable way. The Chilean economy faces the tremendous challenge of ensuring that integration into external markets is achieved in such a way, and to such an extent, that it contributes to development and stability. As said, Chile has had quite diverse economic policy approaches since the 1970s. Thus, it is possible to choose.

In liberalizing the capital account, a dose of prudent selectivity is also in order with regard to outflows, especially from pension funds. Observers and lobbyists argue that these funds are too large for Chile and that investing abroad increases profitability. Chile is a capital-scarce country, however, and the return of capital tends to be higher in Chile than in developed countries. Hence, it is questionable whether funds saved by Chileans and held by pension funds should be encouraged to move abroad rather than preferentially invested domestically. The issue is particularly controversial when microeconomic risk diversification is achieved at the expense of macroeconomic sustainability because of its pro-cyclical nature. What is at stake is to build the capacity to have financial development by *completing* the domestic capital market with a long-term segment and improved access to it of SMEs.

Is it possible to forge ahead with policies that contrast with contemporary economic ideology? Chile in the first half of the 1990s provides evidence that it is indeed possible and can be an efficient and profitable way to insure against costly crises.

References

Agénor, P. and P. Montiel (1996), *Development Macroeconomics*, Princeton University Press, Princeton.

Agosin, M. (2001), "Korea and Taiwan in the financial crisis," in R. Ffrench-Davis (ed.), *Financial Crises in "Successful" Emerging Economies*, ECLAC/Brookings Institution Press, Washington, DC.

Agosin, M. (1998), "Capital inflows and investment performance: Chile in the 1990s," in Ffrench-Davis and Reisen (1998).

Agosin, M. and R. Ffrench-Davis (2001), "Managing capital inflows in Chile," in S. Griffith-Jones, M. Montes and A. Nasution (eds.), *Short-Term Capital Flows and Economic Crises*, Oxford University Press and United Nations University (UNU)/World Institute for Development Economics Research (WIDER), New York.

Akyüz, Y. (1998), "The East Asian financial crisis: Back to the future?", in Jomo (1998).

Akyüz, Y. (1993), "Financial liberalization: The key issues," in Y. Akyuz and G. Held (eds.), *Finance and the Real Economy: Issues and Case Studies in Developing Countries*, ECLAC/UNCTAD/UNU/WIDER, Santiago.

Altimir, O. (2004), "Distributive tensions under the new economic order," in G. Indart (ed.), *Economic Reforms, Growth and Inequality in Latin America: Essays in Honor of Albert Berry*, Aldershot, Ashgate.

Amsden, A.H. (2001), *The Rise of "The Rest": Challenges to the West from Late-Industrializing Economies*, Oxford University Press, New York.

Arrow, K. (1974), "Limited knowledge and economic analysis," *The American Economic Review*, vol. LXIV, No. 1, March; and in R. Ffrench-Davis (1981), vol. I.

Bacha, E. (1986), *El milagro y la crisis: economía brasileña y latinoamericana*, Lectura 57, Fondo de Cultura Económica, Mexico.

Bacha, E. and C. Díaz-Alejandro (1983), "Los mercados financieros: una visión desde la semi-periferia," in Ffrench-Davis (1983).

Baig, I. and T. Goldfajn (2000), "The Russian default and the contagion to Brazil," *IMF Working Paper* 00/160, International Monetary Fund, Washington, DC.

Balassa, B. (1981), *Newly Industrializing Countries in the World Economy*, Pergamon Press, New York.

Balassa, B. (1964), "The purchasing-power parity doctrine: A reappraisal." *Journal of Political Economy*, December; and in R. Ffrench-Davis (1981), vol. II.

Ball, Laurence M. (1999), "Policy rules for open economies," in John Taylor (ed.), *Monetary Policy Rules*, University of Chicago Press, Ill.

Barro, R. and X. Sala-i-Martin (2004), *Economic Growth*, Second Edition, The MIT Press, Cambridge, Mass.

Berry, A. and C. Ruiz (2003), "Firm size and the impacts of financial liberalization and integration," in A. Berry and G. Indart (eds.), *Critical Issues in International Financial Reform*, Transaction Publishers, New Brunswick, NJ.

Bhagwati, J. (2004), *In Defense of Globalization*, Oxford University Press, New York.

Bhagwati, J. (1998), "The capital myth: The difference between trade in widgets and dollars," *Foreign Affairs*, May–June.

Bhagwati, J. (1978), *Foreign Trade Regimes and Economic Development: Anatomy and Consequences of Exchange Control Regimes*, National Bureau of Economic Research, New York; ch. 8, reprinted in Ffrench-Davis (1981), vol. I.

Bosworth, B., R. Dornbusch and R. Labán (1994) (eds.), *The Chilean Economy. Policy Lessons and Challenges*, Brookings Institution Press, Washington, DC.

Bourguignon, F. and Ch. Morrison (2002), "Inequality among world citizens: 1820–1992," in *American Economic Review*, September.

Bouzas, R. and S. Keifman (2003), "Making trade liberalization work," in Kuczynski and Williamson (2003).

Bradford, C. (1992), "The East Asian development experience," in E. Grilli and D. Salvatore (eds.), *Handbook of Economic Development*, North Holland Press, Amsterdam.

Budnevich, C. (2003), "Countercyclical fiscal policy: A review of the literature, empirical evidence and some policy proposals," in Ffrench-Davis and Griffith-Jones (2003).

Buitelaar, R., R. Padilla and R. Urrutia (1999), "The In-bond Assembly Industry and Technical Change", *CEPAL Review*, No. 67, April.

Caballero, R. (2000), "Macroeconomic volatility in Latin America: a conceptual framework and three case studies," *Economia*, vol. 1, No. 1, fall.

Caballero, R. and V. Corbo (1990), "The effect of real exchange rate uncertainty on exports: Empirical evidence," *The World Bank Economic Review*, 3, Washington, DC.

Calvo, G. (1998), "Varieties of capital-market crises," in G. Calvo and M. King (eds.), *The Debt Burden and its Consequences for Monetary Policy*, Macmillan, London.

Calvo, G. and E. Mendoza (2000), "Rational contagion and the globalization of securities markets," in *Journal of International Economics*, 51.

Calvo, G., E. Leiderman and C. Reinhart (1993), "Capital inflows and real exchange rate appreciation in Latin America: The role of external factors," *IMF Staff Papers*, vol. 40, No. 1, March.

Camdessus (1997), "Toward a new generation of structural reforms in Latin America," International Monetary Fund, June.

Cardoso, F.H. (1977), "Originality of a copy: CEPAL and the idea of development," in *CEPAL Review*, No. 4, Spring; and in Ffrench-Davis (1981), vol. II.

Chang, H-J. (2005), "Institutions of macroeconomic management: History, theory and practice," *Working Paper*, IPD at Columbia University, Macroeconomics Task Force.

Corbo, V., O. Landerretche and K. Schmidt-Hebbel (2002), "Does inflation targeting make a difference?", in Loayza and Soto (2002).

Corden, M. (1972), "Economies of scale and customs union theory," *Journal of Political Economy*, vol. 80, No. 3, May–June.

Culpeper, R. (1995), "Resurgence of private flows to Latin America: The role of North American investors," in Ffrench-Davis and Griffith-Jones (1995).

Dean, J. (1998), "Why left-wing moralists and right-wing academics are wrong about Asia," *Challenge*, March–April.

De Long, J.B. and L. Summers (1991), "Equipment investment and economic growth," *Quarterly Journal of Economics*, vol. 106, No. 2, Cambridge, Mass.

Devlin, R. (1989), *Debt and Crisis in Latin America: The Supply Side of the Story*, Princeton University Press, Princeton.

Devlin, R. and R. Ffrench-Davis (1998), "Towards an evaluation of regional integration in Latin America in the 1990s," in J.J. Teunissen (ed.), *Regional Integration and Multilateral Cooperation in the Global Economy*, FONDAD, The Hague.

Devlin, R. and R. Ffrench-Davis (1995), "The great Latin American debt crisis: A decade of asymmetric adjustment," in G. Helleiner (ed.), *Poverty, Prosperity and the World Economy*, Macmillan, London.

Devlin, R. and P. Giordano (2004), "The old and new regionalism: benefits, costs, and implications for the FTAA," in Estevadeordal, et al. (2004).

Díaz-Alejandro, C. (1985), "Good-bye financial repression, hello financial crash," *Journal of Development Economics*, vol. 19, No. 1/2, Amsterdam, December; and in A. Velasco, (ed.), *Trade, Development and the World Economy: Selected Essays of Carlos F. Díaz-Alejandro*, Basil Blackwell, Oxford, 1988.

Díaz-Alejandro C. (1975), "Trade policies and economic development," reproduced in Ffrench-Davis (1981).

Dodd, R. (2003), "Derivatives, the shape of international capital flows and the virtues of prudential regulation," in Ffrench-Davis and Griffith-Jones (2003).

Dornbusch, R. (1991), "Special exchange rates for capital account transactions," in *Exchange Rates and Inflation*, The MIT Press, Cambridge, Mass.

Dornbusch, R. (1989), "Real exchange rates and macroeconomics: A selective survey," *Scandinavian Journal of Economics*, vol. 2.

Easterly, W. (2001), "The lost decades: developing countries' stagnation in spite of policy reform," World Bank, February.

Easterly, W. and R. Levine (2002), "It's not factor accumulation: Stylized facts and growth models," in N. Loayza and R. Soto (eds.), *Economic Growth: Sources, Trends and Cycles*, Central Bank of Chile, Santiago.

Easterly, W. and L. Servén (2003), *The Limits of Stabilization: Infrastructure, Public Deficits and Growth in Latin America*, Stanford University Press, Ca.

Easterly, W., R. Islam and J. Stiglitz (2001), "Volatility and Macroeconomic Paradigms for Rich and Poor Countries," in J. Dreze (ed.), *Advances in Macroeconomic Theory*, Palgrave, London.

Easterly, W.R., N.A. Loayza and P.J. Montiel (1997), "Has Latin America's post-reform growth been dissapointing?", *Policy Research Working Papers*, No. 1708, World Bank, Washington, DC.

Eatwell, J. (1997), "International capital liberalization: The impact on world development," in *Estudios de Economía*, vol. 24, No. 2, Santiago.

ECLAC (2004a), *Productive Development in Open Economies*, Santiago.

ECLAC (2004b), *Economic Survey of Latin America and the Caribbean, 2003–2004*, Santiago.

ECLAC (2004c), *Social Panorama of Latin America, 2004*, Santiago, November.

ECLAC (2004d), *Preliminary Overview of the Economies of Latin America and the Caribbean*, Santiago, December.

ECLAC (2002a), *Globalization and Development*, United Nations, Santiago. Also published by Stanford University Press, 2003, Palo Alto, Ca.

ECLAC (2002b), *Growth with Stability: Financing for Development in the New International Context*, ECLAC Books, No. 67, Santiago.

ECLAC (1998), *Policies to Improve Linkages with the Global Economy*, United Nations, Santiago, 1995. Second revised Spanish edition published by Fondo de Cultura Económica, Santiago, 1998.

ECLAC (1992), *Social Equity and Changing Production Patterns: An Integrated Approach*, United Nations, Santiago, April.

ECLAC, *Economic Survey of Latin America and the Caribbean*, various issues.

ECLAC, *Latin America and the Caribbean in the World Economy*, various issues.

Edwards, S. (1995), *Crisis and Reform in Latin America: From Despair to Hope*, World Bank/Oxford University Press, New York.

Edwards, S. (1989), "The Order of Liberalization of the Current and Capital Accounts of the Balance of Payments," *Essays in International Finance*, No. 156, Princeton University, NJ.

Edwards, S. and A. Cox-Edwards (1987), *Monetarism and Liberalization: The Chilean Experiment*, Ballinger, Cambridge, Mass.

Eichengreen, B. (2003), *Capital Flows and Crises*, The MIT Press, Cambridge, Mass.

Estevadeordal, A., D. Rodrik, A. Taylor and A. Velasco (2004) (eds.), *Integrating the Americas: FTAA and Beyond*, Harvard University, Rockefeller Center for Latin American Studies, Cambridge, Mass.

Fajnzylber, F. (1990), "Industrialization in Latin America: From the 'Black Box' to the 'Empty Box'," *Cuadernos de la CEPAL*, No. 60, Santiago.

Fanelli, J.M. (2003), "Micro-macro interactions, competitiveness and sustainability," in A. Dutt and J. Ros (eds.), *Development Economics and Structuralist Macroeconomics*, Edward Elgar, Aldershot.

Fanelli, J.M. and R. Frenkel (1994), "Macroeconomic policies for the transition from stabilization to growth," in C. Bradford (ed.), *The New Paradigm of Systemic Competitiveness: Toward More Integrated Policies in Latin America*, OECD Development Centre, Paris.

Fanelli, J.M. and J.L. Machinea (1995), "Capital movements in Argentina," in Ffrench-Davis and Griffith-Jones (1995).

Feldstein, M. and C. Horioka (1980), "Domestic saving and international capital flows," *Economic Journal*, 9.

Ffrench-Davis, R. (2005), "Macroeconomics-for-growth under financial globalization: Four strategic issues for Latin America," in R. Ffrench-Davis (ed.), *Seeking Growth Under Financial Volatility*, Palgrave Macmillan, London.

Ffrench-Davis, R. (2003), "Financial crises and national policy issues: An overview," in Ffrench-Davis and Griffith-Jones (2003).

Ffrench-Davis, R. (2002) *Economic Reforms in Chile: From Dictatorship to Democracy*, University of Michigan Press, Ann Arbor.

Ffrench-Davis, R. (2001) (ed.), *Financial Crises in "Successful" Emerging Economies*, Brookings Institution Press/ECLAC, Washington, DC.

Ffrench-Davis, R. (2000), *Reforming the Reforms in Latin America: Macroeconomics, Trade, Finance*, Macmillan Palgrave, London.

Ffrench-Davis, R. (1984), "International private lending and borrowing strategies of developing countries," *Journal of Development Planning*, No. 14, United Nations, New York.

Ffrench-Davis, R. (1983) (ed.), *Relaciones financieras externas. Su efecto en la economía latinoamericana*, Lecturas de *El Trimestre Económico*, No. 47, Fondo de Cultura Económica/CIEPLAN, Mexico.

Ffrench-Davis, R. (1982), "External debt and balance of payments of Latin America. Recent trends and outlook," *Economic and Social Progress in Latin America*, Inter-American Development Bank, Washington, DC.

Ffrench-Davis, R. (1981) (ed.), *Intercambio y Desarrollo*, vols. I and II, Lecturas de *El Trimestre Económico*, No. 38, Fondo de Cultura Económica, Mexico.

Ffrench-Davis, R. (1980), "Distorsiones del mercado y teoría de las uniones aduaneras", *Integración Latinoamericana*, No. 44, Buenos Aires, March.

Ffrench-Davis, R. (1979), *Economía internacional: teorías y políticas para el desarrollo*, Fondo de Cultura Económica, Mexico.

Ffrench-Davis, R. and S. Griffith-Jones (2003) (eds.), *From Capital Surges to Drought*, Palgrave Macmillan, London.

Ffrench-Davis, R. and S. Griffith-Jones (1995) (eds.), *Coping With Capital Surges. The Return of Finance to Latin America*, Lynne Rienner Publishers, Boulder, Colorado.

Ffrench-Davis, R. and G. Larraín (2003), "How optimal are the extremes? Latin American exchange rate policies during the Asian Crisis," in Ffrench-Davis and Griffith-Jones (2003).

Ffrench-Davis, R. and M. Marfán (1988), "Selective policies under a structural foreign exchange shortage," in *Journal of Development Economics*, 29; and in H. Singer, N. Hatti and R. Tandon (eds.), *Adjustment and Liberalization in the Third World*, Indus Publishing Company, New Delhi, 1991.

Ffrench-Davis, R. and J.A. Ocampo (2001), "The globalization of financial volatility," in Ffrench-Davis (2001).

Ffrench-Davis, R. and H. Reisen (1998) (eds.), *Capital Flows and Investment Performance: Lessons from Latin America*, OECD Development Centre/ECLAC, Paris.

Ffrench-Davis, R. and H. Tapia (2005), "The Chilean-style of capital controls: An empirical assessment," Working Paper, ECLAC research project on *Management of Volatility, Financial Globalization and Growth in EEs*.

Ffrench-Davis, R. and H. Tapia (2004), "Macroeconomics-for-growth in emerging economies," *IPD Working Paper*, Columbia University, New York.

Ffrench-Davis, R. and H. Tapia (2001), "Three varieties of capital surge management in Chile," in Ffrench-Davis (2001).

Ffrench-Davis, R. and L. Villar (2005), "Real macroeconomic stability and the capital account in Chile and Colombia," in R. Ffrench-Davis (ed.), *Seeking Growth Under Financial Volatility*, Palgrave Macmillan, London.

Ffrench-Davis, R., O. Muñoz and G. Palma (1998), "The Latin American economies 1950–1990," in L. Bethell (ed.), *Latin America: Economy and Society Since 1930*, Cambridge University Press, Cambridge.

Financial Stability Forum (2000), "Report of the working group," Bank for International Settlements, Basle.

Fischer, S. (1993), "The role of macroeconomic factors in growth," *Journal of Monetary Economics*, vol. 32, No. 3.

Fontaine, J.A. (1989), "The Chilean economy in the 1980s: Adjustment and recovery," in S. Edwards and F. Larraín (eds.), *Debt, Adjustment and Recovery: Latin America's Prospects for Growth and Development*, Basil Blackwell, Oxford.

Forbes, K. (2003), "One cost of the Chilean capital controls: increased financial constraints for smaller traded firms," *NBER Working Paper* 9777, June.

Foxley, A. (1983), *Latin American Experiments in Neo-conservative Economics*, University of California Press, California.

Frenkel, R. (2004), "From the boom in capital inflows to financial traps," ECLAC research project on *Management of Volatility, Financial Globalization and Growth in EEs*, supported by the Ford Foundation, to be published in IPD Capital Account Liberalization volume.

Frenkel, R. (2003), "Globalization and financial crises in Latin America," *CEPAL Review*, No. 80, August.

Frenkel, R. (1983), "La apertura financiera externa: el caso Argentino", in Ffrench-Davis (1983).

Fritsch, W. and G. Franco (1993), "The political economy of trade and industrial policy reform in Brazil in the 1990s", *Reformas de Políticas Públicas*, No. 6, ECLAC, Santiago, June.

Furman, J. and J. Stiglitz (1998), "Economic crises: Evidence and insights from East Asia," *Brookings Papers on Economic Activity*, No. 2, Brookings Institution Press, Washington, DC.

Ganuza, E., R. Paes de Barros, L. Taylor and R. Vos (2001), *Liberalización, desigualdad y pobreza: América Latina en los noventa*, Editorial Universitaria de Buenos Aires.

Gallego, F. and L. Hernández (2003), "Microeconomic effects of capital controls: the Chilean experience during the nineties," *Working Paper* No. 203, Central Bank of Chile, February.

Gelb, S. (2005) "Macroeconomics in post-apartheid South Africa: Real growth versus financial stability," in R. Ffrench-Davis (ed.), *Seeking Growth Under Financial Volatility*, Palgrave Macmillan, London.

Griffith-Jones, S. (2001), "An international financial architecture for crisis prevention," in Ffrench-Davis (2001).

Griffith-Jones, S. (1998), *Global Capital Flows, Should They Be Regulated?*, Macmillan, London.

Griffith-Jones, S. (1995), "European private flows to Latin America: The facts and the issues," in Ffrench-Davis and Griffith-Jones (1995).

Griffith-Jones, S. (1988) (ed.), *Managing World Debt*, Wheatsheaf Books, Sussex, and St. Martin's Press, New York.

Griffith-Jones, S. and A. Persaud, with S. Spratt and M. Segoviano (2005), "The pro-cyclical impact of Basle II on emerging markets and its political economy," ECLAC research project on *Management of Volatility, Financial Globalization and Growth in EEs*, supported by the Ford Foundation, to be published in IPD Capital Account Liberalization volume.

Griliches, Z. and D. Jorgenson (1967), "The explanation of productivity change," *Review of Economic Studies*, 34, July.

Gurría, A. (1995), "Capital flows: The Mexican case," in Ffrench-Davis and Griffith-Jones (1995).

Harberger, A. (1985), "Observations on the Chilean economy, 1973–83," *Economic Development and Cultural Change*, 33, April.

Hausmann, R. and M. Gavin (1996), "Securing stability and growth in a shock-prone region: The policy challenge for Latin America," in R. Hausmann and H. Reisen (eds.), *Securing Stability and Growth in Latin America*, OECD, Paris.

Hawkins, J. (2003), "International bank lending: Water flowing uphill?", in Ffrench-Davis and Griffith-Jones (2003).

Held, G. (1994), "Liberalization or financial development?", *CEPAL Review*, No. 54, Santiago, December.

Helleiner, G. (1997), "Capital account regimes and the developing countries," in *International Monetary and Financial Issues for the 1990s*, vol. VIII, UNCTAD, Geneva.

Helleiner, G., S. Abrahamian, E. Bacha, R. Lawrence and P. Malan (eds.) (1995), *Poverty, Prosperity and the World Economy*, Macmillan, London.

Herrera, C. (1992), "La apertura gradual en Costa Rica a partir de 1983," *Pensamiento Iberoamericano*, No. 21, Madrid, January–June.

Hnatkovska, V. and N. Loayza (2003), "Volatility and growth," World Bank, August.

Hofman, A. (2000), *The Economic Development of Latin America in the Twentieth Century*, Edward Elgar, Cheltenham, UK.

Hofman, A. and H. Tapia (2004), "Potential output in Latin America: A standard approach for 1950–2002," ECLAC, July.

IDB (Inter-American Development Bank) (2004), *Economic and Social Progress in Latin America, 2004 Report. Good Jobs Wanted: Labor Markets in Latin America*, Washington, DC.

IDB (Inter-American Development Bank) (1997), *Latin America After a Decade of Reforms, Economic and Social Progress in Latin America, 1997 Report*, Washington, DC, September.

IEO/IMF (2005), "Appraisal of capital account opening," Independent Evaluation Office, Washington, DC.

IMF (International Monetary Fund) (1998), *International Capital Markets*, Washington, DC, September.

IMF, *International Financial Statistics*, Washington, DC, various issues.

Jomo, K.S. (1998) (ed.), *Tigers in Trouble: Financial Governance, Liberalisation and Crises in East Asia*, Zed Books, London.

Kaplan, E. and D. Rodrik (2001), "Did the Malaysian capital controls work?", *NBER Working Paper*, No. 8142, Cambridge, Mass.

Katz, J. (2001), *Structural Reforms, Productivity and Technological Change in Latin America*, CEPAL, Santiago.

Kenen, P. (1993), "Financial opening and the exchange rate regime," in H. Reisen and B. Fischer (eds.), *Financial Opening*, OECD, Paris.

Kindleberger, C. (1978), *Manias, Panics and Crashes*, Basic Books, New York.

Kochhar, K., L. Dicks-Mireaux, B. Horvath, M. Mecagni, E. Offerdal and J. Zhou (1996), "Thailand – The road to sustained growth," *Occasional Paper*, 146, IMF, Washington, DC, December.

Krugman, P. (2000), "Crises: The price of globalization?", Federal Reserve Bank of Kansas City, *Symposium on Global Economic Integration: Opportunities and Challenges*, Jackson Hole, Wyoming.

Krugman, P. (1999), "Balance sheets, the transfer problem, and financial crises," in P. Izard, A. Razin and A. Rose (eds.), *International Finance and Financial Crises*, Kluwer, Dordrecht, The Netherlands.

Krugman, P. (1990a), *The Age of Diminished Expectations*, The MIT Press, Cambridge, Mass.

Krugman, P. (1990b), *Rethinking International Trade*, The MIT Press, Cambridge, Mass.

Kuczynski, P. and J. Williamson (2003) (eds.), *After the Washington Consensus: Restarting Growth in Latin America*, Institute for International Economics, Washington, DC.

Kuwayama, M. and J. Durán, (2003), "La calidad de la inserción internacional de América Latina y el Caribe en el comercio mundial," *Serie Comercio Internacional*, No. 26, Santiago, Mayo.

Labán, R. and F. Larraín (1997), "Can a liberalization of capital outflows increase net capital inflows?", *Journal of International Money and Finance*, vol. 16, No. 3.

Larrañaga, O. (2001), "Distribución de ingresos: 1958–2001," in R. Ffrench-Davis and B. Stallings, *Reformas, crecimiento y políticas sociales en Chile desde 1973*, LOM Ediciones, Santiago.

Le Fort, G. and S. Lehmann (2003), "The special reserve requirement and net capital inflows: Chile in the 1990s," *CEPAL Review*, No. 81, December, Santiago.

Leiva, P. (2004), *The Strategic Association Chile-European Union*, CELARE, Santiago.

Lessard, D. and J. Williamson (1987), *Capital Flight*, Institute for International Economics, Washington, DC.

Loayza, N. and R. Soto (2002) (eds.), *Inflation Targeting: Design Performance, Challenges*, Central Bank of Chile, Santiago.

Loayza, N., P. Fajnzylber and C. Calderón (2004), "Economic growth in Latin America and the Caribbean: stylized facts, explanations and forecasts," *Working Paper* No. 265, Central Bank of Chile, June.

Lustig, N. (2000), "Crises and the poor: Socially responsible macroeconomics", in *Economía*, vol. 1, No. 1, Brookings Institution, December.

Lustig, N. (1997), "The United States to the rescue: Financial assistance to Mexico in 1982 and 1995," *CEPAL Review*, No. 61, Santiago, April.

Macario, C. (2000) (ed.), *Export Growth in Latin America*, Lynne Rienner Publisher, Boulder, Colo.

Maddison, A. (2001), *The World Economy: A Millennial Perspective*, OECD, Paris.

Mahani, Z., K. Shin and Y. Wang (2005), "Macroeconomic adjustment and the real economy in Korea and Malaysia since 1997," in R. Ffrench-Davis (ed.), *Seeking Growth under Financial Volatility*, Palgrave Macmillan, London.

Marfán, M. (2005), "Fiscal policy efficacy and private deficits: A macroeconomic approach," in J.A. Ocampo (ed.), *Rethinking Development Challenges*, Stanford University Press, Palo Alto, California.

Martin, P. (1997), "Press conference," Meeting of Ministers of Finance of the Americas, reproduced in *El Mercurio*, December 4, Santiago.

Martner, R. and V. Tromben (2004). "Tax reforms and fiscal stabilization in Latin American countries," *Serie Gestión Pública*, No. 45, ECLAC, June.

Massad, C. and R. Zahler (1988) (eds.), *Deuda interna y estabilidad financiera*, Grupo Editor Latinoamericano, Buenos Aires.

McKinnon, R. (1991), *The Order of Economic Liberalization: Financial Control in the Transition to a Market Economy*, Johns Hopkins University Press, Baltimore.

Medina, J.P. and R. Valdés (2002), "Optimal monetary policy rules when the current account matters," in N. Loayza and K. Schmidt-Hebbel (eds.), *Monetary Policy: Rules and Transmission Mechanisms*, Central Bank of Chile, Santiago.

Meller, P. (1994), "The Chilean trade liberalization and export expansion process, 1974–90," in G.K. Helleiner (ed.), *Trade Policy and Industrialization in Turbulent Times*, Routledge, London.

Meller, P. (1991), "Adjustment and social costs in Chile during the 1980s," *World Development*, vol. XIX, No. 11.

Mishkin, F. (1999), "International capital movements, financial volatility and financial instability," NBER Website <http://www.nber.org/papers/w6390>.

Mishkin, F. and K. Schmidt-Hebbel (2002), "A decade of inflation targeting in the world: what do we know and what do we not know," in Loayza and Soto (2002).

Morley, S. (2001), *The Income Distribution Problem in Latin America and the Caribbean*, Libros de la CEPAL, No. 65, Santiago.

Morley, S. (1995), *Poverty and Inequality in Latin America. The Impact of Adjustment and Recovery in the 1980s*, The Johns Hopkins University Press, Baltimore and London.

Morley, S., R. Machado and S. Pettinato (1999), "Indexes of structural reform in Latin America," *Serie Reformas Económicas*, No. 12, ECLAC, January.

Neut, A. and A. Velasco (2003), "Tough policies, incredible policies?", *NBER Working Paper*, No. 9932, September.

Obstfeld, M. (1998), "The global capital market: Benefactor or menace?", *Journal of Economic Perspectives*, vol. 12 (Fall).

Obstfeld, M. (1994), "Risk-taking, global diversification and growth," *American Economic Review*, vol. 84.

Ocampo, J.A. (2004), "Latin America's growth and equity frustrations during structural reforms," *Journal of Economic Perspectives*, vol. 12, No. 2, Spring.

Ocampo, J.A. (2003), "Capital account and counter-cyclical prudential regulations in developing countries," in Ffrench-Davis and Griffith-Jones (2003).

Ocampo, J.A. (2002), "Rethinking the development agenda," *Cambridge Journal of Economics*, vol. 26, No. 3, May.

Ocampo, J.A. (1999), "International financial reform: The broad agenda," *CEPAL Review*, No. 69, Santiago, December.

Ocampo, J.A. (1993), "New theories of international trade and trade policy in developing countries," in M. Agosin and D. Tussie (eds.), *Trade and Growth: New Dilemmas in Trade Policy*. St. Martin's Press, New York.

Ocampo, J.A. and M.A. Parra (2003), "The terms of trade for commodities in the twentieth century," *CEPAL Review*, No. 79, April.

Ocampo, J.A. and C. Tovar (1998), "Capital flows, savings and investment in Colombia, 1990–96," in Ffrench-Davis and Reisen (1998).

Ocampo, J.A. and L. Villar (1992), "Trayectoria y vicisitudes de la apertura económica colombiana", *Pensamiento Iberoamericano*, No. 21, Madrid, January–June.

Ocampo, J.A., S. Zamagni, R. Ffrench-Davis and C. Pietrobelli (2000) (eds.), *Financial Globalization and the Emerging Economies*, ECLAC/Jacques Maritain Institute, Santiago.

Palma, G. (2005), "The 1999 Brazilian financial crisis: how 'exuberant monetarism' led to banking fragility and public sector Ponzi finance," *Working Paper*, IPD at Columbia University, Macroeconomics Task Force.

Parrado, E. and A. Velasco (2002), "Alternative monetary rules in the open economy: a welfare-based approach," in Loayza and Soto (2002).

Perry, G. and D. Lederman (1998), "Financial vulnerability, spillover effects and contagion: lessons from the Asian crises for Latin America," *World Bank Latin American and Caribbean Studies Viewpoints*, The World Bank, Washington, DC.

Persaud, A. (2003), "Liquidity black holes," in Ffrench-Davis and Griffith-Jones (2003).

Pfaff, W. (2000), "A challenge to globalization theory," in Ocampo et al. (2000).

Pietrobelli, C. and S. Zamagni (2000), "The emerging economies in the global financial market: Some concluding remarks," in Ocampo et al. (2000).

Pindyck, R. (1991), "Irreversibility, uncertainty and investment," *Journal of Economic Literature*, 29, vol. 3.

Pinto, A. (1970), "Naturaleza e implicaciones de la heterogeneidad estructural," *El Trimestre Económico*, No. 145, January–March.

Prasad, E., K. Rogoff, S. Wei and M. Kose (2003), "Effects of financial globalization on developing countries: Some empirical evidence," *IMF Occasional Paper*, No. 220, September.

Prebisch, R. (1977), "En torno a las ideas de la CEPAL: problemas de la industrialización en la América Latina," in Ffrench-Davis (1981).

Prebisch, R. (1963), *Hacia una dinámica del desarrollo latinoamericano*, Fondo de Cultura Económica, Mexico.

Radelet, S. and J. Sachs (1998), "The East Asian financial crisis: Diagnosis, remedies, prospects," *Brookings Papers on Economic Activity* 1, Washington, DC.

Ramos, J. (1993), "Macroeconomic equilibria and development," in Sunkel (1993).

Ramos, J. (1986), *Neoconservative Economics in the Southern Cone of Latin America, 1973–83*, Johns Hopkins University Press, Baltimore.

Reisen, H. (2003), "Ratings since the Asian crisis," in Ffrench-Davis and Griffith-Jones (2003).

Reisen, H. (1997), "The limits of foreign savings," in R. Hausmann and H. Reisen (eds.), *Promoting Savings in Latin America*, OECD Development Centre, Paris.

Reisen, H. (1994), *Debt, Deficits and Exchange Rates*, OECD Development Centre/Edward Elgar, England.

Robichek, W. (1981), "Some reflections about external public debt management," *Estudios Monetarios VII*, Central Bank of Chile, Santiago.

Rodríguez, O. (1980), *La teoría del subdesarrollo de la CEPAL*, Siglo XXI, Mexico.

Rodrik, D. (2003), "Growth strategies," draft for Handbook of Economic Growth, NBER *Working Paper*, No. 10050, October.

Rodrik, D. (2001a), "Why is there so much economic insecurity in Latin America?", *CEPAL Review*, No. 73, Santiago, April.

Rodrik, D. (2001b), "The global governance of trade as if development really mattered," UNDP, New York.

Rodrik, D. (1998), "Who needs capital account convertibility?", in P. Kenen (ed.), *Should the IMF Pursue Capital Account Convertibility?*, Princeton *Essays in International Finance*, No. 207.

Rodrik, D. (1992), "Conceptual issues in the design of trade policy for industrialization," *World Development*, vol. 20, No. 3, June.

Rodrik, D. and F. Rodríguez (2001), "Trade policy and economic growth: A Skeptic's guide to the cross-national evidence," in B. Bernanke and K. Rogoff (eds.), *Macroeconomics Annual 2000*, MIT Press for NBER, Cambridge, Mass.

Rodrik, D. and A. Velasco (2000), "Short-term capital flows," *Annual World Bank Conference on Development Economics 1999*, The World Bank, Washington, DC.

Rojas-Suárez, L. and S. Weisbrod (1996), "Building stability in Latin American financial markets", in R. Hausmann and H. Reisen (eds.), *Securing Stability and Growth in Latin America*, OECD, Paris.

Ros, J. (2001), "From the capital surge to the financial crisis and beyond: The Mexican economy in the 1990s," in Ffrench-Davis (2001).

Ros, J. (2000), *Development Theory and Economics of Growth*, The University of Michigan Press, Ann Arbor.

Ros, J. (1993), "La reforma del régimen comercial en México durante los años ochenta: sus efectos económicos y dimensiones políticas," in *Reformas de Política Pública*, No. 4, CEPAL, Santiago, April.

Sachs, J. (1987), "Trade and exchange-rate policies in growth-oriented adjustment programs," in V. Corbo, M. Goldstein and M. Khan (eds.), *Growth-oriented Adjustment Programs*, IMF and The World Bank, Washington, DC.

Sachs, J., A. Tornell and A. Velasco (1996), "Financial crises in emerging markets: The lessons from 1995," *Working Paper Series*, No. 5576, NBER, Cambridge, May.

Santos-Paulino, A. and A.P. Thirwall (2004), "The impact of trade liberalisation on exports, imports and the balance of payments of developing countries," *The Economic Journal*, vol. 114, February.

Schmidt-Hebbel, K., L. Servén and A. Solimano (1996), "Saving and investment: Paradigms, puzzles, policies," *The World Bank Research Observer*, vol. 11, No. 1, World Bank, Washington, DC.

Servén L. and A. Solimano (1993), "Economic adjustment and investment performance in developing countries: The experience of the 1980s," in L. Serven and A. Solimano (eds.), *Striving for Growth After Adjustment. The Role of Capital Formation*, World Bank, Washington DC.

Shiller, R. (2000), *Irrational Exuberance*, Princeton University Press, Princeton, NJ.

Singh, A., A. Belaisch, C. Collyns, P. De Masi, R. Krieger, G. Meredith and R. Rennhack (2005), "Stabilization and reform in Latin America: A macroeconomic perspective on the experience since the early 1990s," *Occasional Paper*, 238, IMF, February, Washington, DC.

Solow, R. (2001), "From neoclassical growth theory to new classical macroeconomies," in J. Drèze (ed.), *Advances in Macroeconomic Theory*, IEA/Palgrave, London.

Solow, R. (1957), "Technical change and aggregate production function," *Review of Economics and Statistics*, 39, August.

Stallings, B. and R. Studart (2005), *Finance for Development: Latin America's Banks and Capital Markets after Liberalization*, Brookings Institution, Washington, DC, forthcoming.

Stallings, B. and W. Peres (2000), *Growth, Employment, and Equity: The Impact of the Economic Reforms in Latin America and the Caribbean*, Brookings Institution Press/ECLAC, Washington, DC.

Stewart, F. (1997), "John Williamson and the Washington Consensus revisited," in L. Emmerij (ed.), *Economic and Social Development into the XXI Century*, IDB, Washington, DC.

Stiglitz, J. (2005), "Responding to economic crises: policy alternatives for equitable recovery and development," *Working Paper*, IPD at Columbia University, Macroeconomics Task Force.

Stiglitz, J. (2002), *Globalization and its Discontents*, W.W. Norton, New York, May.

Stiglitz, J. (2001), "More instruments and broader goals: Moving toward the post-Washington Consensus", in H-J. Chang (ed.), *The Rebel Within*, Wimbledon Publishing Company, London. Originally presented as the 1998 WIDER Annual Lecture, Helsinki, January.

Stiglitz, J. (2000), "Capital market liberalization, economic growth and instability", *World Development*, vol. 28, No. 6, June.

Stiglitz, J. (1998), "The role of the financial system in development," Presentation at the Fourth Annual Bank Conference on Development in Latin America and the Caribbean (LAC ABCDE), San Salvador, El Salvador, June 29, 1998.

Stiglitz, J. (1994), "The role of the state in financial markets," *Proceedings of the World Bank Annual Conference on Development Economics*, vol. 2, World Bank, Washington, DC, May.

Sunkel, O. (1993) (ed.), *Development from Within: Toward a Neostructuralist Approach for Latin America*, Lynne Rienner Publishers, Boulder and London.

Ten Kate, A. (1998), "The response of manufacturing exports to import liberalization in Mexico: Is there a second wave?", in M.J. Lord (ed.), *The Handbook of Latin American Trade in Manufactures*, Edward Elgar, Cheltenham and Northampton.

Teunissen, J.J., J. Williamson et al. (1992), *Fragile Finance*, FONDAD, Den Hague.

Tobin, J. (1984), "On the efficiency of the financial system," *Lloyds Bank Review*, No. 153, July.

Tokman, V. (2004), *Una voz en el camino. Empleo y equidad en América Latina: 40 años de búsqueda*, Fondo de Cultura Económica, Santiago.

Turner, P. (2000), "Procyclicality of regulatory ratios?", in J. Eatwell and L. Taylor (eds.), *Global Finance at Risk: The Case for International Regulation*, The New Press, New York.

Tytell, I. and S-J. Wei (2004), "Does financial globalization induce better macro-economic policies?", Working Paper 04/84, International Monetary Fund, May.

UNCTAD (2004), *Foreign Investment Report 2004*, United Nations, Geneva.

United Nations (1999), Towards a New International Financial Architecture. Report of the Task Force of the Executive Committee on Economic and Social Affairs. Santiago: Economic Commission for Latin America and the Caribbean (ECLAC).

Uthoff, A. and D. Titelman (1998), "The relation between foreign and national savings under financial liberalization," in Ffrench-Davis and Reisen (1998).

Velasco, A. (2000), "Exchange rate policies for developing countries: What have we learned? What do we still not know?", UNCTAD/CID, Harvard University.

Wade, R. (1990), *Governing the Market – Economic Theory and the Role of Government in East Asian Industrialization*, Princeton University Press, Princeton, NJ.

Wang, Y. (2000),"Getting the sequencing right: lessons from the Korean experience with capital market liberalization," Korea Institute for Economic Policy, Seoul.

Weller, J. (2001), *Economic Reforms, Growth and Employment: Labour Markets in Latin America and the Caribbean*, ECLAC, Libros de la CEPAL, No. 66, Santiago.

Westphal, L.E. (1992), "La política industrial en una economía impulsada por las exportaciones: lecciones de la experiencia de Corea del Sur," *Pensamiento Iberoamericano*, No. 21, Madrid, January–June.

Williamson, J. (2003a), "Proposals for curbing the boom-bust cycle in the supply of capital to emerging markets," in Ffrench-Davis and Griffith-Jones (2003).

Williamson, J. (2003b), "Overview: an agenda for restarting growth and reform," in Kuczynski and Williamson (2003).

Williamson, J. (2003c), "Appendix," in Kuczynski and Williamson (2003).

Williamson, J. (2000), "Exchange rate regimes for emerging markets: reviving the intermediate option," *Policy Analysis in International Economics*, 60, Institute for International Economics, Washington, DC.

Williamson, J. (1993), "A cost-benefit analysis of capital account liberalization," in H. Reisen and B. Fischer (eds.), *Financial Opening*, OECD, Paris.

Williamson, J. (1990) (ed.), *Latin American Adjustment*, Institute for International Economics. Washington, DC.

Williamson, J. (1981) (ed.), *The Crawling-peg: Past Performance and Future Prospects*, Macmillan, "Introductory survey," London.

Winters, A. (2004), "Trade liberalisation and economic performance: an overview," *The Economic Journal*, vol. 114, February.

Winters, A. (1998), "Assessing regional integration arrangements," in S.J. Burki, G. Perry and S. Calvo (eds.), *Trade: Toward Open Regionalism*, World Bank, Washington, DC.

Wionczek, M.S. (1985) (ed.), *Politics and Economics of External Debt Crisis: The Latin American Experience*, Westview Press, Boulder.

World Bank (2003), *Inequality in Latin America & the Caribbean: Breaking with History?*, Washington, DC.

World Bank (1997), *The Long March: a Reform Agenda for Latin America and the Caribbean in the Next Decade*, Washington, DC.

Zahler, R. (2005), "Macroeconomic stability and investment allocation of domestic pension funds: the case of Chile," in R. Ffrench-Davis (ed.), *Seeking Growth under Financial Volatility*, Palgrave Macmillan, London.

Zahler, R. (1998), "The Central Bank and Chilean macroeconomic policy in the 1990s," *CEPAL Review*, No. 64, April.

Zahler, R. (1988), "Estrategias financieras latinoamericanas: la experiencia del Cono Sur," *Colección Estudios CIEPLAN*, 23, Santiago, March.

Index

Note: Page numbers followed by tab, fig and n refer to tables, figures and notes.